Foreword

The Bretton Woods conference of July 1944 was of incalculable importance for the world economy. It demonstrated and gave life to a remarkable spirit of international economic cooperation; produced agreements that made possible the reconstruction of war-torn economies and an unprecedented growth of output and trade in the following decades; and created two institutions, which we now have the honor to lead, that have been central in the effort to achieve those goals. It was thus natural for the International Monetary Fund and the World Bank to join forces to help their membership commemorate the fiftieth anniversary of that important milestone in the evolution of the world economy.

That this anniversary was a time for celebration was clear, but more importantly it was an opportunity for reflection and for reassessing the roles of our institutions as we approach the twenty-first century. The Cold War has ended, and with it have vanished the divisions that long prevented the Fund and the World Bank from becoming truly global in scope and in membership. International markets in goods and financial assets have grown dramatically. Throughout much of the developing world, a "silent revolution" has brought increasing acceptance of the benefits of financially disciplined and outwardly directed economic policies. The operations, though not the essential purposes, of the Fund and the Bank have changed considerably over the past 50 years to respond to these developments, but much more adaptation is and will continue to be required.

We chose the occasion of the 1994 Annual Meetings of the Boards of Governors of the Fund and the World Bank in Madrid, Spain, to hold a conference on the future of the Bretton Woods institutions that would bring together policymakers, academic economists, representatives of nongovernmental development organizations, and many of the journalists who have covered the institutions over the years. For two days before the meetings officially opened, several hundred of these eminent individuals gathered at the conference to speak, to listen, and to discuss. In our view, they succeeded wonderfully in stimulating thinking and in bringing good and practical ideas to the fore. At the end of the conference, while there may not have been agreement on all of the key issues, we believe that, as this volume shows, we were in many ways closer to a consensus than might have been expected.

We would like to take this occasion to thank all of those who came from around the globe to participate in the Madrid conference and who contributed to this book: the keynote speakers, the panelists, the session chairs, and members of our distinguished audience. Our thanks also to the staff who made it all possible. Under the general direction of

Leo Van Houtven and Armeane M. Choksi and with the assistance of many others from the Fund and the World Bank, James M. Boughton and K. Sarwar Lateef organized and ran the conference and were the principal editors of this volume. Finally, we offer our heartfelt thanks to the Spanish Government, which not only was our gracious host in Madrid but whose officials also participated so actively in the conference.

MICHEL CAMDESSUS
Managing Director
International Monetary Fund

LEWIS T. PRESTON
President
World Bank Group

Fifty Years After Bretton Woods
The Future of the IMF and the World Bank

pain

Reprinted June 1995

This book was designed and produced by the IMF Graphics Section.

Front cover photographs: The Mount Washington Hotel, Bretton Woods, New Hampshire, U.S.A., IMF archives: and Palacio Municipal de Congresos, Campo de las Naciones, Madrid, Spain, IMF photo by Denio Zara.

Cataloging-in-Publication Data

Fifty Years after Bretton Woods : the future of the IMF and the World Bank : proceedings of a conference held in Madrid, Spain, September 29–30, 1994 / James M. Boughton and K. Sarwar Lateef, editors. — Washington : International Monetary Fund : World Bank Group, 1995.

ISBN 1-55775-487-X

1. International finance — Congresses. 2. International Monetary Fund — Congresses. 3. World Bank — Congresses. I. Boughton, James M. II. Lateef, K. Sarwar.

HG3881.F4 1995

Price: US$21.00

Please send orders to:
International Monetary Fund, Publication Services
700 19th Street, N.W., Washington, D.C. 20431, U.S.A.
Tel.: (202) 623-7430   Telefax: (202) 623-7201
Internet: publications@imf.org

Preface

This volume is the record of a conference held at the splendid setting of the Palacio Municipal de Congresos, Campo de las Naciones, Madrid, Spain, on September 29–30, 1994. The conference was sponsored jointly by the International Monetary Fund and the World Bank, and it was held in conjunction with the Annual Meetings of the Boards of Governors of the two institutions. All delegates, special guests, staff, and visitors attending the meetings were invited to attend the conference and to participate in the general discussion; that several hundred did attend made the conference a great success. The speakers were chosen from among the policymakers, academic economists, and other influential leaders from all regions of the world who have been actively involved in the key issues facing the Bretton Woods institutions.

The papers and statements included in this volume are based on the presentations made at the conference; each chapter corresponds—in chronological order—to a conference session. In addition, Chapter 1 includes an overview of the discussion on major issues; in many cases, the same issue arose in more than one session, and the overview is intended to help guide the reader to the appropriate chapters that follow.

The contributions took a variety of forms: keynote addresses, formal papers, panel discussions, statements by session chairs, and comments and questions from the audience. Where no written statement was submitted, the text has been derived from the verbatim transcript. When presentations were not made in English, the text was derived either from versions submitted by the authors or from translations made by the conference secretariat.[1] Regardless of their source, all statements have been edited with the aim of assembling a comprehensive permanent record, and several authors revised their statements after the conference to clarify specific points.

The views expressed in this volume are those of the individual authors and participants, subject to any misinterpretation that might have crept in through the editorial process, for which we alone are responsible. The opinions expressed are not necessarily those of the International Monetary Fund, the World Bank, or any institution with which an individual author is affiliated.

Both the conference and this volume were the product of many people in addition to the authors. We extend a special note of thanks to

---

[1]The statements of Felipe González and Pedro Solbes Mira were translated from Spanish by the secretariat. English translations of Liu Zhongli's statement (delivered in Chinese) and that of Pedro Aspe Armella (delivered in Spanish) were provided by the ministers' offices. All other presentations were made in English.

Armeane M. Choksi and Leo Van Houtven for their guidance in directing this project; to Angel Torres, our liaison with the Spanish authorities, and to Joaquín de la Herrán and Isabel Riano of the Spanish Ministry of Economy and Finance; to Chris Clarke for his tireless and invaluable service at every stage, including as rapporteur for the conference discussion; to Sonia Benavides, Mary Helen O'Brien, and Kristen Schubert for their work on the conference and on this volume; to Paul Rabé and Marta Vindiola for greatly valued and varied assistance; to the members of the Fund-Bank working group that was responsible for the initial planning of the conference, notably including (in addition to ourselves) Morris Goldstein and Ian McDonald, from the Fund, and to Jochen Kraske, Timothy Cullen, and Michael Walton, from the Bank; to Erik Friis, Patricia Davies, Enrique Alejo González, and the rest of the Annual Meetings secretariat and the Madrid '94 Task Force for their assistance in the smooth running of the conference; and, finally, to Elin Knotter for her skillful job of style editing the manuscript and to Tom Walter for seeing the book through to publication.

JAMES M. BOUGHTON
K. SARWAR LATEEF

CONTENTS

The following symbols have been used in this book:

...   to indicate that data are not available;

—   to indicate that the figure is zero or less than half the final digit shown, or that the item does not exist;

–   between years or months (e.g., 1992–93 or January–June) to indicate the years or months covered, including the beginning and ending years or months;

/   between years (e.g., 1992/93) to indicate a crop or fiscal (financial) year.

"Billion" means a thousand million.

Minor discrepancies between constituent figures and totals are due to rounding.

All references are to U.S. dollars unless noted otherwise.

Conference Participants

Featured Speakers

Fazle Hasan Abed is founder and Executive Director of the Bangladesh Rural Advancement Committee, established in 1972. Prior to this, he served as Treasurer and Head of Finance of the Pakistan Shell Oil Company, Ltd.

Abdlatif Y. Al-Hamad has been Director General and Chairman of the Board of Directors of the Arab Fund for Economic and Social Development since 1985. He served previously as Minister of Finance and Minister of Planning of Kuwait and as Chairman of the Boards of Governors of the International Monetary Fund and the World Bank. Mr. Al-Hamad is a member of the Banking Advisory Board Group of the International Finance Corporation and the Commission on Global Governance.

Pedro Aspe Armella was appointed Secretary of Finance and Public Credit of Mexico by President Salinas de Gortari in 1988. He served previously as Under Secretary of Planning and Budget.

Leszek Balcerowicz is a professor at the Warsaw School of Economics. He is also Chairman of the Center for Social and Economic Research Scientific Foundation and Chairman of the Advisory Board of the Foundation for Economic Education. Dr. Balcerowicz was Deputy Prime Minister and Minister of Finance of Poland from 1989 to 1991.

C. Fred Bergsten has been Director of the Institute for International Economics since its creation in 1981. He is also the U.S. representative and Chairman of the Eminent Persons Group created in 1992 by the Asia Pacific Economic Cooperation forum, having served previously as Assistant Secretary of the U.S. Treasury for International Affairs.

Kwesi Botchwey has served as Minister of Finance of Ghana since 1982. Dr. Botchwey was previously a lecturer in law at the universities of Zambia, Dar-es-Salaam, and Ghana and has taught foreign investment, international trade, and economic development.

Michel Camdessus has been Managing Director of the International Monetary Fund since 1987. Mr. Camdessus was Director of the French Treasury and Chairman of the Paris Club between 1982 and 1984 and served as Governor of the Bank of France from 1984 until his appointment to the Fund.

Note: The affiliations and titles are those as of the time of the conference.

Kenneth Clarke was appointed Chancellor of the Exchequer of the United Kingdom in 1993. Mr. Clarke has been a Member of Parliament since 1970 and has served as Secretary of State at the Home Office and Minister of Health.

A.W. Clausen is the retired Chairman and Chief Executive Officer of Bank America Corporation and its subsidiary, Bank of America N.T. & S.A. He serves as an Honorary Director on both boards. Mr. Clausen was President of the World Bank Group from 1981 to 1986.

Jacques de Larosière has been the President of the European Bank for Reconstruction and Development since September 1993. He served as Director of the French Treasury and Chairman of the Paris Club before becoming Managing Director of the International Monetary Fund in 1978. Mr. de Larosière was Governor of the Bank of France from 1987 to 1993.

Lamberto Dini was appointed Minister of the Treasury of Italy in May 1994. He served previously as Director General of the Bank of Italy and Chairman of the Group of Ten Deputies. Mr. Dini was on the staff of the International Monetary Fund from 1959 to 1976 and served as Executive Director for Italy from 1976 to 1980.

Wendy Dobson is Professor of Economics at the University of Toronto. She served as Associate Deputy Minister of Finance in Canada from 1987 to 1989 and has headed Canada's leading independent policy institute.

Wim Duisenberg has been President of De Nederlandsche Bank since 1982. He was Minister of Finance of the Netherlands between 1973 and 1977 and served previously as Special Advisor to De Nederlandsche Bank. Dr. Duisenberg was on the staff of the International Monetary Fund from 1966 to 1969.

Albert Fishlow is Professor of Economics at the University of California at Berkeley and Coeditor of the *Journal of Development Economics*. Until 1983, he was Professor of Economics and Director of the Center for International and Area Studies at Yale University. Professor Fishlow was Deputy Assistant Secretary of State for Inter-American Affairs in 1975 and 1976 and has been a member of many U.S. task forces on Latin American affairs.

Jacob A. Frenkel was appointed Governor of the Bank of Israel in 1991, having served as Economic Counsellor and Director of the Research Department of the International Monetary Fund since 1987. He held the David Rockefeller Chair in International Economics at the University of Chicago and was on the faculty of Jerusalem and Tel Aviv universities.

Richard N. Gardner has been the U.S. Ambassador to Spain since 1993. Ambassador Gardner is on leave from the Faculty of Law at Columbia University, where he holds the Chair in Law and International Organization. He was Deputy Assistant Secretary of State for International Organization Affairs under Presidents Kennedy and Johnson.

Victor Gerashchenko was Chairman of the Central Bank of the Russian Federation from 1992 to 1994. After a career with the Moscow Narodny Bank in Beirut, London, and Singapore and the Ost-West Handelsbank in Frankfurt, he served as head of the State Bank of the U.S.S.R. and First Deputy Chairman of the Vneshtorgbank of the U.S.S.R.

Felipe González has been Prime Minister of Spain since 1982. He has been Secretary-General of the Partido Socialista Obrero Español since 1979.

Toyoo Gyohten has been Chairman of the Board of Directors of the Bank of Tokyo, Ltd., since 1992. Prior to his current position, he was a visiting professor at Harvard and Princeton universities and the University of St. Gallen in Switzerland. Dr. Gyohten served as Japan's Vice Minister of Finance for International Affairs from 1986 to 1989.

Gerald K. Helleiner has been Professor of Economics at the University of Toronto since 1965. He is also the Research Coordinator of the Group of Twenty-Four Developing Countries.

Peter Kenen has been Professor of Economics and International Finance at Princeton University since 1971. He has also served as consultant to the Council of Economic Advisers, the U.S. Treasury, the Office of Management and Budget, and the International Monetary Fund.

Tony Killick has been with the Overseas Development Institute in London since 1979, where he has held the position of Director and, most recently, Senior Research Fellow. He is also a Visiting Professor at the University of Surrey and has been a consultant to many international organizations and governments. Professor Killick has also held teaching and research posts at the universities of Ghana and Nairobi and at Harvard University.

Liu Zhongli has held the position of Minister of Finance of the People's Republic of China since 1992. He previously served as Deputy Secretary-General of the State Council, Vice Minister of Finance, and Deputy Governor of Heilongjiang Province.

Jean-Claude Milleron is Under Secretary-General of the United Nations for the Department of Economic and Social Information and Policy Analysis. Previously, he served in France as Director General of INSEE and Director of Planning and as Chairman of the Monetary Committee of the European Communities.

Musalia Mudavadi was appointed Minister of Finance of Kenya in 1993. He previously served as Minister for Supplies and Marketing and was Director of Tysons, Ltd., until 1989.

Moisés Naím is currently a Senior Associate and the Director of Latin American Programs at the Carnegie Endowment for International Peace. Mr. Naím served previously as an Executive Director of the World Bank Group and as Minister of Industry and Trade of Venezuela.

Alassane Ouattara has been Deputy Managing Director of the International Monetary Fund since July 1994. He served previously as Prime Minister of Côte d'Ivoire, Governor of the Central Bank of West African States, and Counsellor and Director of the African Department of the International Monetary Fund.

Richard Portes has been Director of the Centre for Economic Policy Research since 1983. He has also held the position of Secretary-General of the European Economic Association since 1992.

Lewis T. Preston has been President of the World Bank Group since 1991. Mr. Preston was Chairman of the Board and Chief Executive Officer of J.P. Morgan and Co., from 1980 to 1991, having served as a member of the Corporate Office and the Board of Directors since 1976.

Moeen Qureshi is Chairman and Managing Partner of Emerging Markets Corporation. He was Executive Vice President and Chief Operating Officer of the International Finance Corporation from 1977 to 1981 and was Senior Vice President of the World Bank from 1980 to 1991. Mr. Qureshi served as Prime Minister of Pakistan for an interim period in 1993.

M. Saifur Rahman has served as Minister of Finance of Bangladesh since 1991 and as Chairman of the Boards of Governors of the International Monetary Fund and the World Bank for 1993–94. He served as Minister of Finance, Commerce, and Foreign Trade from 1976 to 1982. Mr. Rahman has been a consultant with Price Waterhouse, Asia Pacific; Arthur D. Little, Boston; and KPMG Peat Marwick International.

Luis Angel Rojo has been Governor of the Bank of Spain since 1992, having served as Deputy Governor since 1988. He is Professor of Economic Theory on the Faculty of Economics of the Complutense University of Madrid.

Maria Schaumayer has been Governor of the Austrian National Bank since 1990. Dr. Schaumayer was previously a member of the Board of Management and Executive Director of Finance of ÖMV Aktiengesellschaft and a member of the Board of Management of the Österreichische Kommunalkredit AG, both in Austria.

Manmohan Singh has been Minister of Finance of India since 1991. He was appointed Economic Advisor to the Prime Minister of India in 1990, having served previously as Secretary-General of the South Commission in Geneva, Governor of the Reserve Bank of India, and Secretary of the Ministry of Finance.

Pedro Solbes Mira has been Minister of Economy and Finance of Spain since 1993. Mr. Solbes previously held positions as Minister of Agriculture and Secretary of State for the European Communities.

Hans Tietmeyer has been President of the Deutsche Bundesbank since October 1993, having served as Vice President since 1991. He previously held the position of State Secretary in the German Ministry of Finance.

Paul Volcker is Chairman of James D. Wolfensohn, Inc., and Professor of International Economic Policy at Princeton University. He has been Convener of the Bretton Woods Commission since its creation in 1992. Mr. Volcker served as Chairman of the Board of Governors of the U.S. Federal Reserve System from 1979 to 1987.

Widjojo Nitisastro is Economic Advisor to the Government of Indonesia. He served previously as Chairman of the National Planning Agency and Coordinating Minister of State for Economics, Financial, and Industrial Affairs. Dr. Widjojo was Dean of the School of Economics at the University of Indonesia in Jakarta.

Other Senior Officials

IMF

Stanley Fischer
First Deputy Managing Director

P.R. Narvekar
Deputy Managing Director

Leo Van Houtven
Secretary and Counsellor

Manuel Guitián
Associate Director, Monetary and Exchange Affairs Department

K. Burke Dillon
Chief Economist, Resident Representatives' Office in Moscow

World Bank

Attila Karaosmanoglu
Managing Director

Sven Sandstrom
Managing Director

Ernest Stern
Managing Director

Michael Bruno
Vice President, Development Economics and Chief Economist

Armeane M. Choksi
Vice President, Human Resources Development and Operations Policy

Ismail Serageldin
Vice President, Environmentally Sustainable Development

Ishrat Hussain
Chief Economist, Africa Regional Office

Other Participants in the General Discussion

Nancy Alexander
Director of Issues,
Bread for the World

Peter Bod
President, National Bank of Hungary

Ariel Buira
Deputy Director, Bank of Mexico

Klaus Engelen
International Correspondent,
Handelsblatt

Jo Marie Griesgraber
Project Director, Center of Concern

Jacques Polak
President, Per Jacobsson Foundation

Layeshi Yaker
Executive Secretary, UN Economic
Commission for Africa

Salvatore Zecchini
Assistant Secretary-General,
Organization for Economic Cooperation
and Development

Conference Secretariat

IMF

James M. Boughton
Historian

Christopher P. Clarke
Recording Officer

Marta E. Vindiola
Editorial Assistant

World Bank

K. Sarwar Lateef
Staff Director, 50th Anniversary
Secretariat, Human Resources
Development and Operations Policy

Paul E. Rabé
50th Anniversary
Secretariat, Human Resources
Development and Operations Policy

1

Introduction and Overview

James M. Boughton and K. Sarwar Lateef

[1] On July 1–22, 1944, delegates from 44 nations met at Bretton Woods, New Hampshire, to design a framework for future international economic cooperation. Faced with an exceedingly ambitious agenda—to agree on fundamental principles, to design a set of institutions capable of furthering those principles, and to draft the Articles of Agreement to govern those institutions—these delegates managed in just three weeks to realize nearly all of their goals. That "political miracle," as Richard Gardner calls it (in Chapter 4 of this volume), was all the more remarkable for having been accomplished in the midst of a global war by delegates from countries with broadly diverse experiences and objectives. The design of the Articles was largely the product of the British and U.S. delegations, but many other countries—China, France, and India are prominent examples—put their stamp on the final product. As Jacques Polak—one of several veterans of Bretton Woods who gathered 50 years later in Madrid—noted in a tribute (see Box), for all who were there in 1944 it was one of the most intense experiences, perhaps the defining experience, of their professional lives. And "Bretton Woods" entered the lexicon as a symbol of international economic cooperation and stability.

The two institutions created at Bretton Woods—the International Monetary Fund (IMF) and the International Bank for Reconstruction and Development (IBRD, or the World Bank)—have helped shape the world economy for 50 years in which the economic, political, and social environment has undergone frequent and ultimately fundamental change. The institutions have faced numerous challenges and innovations:

- the complex and evolving needs of developing countries;
- the trend toward greater symmetry in economic size and power among the large industrial countries;
- the growing interdependence of industrial and developing countries;
- the integration of former centrally planned economies into the world market system;

1

- the increased international integration of markets;
- the evolution of a market-friendly development paradigm; and
- the acceleration of technological innovation and diffusion.

This evolution has stimulated international trade and has contributed to an unprecedented rate of economic growth and development throughout the world, but it has also made the task of maintaining stabil-

---

A Toast to the Twins

Jacques J. Polak was an Expert Economist in the delegation of the Netherlands at the Bretton Woods conference in July 1944. Subsequently, he served as Economic Counsellor and Director of Research at the IMF. Following his retirement from those positions in 1979, he was elected Executive Director in the IMF from the Netherlands. He "retired" again in 1986, and since that time has served as President of the Per Jacobsson Foundation. At the dinner for conference participants at the Castillo de Viñuelas outside Madrid on September 29, Polak introduced his fellow veterans who were in attendance: Abol Hassan Ebtehaj, who had been the Governor of the National Bank of Iran and Chairman of the Iran delegation at Bretton Woods; Aron Broches, who had been Secretary of the delegation of the Netherlands; and J. Burke Knapp, then an economist in the U.S. Federal Reserve System. Polak then offered the following toast:

All of us, I am sure, are happy to be here tonight to join in this celebration of the Bretton Woods conference. This meeting in Madrid is an exceptional event, but frankly it cannot begin to compete with the real thing as we remember it—the conference 50 years ago in that wonderful setting at the foot of Mount Washington. To all those who were there that experience can, I believe, best be described as a happening—the most exhilarating experience of their professional lives. That experience included

- an overarching common desire to make sure that the postwar world would not repeat the disastrous national and international economic mismanagement of the interwar period;
- splendid preparation, mostly, but not exclusively, by the technicians of the United States and the United Kingdom;
- the close togetherness, in a single hotel, with few distractions— no spouses allowed—of many brilliant economists from the allied countries; and
- extremely hard work.

This—I believe—is how Bretton Woods brought into the world the Bretton Woods twins. On behalf of some of the remaining proud parents, may I propose a toast to the Twins' fiftieth birthday.

ity far more daunting and complex. The international financial system that emerged from Bretton Woods and that matured through the 1950s and 1960s—a system that promoted stable exchange rates between convertible currencies—collapsed in the early 1970s. The conditions that made that system possible—the predominance of a single economic superpower committed to being the stable core of the system and the limited role of private capital flows—vanished and are unlikely to be seen again. In the wake of that collapse, the IMF lost the linchpin of its strategy, but its underlying mandate established at Bretton Woods in Article I of the Articles of Agreement remained intact:

- to promote international monetary cooperation;
- to facilitate the expansion and balanced growth of international trade;
- to promote exchange stability;
- to assist in the establishment of a multilateral system of payments; and
- to make its resources temporarily available to its members, under adequate safeguards, thereby helping members to correct maladjustments in their balance of payments without resorting to measures destructive of national or international prosperity.

Adhering to these purposes while adapting to the ever-changing needs of a diverse and growing membership has constituted the principal challenge to the Fund for more than two decades.

Since Bretton Woods, the IBRD has added new affiliates to accommodate shifting development priorities and has become the World Bank Group: the International Finance Corporation (IFC) in 1956 to promote private investment; the International Development Association (IDA) in 1960 to provide donor-funded concessional resources to the poorer member countries; the International Centre for Settlement of Investment Disputes (ICSID) in 1966 to provide conciliation and arbitration services for disputes between foreign investors and host governments; and the Multilateral Investment Guarantee Agency (MIGA) in 1988 to provide noncommercial investment risk insurance and related technical services.

This institutional evolution has been matched by a changing approach to development. The early focus on discrete projects has evolved into a broader emphasis on policies, strategies, and institutions, and a more holistic approach to development. Despite the evolving role of the World Bank Group, its fundamental objectives as set out in the charters of its institutions remain valid. Within these objectives, the Group's primary concern is to help borrowers reduce poverty and improve living standards by promoting sustainable growth and investment in people. To do this, the Bank Group helps borrowers through its financial and advisory roles to

- pursue economic reforms aimed at enhancing growth and reducing poverty;
- invest in the health and education of their people;
- protect the environment;
- stimulate the private sector; and
- reorient their governments toward core functions.

As the fiftieth anniversary of Bretton Woods approached, not only the two institutions (see Camdessus, 1994, and World Bank Group, 1994) but also interested groups around the world began planning independently to commemorate the occasion. These events took a variety of forms, but they all sought in their own way to re-examine the roles of the Bretton Woods institutions in the light of the world that we live in today.[1]

In September 1993, the North-South Roundtable met at Bretton Woods under the chairmanship of Richard Jolly, with the aim of developing—as the conference report put it—"an integral view of the United Nations and the Bretton Woods institutions taken together" (p. 2). The conference report (Bretton Woods Commission, 1994, pp. 12–13) called for the creation of a Development Security Council within the United Nations, whose responsibilities would include a review of the Bretton Woods institutions and regional economic agencies. The report (p. 15) also called for "reviving the issue of SDRs," canceling debts of low-income countries to multilateral institutions, and establishing a new lending window within the World Bank Group with terms intermediate between those of IDA and the IBRD.

In April 1994, the Group of Twenty-Four developing countries sponsored a conference of scholars and policymakers in Cartagena, Colombia, organized by Gerald K. Helleiner. The suggestions and recommendations made by participants at the Cartagena conference included increased participation by developing countries in the Fund and the World Bank; longer-term orientation in the design of conditionality for financial arrangements; a new allocation of SDRs and other sources of financing, especially for low-income countries; consideration by the Bretton Woods institutions of a partial writing down of their claims on low-income countries; a review of the functioning of the Interim and Development Committees; and greater consistency between Fund and Bank activities (see Helleiner's introductory chapter in United Nations Conference on Trade and Development, 1994).

In May 1994, the Institute for International Economics held a conference in Washington, D.C., organized by C. Fred Bergsten. One of the

---

[1]The following summary is selective. It omits a number of conferences dealing with specific topics or with issues related to a specific country, and it is limited to conferences that provided substantive rather than mainly political discussions of the issues.

main themes that emerged from that conference (see Kenen, 1994) was that the success of Bretton Woods may be attributable more to the principles that were established there—the "institutions" in a broad sense—than to the formal organizations that were created. Participants lamented the Fund's lack of influence over countries' exchange rate policies in the system that had developed since Bretton Woods and noted that the "privatization of the development process" (Kenen, 1994, p. 397) had marginalized the World Bank's financing role. Though there was not yet a consensus on specific proposals (for illustration, see the discussion below of proposals for reforming the international monetary system), the challenge that emerged from that discussion was to find "modest reforms" (Kenen, 1994, p. 405) that would enable the institutions to evolve so as to cope more effectively with changes in the world economy.

In June 1994, the Center of Concern, a Washington-based coalition of nongovernmental organizations, held a forum aimed at reforming the Bretton Woods institutions according to "the principles of participation, transparency, accountability, and subsidiarity" (Griesgraber, 1994, p. ix). The report of that conference concluded that the people most directly affected by the policies promoted by the institutions, primarily the poor, should have more influence over those policies and more control over the institutions themselves; that to further that goal, the institutions should make more information publicly available; and that the Bretton Woods institutions should defer to local or regional institutions whenever appropriate. More specifically, it called for a complete overhaul of structural adjustment programs, which it found to have been largely ineffective and inimical to development.

In July 1994, on the anniversary of the original conference, the Bretton Woods Commission[2] held a plenary session that culminated more than a year of meetings and brought together the authors of numerous background reports and other papers on issues of relevance to the future of the institutions. The Commission's own report, released shortly before, had concluded that the international monetary system was unsatisfactory and could be improved. In particular, it recommended that the large industrial countries should move now to achieve better coordination of economic policies and conditions; only when a good degree of convergence of fiscal and monetary policies was attained would conditions be ripe for implementing reforms aimed at institutionalizing the resulting exchange rate stability. At the plenary session, that proposal was criticized from both sides: by those (notably Fred Bergsten) who believed that effective international cooperation was practically impossible without first securing

---

[2] The Bretton Woods Commission (formally, the Commission on the Future of the Bretton Woods Institutions) was commissioned by the Bretton Woods Committee. It was convened by Paul A. Volcker and was chaired by Richard Debs, Wilfried Guth, and Yusuke Kashiwagi.

systemic reform and by those (including senior officials from the three largest industrial countries) who believed that the current system was working acceptably well.

The Bretton Woods Commission also supported continued funding of IDA but recommended that the World Bank Group should shift much more of its activity toward the private sector and make greater use of cofinancing, guarantees, and innovative financing techniques. More generally, the Commission recommended that the Fund defer more to the Bank on matters related to structural adjustment in developing countries. That proposal was criticized at the plenary session by the IMF's Managing Director, Michel Camdessus, who questioned the underlying premise that the Fund should not be concerned with development. Neither was it generally supported by other officials who participated, either from industrial or developing countries.

As a culmination of this season of reflection, the IMF and the World Bank decided jointly to hold an anniversary conference that would provide a forum in which policymakers, academic economists, and other analysts and practitioners from all regions of the world could discuss the major issues confronting the institutions. The 1994 Annual Meetings in Madrid, Spain, provided an occasion when many of the world's finance ministers and central bank governors would be present. A large number of ministers and governors participated in this milestone conference, along with a number of leading academics, representatives of nongovernmental organizations, and many of the senior officers of the Fund and the Bank.

The Madrid conference, it must be stressed, was in no sense "Bretton Woods II." Its purpose was neither to revisit the past—though many participants naturally reflected on the lessons of Bretton Woods and the experience of the past 50 years—nor to redesign the institutions. Rather, its much more modest objective was to provide a forum for discussion of how the institutions could adapt more effectively to the conditions and issues of the 1990s and beyond. Its success should perhaps be judged not by whether it produced definitive answers but by its having helped in getting the right questions asked and in suggesting answers that point in the right direction.

The Issues

The following summary of the discussion of specific issues focuses on the roles of the Bretton Woods institutions in the areas of global economic management; economic reforms, in both developing countries and the transition economies; poverty reduction; and finance for development. It concludes with a review of the discussion of the more general functioning and structure of the two institutions.

Strengthening Surveillance and the International Monetary System

The effectiveness of IMF surveillance, especially with regard to the functioning of the international monetary system, was a recurring theme throughout the anniversary year. The range of views on this topic had been clearly illustrated at the Institute for International Economics conference in Washington. On one side was a proposal by John Williamson and Randall Henning, which called on the large industrial countries to accept a "blueprint" for coordinating monetary and fiscal policies in a medium-term, IMF-monitored, framework, to stabilize exchange rates and reduce current account imbalances.[3] Although the proposal was praised by many participants at that conference for its intellectual underpinnings, it failed to generate any political support. Lawrence Summers, the U.S. Under Secretary of the Treasury for International Affairs, characterized the proposal as "unrealistic" and concluded that there was "little prospect" of its implementation (Kenen, 1994, p. 423). The late Horst Schulmann—President of the Landeszentral Bank in Hesse, Germany—opposed any effort, "formal or informal," to keep exchange rates within specified ranges, arguing that flexible exchange rates serve as a safety valve when countries are affected differently by circumstances. In these conditions, he concluded, it "has become more difficult to argue that we need the IMF."[4]

By the time of the Madrid conference, a consensus began to emerge, well inside the extremes: neither laissez-faire nor dirigiste, but aimed at achieving what Maria Schaumayer called "flexible stability" (Chapter 11). In the course of the two days of meetings, several speakers advocated moving toward a target zone system or some other formalization of exchange rate rules or procedures, though they differed both in motivation and detail:

- C. Fred Bergsten (Chapter 3) set aside the ambitious coordination scheme that he had advocated earlier in favor of a more modest proposal for stabilizing exchange rates. He argued that the major countries will not adopt better macroeconomic policies without the discipline of an exchange rate rule, and he concluded that the Fund should become "the steward" of a system of target zones.
- Peter Kenen (Chapter 5) championed the approach of the Bretton Woods Commission, arguing that better policies have to precede

---

[3]Specifically, the blueprint suggests coordinating policies with regard to government saving or dissaving over the medium term, based on an understanding of the linkages between those policies and current account positions; and aiming monetary policies at maintaining domestic price stability, but occasionally departing from the medium-term path when necessary to stabilize exchange rates. See Kenen (1994), Chap. 2.

[4]Kenen (1994, p. 388). On the next page, Schulmann softens his criticism slightly, saying he "would be content to maintain the IMF as a fleet in drydock."

systemic reform but also that the goal of exchange rate stability can provide a beacon for those trying to implement better policies.

- Jacques de Larosière (Chapter 10) also backed the Commission's approach. He argued that the Fund should oversee both the convergence criteria in the first stage (while policies are being strengthened) and the exchange rate bands in the second stage. This role should be part of a more general restoration of the Fund's "mandate to be the global monetary authority."
- Paul Volcker (Chapter 12) contended that improvements in fiscal policy would have to precede any effort to stabilize exchange rates, but he also argued that policies could not be coordinated effectively unless exchange rates were the central focus. Thus Kenen, de Larosière, and Volcker all agreed with Bergsten that exchange rates should be stabilized and that steadier and more prudent policies were the means of achieving that goal, but each differed slightly in his assessment of the sequence of steps for getting there. Volcker concluded that the Fund should identify ranges outside which exchange rates would be considered to be misaligned, and that countries should then make a general commitment to manage policies to prevent such a misalignment.
- Several speakers from developing countries, including M. Saifur Rahman, Moeen Qureshi, and Kwesi Botchwey, called for the Fund to find a better means of promoting stable macroeconomic policies in the large industrial countries. Qureshi tempered that point, however, by concluding that developing countries should worry less about stability in the large countries (which they can do little to influence anyway) and more about their own policies. Ariel Buira supported Bergsten's view that floating has weakened fiscal discipline.
- Stanley Fischer and Michael Bruno questioned the view that target zones would provide any real incentive for improving macroeconomic policies, but Fischer concluded that a target zone system might nonetheless provide a "slight improvement" over the present system if it could help avoid major misalignments such as the overvaluation of the U.S. dollar in the mid-1980s.

The most thorough skepticism about target zones for exchange rates came from Wendy Dobson, on two grounds (Chapter 11). First, she argued that the Group of Seven major industrial countries are incapable of coordinating policies, because officials of those countries disagree among themselves both on the strategy for stabilizing exchange rates and on the analytical linkages between policies and economic performance. Second, in her view the weight of empirical evidence does not suggest that either volatility or even misalignment of exchange rates is especially costly. The only feasible anchor in today's world, she concluded, is "prudent policies." Lamberto Dini (Chapter 3) and Jacob Frenkel (Chapter 11) were also skeptical, though they did not go so far as Dobson. Dini warned against attempting to "subordinate . . . domestic policy objectives to the pursuit of stable exchange rates" or setting "overly ambitious targets," while Frenkel cautioned that no system could guarantee good performance; officials would have to "earn" good performance through good policymaking.

In any event, skepticism about target zones for exchange rates did not imply skepticism about the role of Fund surveillance. Several speakers, including Bergsten, Dobson, and Toyoo Gyohten, appealed to the major countries to ensure that participation in the process "be as senior as possible" (Gyohten, Chapter 11) so that it could have the maximum possible impact.

Economic Reform and Conditionality

A recurring theme in Madrid was the recognition that the Bretton Woods institutions could take some credit for the emerging consensus on the need for reform in economic policies and that their role in providing policy advice was important. Attention focused heavily on the nature both of their advice in relation to the design of adjustment programs (in developing as well as in transition countries) and of World Bank and Fund conditionality.

Tony Killick led off the discussion (Chapter 8) by posing a paradox. The types of reform policies generally advocated by the two institutions appeared to be responsible for the significant improvement in economic performance of many countries. Yet the direct economic results of specific measures contained in structural adjustment programs supported by the two institutions were "patchy, at best." Programs appeared to strengthen the balance of payments but not to promote either price stability or growth. Killick explained this paradox in part by what he regarded as a tendency by the Fund and the Bank to view adjustment as "catharsis" rather than "continuous adaptation." This tendency led to programs that were too narrowly conceived and too short term and that gave insufficient emphasis to such factors as creating human skills, strengthening technological capabilities, and promoting institutional development.

In the subsequent discussion (Chapter 8), Manuel Guitián maintained that the Fund does view adjustment as a continuous process and accordingly conducts a regular dialogue on policies with member countries. Ishrat Hussain felt that the distinction between adjustment as a transition and adjustment as a continuous adaptation was better understood if one allowed for the large variations in initial conditions. Countries that had delayed adjustment and had therefore suffered serious distortions and large fiscal deficits inevitably needed large and fundamental policy changes. Once those changes had been made, it was easier to pursue a continuous adaptation approach to adjustment. Buira argued that the short-term view was driven by the constraint on external funding for adjustment programs. Longer-term programs required more funding, a view shared by Manmohan Singh (Chapter 3).

Killick's second explanation for his paradox was the "overuse of conditionality" by the Fund and the World Bank. Excessive conditionality, in his view, tended to undermine local "ownership" or endorsement of programs, a quality that Bank studies had shown to have a strong positive correlation with successful outcomes. Killick's view on this point was shared by a number of speakers. Rahman (Chapter 2) argued that successful external support for development involved "moving at the pace of the people" by responding to the needs of the population, reflecting the degree of conviction that was present, and designing programs in a manner that seemed equitable to the people concerned. Supporting the view that adjustment programs needed to be seen to be home-grown to be fully acceptable, Qureshi (Chapter 12) recounted that he had been able to take tough measures as Prime Minister of Pakistan, particularly in the governance area, because those measures had not been taken at the behest of the Bank or the Fund.

Liu Zhongli argued that the World Bank and the Fund had a positive role to play in supporting reforms, as long as the institutions respected member countries' decision making and took into account each country's situation and needs (Chapter 6). Botchwey (Chapter 12), while agreeing with this view, pointed to the danger that the "perfectly agreeable aphorism" relating to home-grown programs was likely to be "intoned by the parties as they walk to the negotiating table, like an incantation, designed—as most incantations are—to free them from the tedious obligation of thinking through what they are saying." To him, ownership meant that the authorities see the program objectives as being fully consistent with their own objectives, and as something they need to do on their own, and "not as some imposition that they must accept because they 'need the money' and have no other choice."

It is this latter phenomenon that Killick described as "paper conditionality": programs that all parties recognize will not be implemented and that merely satisfy the need to "keep the money moving," thus undoing the credibility of the process. He suggested that the Bank and the Fund should be willing to say "no" more often to governments with a weak commitment to reform, and he saw as a minimum test of commitment the willingness of governments to draft letters of intent or letters of development policy, which should never be prepared by staff in Washington. This would enable the institutions to reallocate funds to countries that were seriously pursuing reforms. Botchwey also expressed his dissatisfaction with the way conditionality worked. He argued that where conditionality had not been met, one should not automatically blame the lack of political will; rather, there should be a careful evaluation of the causes of the problem, and waivers should be granted whenever circumstances warrant.

Alassane Ouattara acknowledged the danger of approving paper programs, but he maintained that ownership was not a sufficient safeguard (Chapter 8). It was important to understand local conditions, the political process, and what could reasonably be expected from low-paid civil servants. Issues of governance were also critical. It was important, he argued, to make sure that the public understood the problems and why the measures were needed. He also pointed to the difficulties facing those adjusting countries with high internal and external debt.

The issues raised by Ouattara found agreement among other speakers. Qureshi contended (Chapter 12) that the World Bank must be prepared to take a strong stand on governance issues and to deny its support to those countries where an unwillingness or inability to improve governance was an obstacle to economic progress. A.W. Clausen noted (Chapter 4) that even the most brilliant idea could not be imposed on a society or culture by mandate. It could be implemented only "by a process of education, example, visible successes, and clear and continual communication." He felt the world needed success stories—evidence of what could happen if governments adopted the right policies; Chile, Mexico, China, and the Republic of Korea might be good examples even if the "mountain of development" had not been conquered.

Leszek Balcerowicz strongly agreed with Killick that the Bank and the Fund should recognize that their main contribution to successful adjustment was their influence on contemporary thinking about policy (Chapter 12). He felt that in the future the voice of the two institutions would depend less on their financial role and more on recognition of their expertise. There was room for a program of mass economic education financed and launched by these institutions. Similarly, Clausen submitted that the institutions had a role to play in educating political leaders in managing reforms (Chapter 4). Such advice would be an important input into democratic decision making. Rahman proposed that the two institutions should participate in and contribute to the open economic debate in member countries to help develop implementable policies (Chapter 2).

Layeshi Yaker, while agreeing on the need for adjustment, questioned whether the present programs in Africa—which he implied had largely failed—were an adequate framework for adjustment. He advanced an alternate framework (Chapter 8) that would include a resolution of Africa's debt crisis, trade policies that favored Africa, and a massive international plan for human and technological development. Botchwey, commenting on the "unrelenting gloom" about Africa, wondered "if the African lion is condemned perpetually to lag behind the general advance" (Chapter 12). He believed it was not; there were no iron laws at work. Change or turnaround, he maintained, was not only possible but was already happening in Ghana and other African countries.

Management of the Transition to a Market Economy

The issue of the role of the Bretton Woods institutions in transition economies generated a lively debate. Liu argued (Chapter 6) that the initially low level of development in China and the country's highly centralized planned economy required a gradualist approach to transition. China's reforms had been implemented with a balanced combination of short-term and long-term objectives and with proper linkages between reform, development, and stability to ensure irreversibility. The program did not try to crush the old system overnight but chose to move from the periphery to the center, and from the individual to the whole, using a range of short-term objectives as stepping stones to long-term goals. From his perspective, the World Bank and the Fund should give greater consideration to the relationship between efficiency and equity. Reforms should not only improve efficiency of economic activities but also bring benefits to the majority of the people so as to ensure their sustainability.

Richard Portes (Chapter 6), while arguing against the use of labels and pleading for a pragmatic approach to transition, identified three errors in the approach taken to transition: overemphasis on macroeconomic policy, underestimation of the role of state enterprises in the transition period, and neglect of the need to strengthen financial intermediaries. He acknowledged that a country in transition from socialism must begin with a bold enough move to make the change in regime credible, but he maintained that structural reform could take place only gradually over time, and that price stabilization was not a prerequisite for such reform. Portes noted that it was appropriate for the Fund to be preoccupied with financial stability, but he was concerned that the countries were forced to reorient their own priorities to match those of the Fund. What he regarded as the overemphasis on stabilization had come about because "all other aid" was conditional on satisfying the IMF.

Viktor Gerashchenko supported Portes's warning about trying to do too much all at once and his call for more attention to the need to develop the banking system. Later in the conference (Chapter 12), however, Balcerowicz vigorously refuted a number of Portes's arguments. Noting that the transition countries could not be treated as a homogeneous group, Balcerowicz averred that calling for less emphasis on stabilization was bad advice. He also warned that too much emphasis on reforms at the microeconomic level could lead to more state intervention.

Sustainable Poverty Reduction

Widjojo Nitisastro (Chapter 9) initiated the discussion on sustainable poverty reduction by describing Indonesia's successful efforts to reduce poverty. He attributed this success to sustained, broadly based, and labor-intensive growth; investment in rural infrastructure and appropriate price incentives for agricultural products; rapid growth of labor-intensive exports; and reduction of the population growth rate. Indonesia's strong performance had helped it to withstand the large external shocks from the depreciation of the U.S. dollar and the oil price decline in the mid-1980s without significantly affecting the pace of poverty reduction. Lessons from this experience for other countries included the need for strong political commitment to poverty reduction, the need to develop both individual and institutional capacity to fight poverty, and the need for broad-based and equitable growth along with investment in education and health. Industrial countries could help by reducing volatility in exchange rates, ensuring market access, and providing generous debt relief.

Albert Fishlow (Chapter 9) broadly endorsed Widjojo's analysis on poverty reduction. He stressed the importance of policy in averting income inequality, the two most critical issues being land reform and the development of human capital. He recognized that it was not popular to discuss land reform, but there was no question that a "fairer allocation of this basic asset" can serve as an important stimulant to broad-based development, as demonstrated by both the Latin American experience (in a negative sense) and that of the Republic of Korea and of Taiwan Province of China (in a positive sense). This view was strongly supported by Fazle Hasan Abed, who stressed the importance of destroying the power of the landed elite. Bangladesh, he believed, by not undertaking meaningful land reform, had reduced the access of the disadvantaged section of the population to the opportunities from growth.

In discussing the development of human capital, Fishlow noted the high social returns to be gained from education and that it was the variable that in country after country explained the largest proportion of the variance in income distribution. The effects of investment in nutrition, health, and other social sectors were similar.

Fishlow argued that to the two primary approaches to poverty reduction—market-oriented policies augmented by safety nets and the basic needs approach—a third should be added: reliance on local self-governing institutions and community involvement to improve the material conditions and autonomy of the poor. In this context, decentralization would help reach the poor (a view shared by Rahman, Chapter 2), as would greater reliance on nongovernmental organizations. Abed supported this view (Chapter 9) and noted that governmental neglect had compelled nongovernmental organizations to mobilize and organize the poor. Although governments were often threatened by this reaction, they needed to recognize that nongovernmental organizations were there to supplement and not supplant government programs. He concluded that the World Bank should make these organizations an element in the adjustment process, since they would be effective partners in directing resources to the rural areas, empowering the poor, and democratizing purchasing power.

Finance for Development

The relevance of the financing roles of the Fund and the World Bank in light of the growing importance of private capital flows was a strong undercurrent to the discussion throughout the Madrid conference. Singh argued that although the Fund's financial role may have become irrelevant for the industrial countries, it remained highly relevant for the vast majority of developing countries and economies in transition. It would take some time for these countries to gain access to the world's capital markets on reasonable terms. Moreover, although private capital flows had become an important source of finance for developing countries, they were still highly concentrated in a few countries. For all others, "substantial lending by the World Bank will remain essential for many years to come." Singh did not see any contradiction in the expansion of the World Bank Group and expansion of private sector lending or private investment flows. Rather, he saw these developments as complementary and mutually reinforcing. In this context, he noted with regret that Bank lending had not risen since the early 1980s and that net resource flows had turned negative (Chapter 3). Qureshi also felt that the World Bank Group was in a position to play a major catalytic role by providing partial guarantees and taking small participations in large private investments, thus raising the threshold of confidence and making possible large private capital flows into emerging markets (Chapter 12). Volcker was more skeptical on this issue. There were inherent difficulties in a public bureaucracy lending to private enterprise, and he believed that this dilemma posed problems for the Bank in how it arranged its operations.

There was strong support for a financial role for the World Bank and the Fund in low-income countries (Helleiner, Chapter 5; Botchwey and Balcerowicz, Chapter 12) and on the need for IDA to concentrate attention on the poorest countries (Rahman, Chapter 2). Jean-Claude Milleron (Chapter 13) saw mobilizing resources for development as the overriding challenge facing international organizations.

With respect to the IMF, three issues were raised in this area. First, was an allocation of SDRs an appropriate means of supplementing the existing stock of liquid assets available to member countries? Although there had been no such allocations since 1981, this was still one of the principal policy options being discussed; just two days after the Madrid conference, the Interim Committee was scheduled to consider proposals for a general allocation of SDRs plus a special allocation that would go largely to countries that had joined the Fund since 1981. Hans Tietmeyer (Chapter 10) questioned the appropriateness of a general allocation, warning against what he saw as efforts "to circumvent the economic and political limitations of the global transfer of real resources by ingenious financial engineering." In contrast, Qureshi (Chapter 12) argued that SDR allocations are an important link between international financial stability and development.

The second issue was equally topical. Shortly before the conference, the Government of the United Kingdom had advanced a proposal for the IMF to sell a portion of its 103 million ounces of gold, to invest the proceeds in interest-bearing securities, and to earmark the income from those investments for relief of the debt burden of low-income countries. Kenneth Clarke (Chapter 12) made a brief case for that proposal and was supported by Helleiner (Chapter 5) and Jo Marie Griesgraber (Chapter 8).

A third idea, stemming from a suggestion put forward by the Managing Director earlier in the year, called for "a fast-disbursing, very short-term facility" to help countries cope with speculative shifts in capital flows. That preliminary suggestion was not formally on the table in Madrid, and Camdessus did not mention it in either of his addresses to the conference. It had, however, been considered at the Cartagena conference and was still an option; accordingly, Helleiner recalled it here (Chapter 5), noting that many analysts in developing countries considered the proposal for such a short-term facility inappropriate and felt that it could absorb too large a portion of available resources.

Governance of the Institutions

The issue of the system of governance of the two institutions was raised by several speakers and was the central theme of Moisés Naím's presentation (Chapter 5). He noted that previous conferences relating to the Bretton Woods anniversary had concluded that the Fund and the World Bank suffered from the lack of a precisely defined mission. Although the two institutions had "reinvented themselves several times" in response to new challenges, the most recent example of which was the assistance to countries in transition, the "downside of this flexibility" was a "significant dose of strategic ambiguity" and goal congestion. A primary cause of this problem was the pressure that the two institutions faced from influential constituencies regarding their fundamental role.

The role of shareholders in this "blurred mission" was commented on by several speakers. Singh (Chapter 3) noted the tendency among industrial countries to introduce new objectives under pressure from domestic political constituencies. Many of these new concerns were unobjectionable in themselves but taken together had led to a diffused pattern of World Bank lending. Clausen and Qureshi were equally concerned. Clausen felt (Chapter 4) that the tendency of industrial countries to impose their political agenda on the World Bank could be "disastrous in the extreme," because the true magic of the Bank was its apolitical nature. Qureshi (Chapter 12) argued that in each country the Bank must remain focused on the strategic tasks that will advance its central development role and not pander to political pressures. Lewis T. Preston, in his closing remarks (Chapter 13), responded that this was precisely why selectivity was the first of the Bank's new guiding principles and agreed with Singh that, for this principle to be applied effectively, "we will need the support of our shareholders."

Naím, however, contended that while external pressures were important, an equally important factor was the way decision making at the top was organized in the two institutions. Although the system of governance had undoubtedly resulted in organizations with a high level of technical competence, it was still a candidate for attention and reform. He contended that the balance between shareholders and management was fragile. The Governors of the Fund and the Bank tended to be senior ministers in their governments and too busy to devote attention to the two institutions. The boards of Executive Directors suffered from a "ritualized and symbolic decision-making process in which management receives very little strategic direction." Naím called for reform in the preparation and selection of Executive Directors and for a lower turnover rate. This advice also applied to the President of the World Bank, whose five-year term he saw as too short. Qureshi also questioned the present arrangement whereby "the President of the Bank is always an American and the Managing Director of the Fund is always a European," arguing that it detracted from the "international character and global legitimacy" of the two institutions. Naím observed that the shareholders continued to behave like "absentee owners," becoming interested in their collective property only when they realized that it was under great and evident danger, when it was frequently too late to do anything about it. Preston concurred with the need for greater attention from shareholders, arguing that it was in the Bank's interest for them to play an active role in shaping its future direction.

Some speakers counseled that reform of the Bretton Woods institutions should be pursued within the context of a larger review of the "functioning, role, and coordination of multilateral institutions as a whole" (Solbes, Chapter 13). Following such a review, Solbes suggested, the Bretton Woods institutions would have "a new role in driving and guiding a new concept of global multilateralism with a distribution of political and economic weight quite different from the one that prevailed at Bretton Woods." Helleiner argued (Chapter 5) that such a review should focus on the entire system of international governance. Later, Qureshi (Chapter 12) seemed to agree, arguing that if the United Nations were to be revitalized and restructured, it would become necessary to re-examine how the Bretton Woods institutions could be realigned with the UN system to form a more dynamic alliance to preserve and promote human security. Helleiner maintained that the review currently being undertaken by the Group of Seven on the multilateral system would carry neither a broad sense of ownership nor real legitimacy, and he suggested instead that a representative intergovernmental review along the lines of the 1972–74 Committee of Twenty be undertaken, or at any rate that there be a much more open and consultative process.

The need to strengthen the Interim and Development Committees was also noted. Bergsten (Chapter 3) offered perhaps the most fully formed vision for institutional reform, especially with respect to the IMF. He would reconstitute the Interim Committee as the Council that had been envisaged in the 1978 Amendment to the Articles of Agreement ("twenty years is enough" for an Interim Committee, he proclaimed at the conference); reconstitute the Executive Board as a board of ministerial deputies, meeting several times a year to deal with major policy issues; and establish a board of Alternate Executive Directors, at the same level as the current Executive Board, to conduct the daily business of the Fund. The Development Committee, however, was seen as having been "ineffective and irrelevant" (Helleiner, Chapter 5).

The dominance of the Group of Seven countries in global economic decision making was another major concern. Dobson (Chapter 11) noted that the group is a relatively effective one but lacks political legitimacy, whereas the Interim Committee is relatively legitimate but largely ineffective. She submitted that the Group of Seven could strengthen its own role if it sought to include major developing countries such as India and China within its ranks. Helleiner (Chapter 5) pressed developing countries to seek more influence within the Interim Committee and predicted that the Fund would support such a move.

Conclusions: The Global Roles of the Bretton Woods Institutions

Remarkable consensus emerged among participants that the world owed a debt of gratitude to the founders of the Bretton Woods institutions for establishing "the basic principles . . . that have enabled the institutions to remain . . . flexible and thus to contribute positively to a world inevitably different from the one they expected" (Rahman, Chapter 2), and for creating a "durable framework of multilateral cooperation" in trade and finance (Singh, Chapter 3). Speakers noted the remarkable gains in the developing world in the past 50 years, in both social and economic terms.

"If these institutions are to be judged solely on the basis of the postwar performance of the world economy," Singh noted, "they can legitimately claim credit for a job well done" (Chapter 3).

Several speakers commented on the flexibility that the institutions had shown in response to the diverse challenges they faced. They noted the increased level of coordination as the IMF had accepted greater responsibilities in developing countries, both institutions' close involvement in the problems of the countries in transition from central planning to market economics, and the World Bank's evolution toward support for the private sector and the environment. These evolving roles, "even if not devoid of aspects that are not fully satisfactory" (Solbes, Chapter 13), ensured the continuing relevance of the institutions; indeed, as Prime Minister Felipe González noted in his opening address, "if these institutions did not now exist, they would have to be created" (Chapter 2).

Notwithstanding this praise, many speakers also noted that the institutions must continue to change. Reforms were needed in both institutions if they were to play a positive role and adapt to the vastly changed external environment. Volcker, for example, noted that there "has been a certain loss of youthful enthusiasm and vigor," and a condition has emerged that some describe as "encroaching arteriosclerosis" and others as a "mature recognition of the complexities of the world." He believed that the implied passivity was not justified, and he called for a more prominent role for the two institutions in the years ahead (Chapter 12).

Among the challenges facing the global community that the Bretton Woods institutions were seen as well placed to address (see the remarks by Rahman, Singh, and Solbes in Chapters 2, 3, and 13, respectively) were

- adapting to a global economy characterized by an increasingly open trading system;
- improved monetary coordination and more stable exchange rates;
- continued pursuit of "arduous programs" of stabilization and structural adjustment in many developing economies and countries in transition;
- rapid reduction of poverty in Africa and South Asia;
- protection of the environment; and
- encouragement of private flows to developing countries while reducing the systemic risk of volatility, particularly in portfolio flows.

In examining how the institutions can best meet these challenges, several participants noted both the importance and the difficulty of distinguishing and coordinating the roles of the IMF and the World Bank. Pedro Aspe clearly encapsulated this problem (Chapter 7). The Fund, in his view, should concentrate on "short-term macroeconomic situations," whereas the Bank should focus on "long-term structural transformations," but in doing so, the institutions must recognize that most "macroeconomic imbalances are the result of long-term structural problems." To cope with this increased functional integration, Clausen called for the Fund and the Bank "to develop even stronger ties of cooperation . . . and to work more transparently and more closely with the other development banks" (Chapter 4).

The Bretton Woods institutions, in spite of the enormous volume of material that they publish each year, are not well understood. To counteract that difficulty and to stimulate more open debate, several speakers favored publication of staff reports on consultations between the IMF and member countries. Frenkel (Chapter 11) speculated that countries not wishing to have reports published would quickly come to feel ostracized and would want to join the "club." More fundamentally, Balcerowicz (Chapter 12) argued that the Bretton Woods institutions should see themselves as agents for positive change in open and pluralistic societies. They should not see governments as their exclusive partners but should develop a partnership more broadly with "civil society." On this issue, at least, there was no disagreement. Camdessus observed in his closing address to the conference that the IMF "must be more transparent and open in our work than we have been so far." And Clausen may have best captured the mood of the conference on this issue in concluding that "the world would benefit if both institutions were to extol their virtues a bit more aggressively than their modesty currently permits!"

In sum, the participants in the Madrid conference pointed to a vision in which the Bretton Woods institutions would become clearer and more open in their joint pursuit of the twin objectives of financial stability and sustainable development. Although the separate identities of the Fund and the World Bank are not always easy to discern, each institution was seen as having a vital role to play in assisting governments to cope with the massive changes still under way in the world economy. The two institutions were generally viewed as having responded to the crises of the past half century with skill and flexibility, and the overriding challenge to them now was to retain and strengthen that ability without losing sight of their basic mandates.

References

Bretton Woods Commission, *Bretton Woods: Looking to the Future*, Vol. 1, Commission Report, Staff Review, and Background Papers; and Vol. 2, Conference Proceedings (Washington: Bretton Woods Committee, July 1994).

Camdessus, Michel, *The IMF at Fifty: Facing the Challenges Ahead* (Washington: International Monetary Fund, October 1994).

Griesgraber, Jo Marie, *Rethinking Bretton Woods: Toward Equitable, Sustainable and Participatory Development* (Washington: Center of Concern, 1994).

Kenen, Peter B., ed., *Managing the World Economy: Fifty Years After Bretton Woods* (Washington: Institute for International Economics, 1994).

North-South Roundtable, *The United Nations and the Bretton Woods Institutions: New Challenges for the 21st Century* (New York: Society for International Development, 1993).

United Nations Conference on Trade and Development, *International Monetary and Financial Issues for the 1990s: Proceedings of a Conference Sponsored by the Group of Twenty-Four on the Occasion of the Fiftieth Anniversary of the Bretton Woods Conference* (New York: United Nations, 1994).

World Bank Group, *The World Bank Group: Learning from the Past, Embracing the Future* (Washington: World Bank Group, July 1994).

2

Global Perspectives on the Issues

The opening session of the conference was designed to introduce the issues for discussion from the perspective of the institutions and major policymakers. The conference was convened by M. Saifur Rahman, the Minister of Finance of Bangladesh and the 1994 Chairman of the Boards of Governors of the Fund and the World Bank. His statement was followed by those of the heads of the two Bretton Woods institutions: Michel Camdessus, Managing Director of the IMF, and Lewis T. Preston, President of the World Bank Group. The conference was then officially opened by the Prime Minister of Spain, Felipe González.

M. Saifur Rahman

It is my pleasure as Chairman of the Boards of Governors to welcome all of you to this fiftieth anniversary conference to discuss the future of the IMF and the World Bank. Facing the future and meeting the new challenges call for a review of past experiences and the lessons learned.

Today, we look back over a 50-year period, starting from the point when the most destructive war of all time was just beginning to wind down. Unquestionably, there has been enormous progress. The United Nations Development Program has estimated that the developing countries as a whole achieved a pace of human development in this period three times that attained by the industrial countries a century ago (United Nations Development Program, 1994, p. 1). Significant progress has been achieved on key indicators like infant mortality, overall life expectancy, and adult literacy, with a steady growth in global GDP, which has increased sevenfold. Even though the world population has somewhat more than doubled, per capita GDP has trebled over the course of these 50 years.

Within that overall picture of progress, several aspects most clearly reflect the impact of the Bretton Woods institutions: coordinating management of economic crises, such as the oil shocks of 1973 and 1979 and the Latin American debt crisis of the early 1980s; the rapid spread of physical infrastructure and agricultural technology; the response to changing political environments; and the contributions to the much greater consensus on the merits of the market economy.

We must give great recognition to the wisdom of our forebears at Bretton Woods and our predecessors on the Boards of Governors over the last half century: to the former for establishing the basic principles of organization that have enabled the institutions to remain adaptable and flexible and thus to contribute positively to a world inevitably different from the one they expected, and to the latter for ensuring that the lessons of experience were continuously learned and that adjustments were made in the institutions' policies and procedures.

Fully consistent with the original intent of our architects and illustrative of their success has been the progressive graduation of members from borrower status as they ceased to need direct support for their financial operations. The great expansion of private equity flows to a number of developing countries in recent years can also be seen as the eventual realization of a dream our founders had half a century ago.

Despite dramatic improvements in living standards throughout much of the world over the last 50 years, poverty continues to dominate the lives of more than a billion people. As Lewis Preston has so aptly observed, "the development agenda remains unfinished" (Preston, 1994). Thus, the task ahead is to contribute to the rapid reduction of poverty and to the gradual convergence of living standards and opportunities across the world by assisting lagging countries to meet their peoples' aspirations to attain—and sustain—acceptable levels of human welfare. Accordingly, strategies to address poverty should have a central place in plans for the future of the Bretton Woods institutions.

Within this overriding objective there are of course several interrelated tasks: fulfillment of equal rights and welfare for women; successful management of the vast wave of urbanization that is in store for many of the poorer developing countries; modernization of inefficient systems of public administration to deliver good governance; prevention of Malthusian outcomes from the pressure of rising populations and economic activity on limited natural resources; and resolution of the interstate disputes that arise from increasing economic interdependence and pressure on common resources.

Success in these formidable tasks will demand much more than stock solutions. The history of the past generation has demonstrated dramatically the power and significance of ideas transmitted from one country to another but adapted to the particular situation of the recipient. The rising demand from people in all parts of the world for recognition and participation underscores that such adaptation to local circumstances will be even more important in the future.

From our institutions' experience in helping member countries develop policies and institutions that make investments sustainable, promote growth, and reduce poverty, a number of broad guiding principles have emerged for the future. I would like to spell out a few of them, on which I believe convergence of views between the institutions and the member countries—and between the World Bank and the Fund—will contribute significantly to fulfilling their mandate successfully.

Both institutions should contribute substantially to the open economic debate that is ever more essential in member countries to develop implementable policies. The Bank and the Fund are in a unique position to help because they alone combine familiarity with both the problems that preoccupy us at any particular moment and the persons who have recently wrestled with similar problems in other countries.

Both institutions should give greater attention to local government systems and to legal systems to support member countries' efforts to better protect the rights and interests of the poor and to better reflect them in the design and implementation of development programs. Strengthening local government is critical to the reduction of poverty and to the establishment of a system that is truly accountable to the local electorate. It is also necessary to develop better arrangements for consulting the people potentially affected by the design and impact of programs to be undertaken. I welcome efforts by both the Fund and the Bank in these directions.

'As brought out by the recent debates on what has come to be called "ownership," both institutions must always bear in mind the invaluable lessons of experience: that successful outside intervention in development involves moving at the pace of the people, responding to their needs as they understand them, and reflecting the degree of conviction generated. Also, the intervention should be designed in a manner that seems equitable to the people. The process of preparing such intervention has therefore to be flexibly phased and suited to the institutional, political, and cultural context of the people. '

The fiftieth anniversary of the Bretton Woods institutions has generated widespread interest and has stimulated debates about their achievements and the tasks they have to face to meet the challenges of an increasingly integrated global economic order. These deliberations have spawned a number of useful ideas. Strengthening the governance of the Bretton Woods institutions, increasing their internal efficiency and effectiveness, streamlining the design and processing of projects and programs, emphasizing beneficiary participation, supporting environmentally sustainable development, and promoting private sector and market-oriented development are all desirable goals. We are happy to observe that both the Fund and the Bank have taken commendable steps in these directions.

. As the world economy becomes more integrated, the global financial system is increasingly influenced by the economic policies of major industrial nations. Unsatisfactory international economic situations in the recent past can be attributed to weak policy coordination among the major industrial countries. I support the view that these countries should strengthen their fiscal and monetary policies, achieve greater macroeconomic convergence, and establish a more formal system of coordination. The IMF should undertake this coordination function by exercising effective surveillance over the macroeconomic policies of these countries (Bretton Woods Commission, 1994, p. A-1).

Although private equity flows to a number of developing countries have increased in recent years, the poorest among them have yet to benefit from such a resource flow. These countries continue to need official development assistance for investment in infrastructure and human resource development. I therefore strongly support the view that International Development Association resources should be solely devoted to the poorest and least developed countries with weak institutional and technical capabilities (Bretton Woods Commission, 1994, p. A-9).

The success of the programs and projects of both the World Bank and the Fund will largely depend on the commitment of the member country concerned to the pace of social and economic changes. Our vision of the future is inspired by our firm and unequivocal commitment to freeing the vast masses of humanity from the curse of poverty and the pains and indignity that it entails, and to preserving and indeed enriching the global environment to make our planet more habitable.

In conclusion, I would like to thank those who have organized this conference and congratulate them on the preparation of a stimulating agenda, which will, I hope, generate many new and bright ideas for the meaningful future of these remarkable institutions. I look forward very much to the outcome of these deliberations.

References

Bretton Woods Commission, *Bretton Woods: Looking to the Future*, Vol. 1, Commission Report, Staff Review, and Background Papers (Washington: Bretton Woods Committee, July 1994).

United Nations Development Program, *Human Development Report, 1994* (New York: Oxford University Press for the United Nations Development Program, 1994).

Preston, Lewis T., President, the World Bank, Opening Remarks to Press Conference, "Learning from the Past, Embracing the Future" (July 19, 1994).

Michel Camdessus

It is my pleasure to welcome you to this conference on behalf of the IMF. We are commemorating an international economic conference that has proved to be of unrivalled importance because of both the agreement it produced and the benefits that the working out of that agreement have brought to the world. Mr. Rahman has mentioned the unprecedented economic progress of the past 50 years, and few would question that the multilateral economic cooperation born at Bretton Woods has contributed vitally to it. In fact, it now seems so obvious that the institutional structure created at Bretton Woods was needed by the

world that it is difficult to comprehend, and easy to forget, the oppo
tion the founders faced. A distinguished historian of the negotiations
who is with us here today—Ambassador Gardner—has called the
agreement a "miracle" because of the opposition to multilateral economic cooperation that was prevalent at the time on both sides of the
Atlantic. As he has written, the agreement was made possible in part by
leaders of vision "surrounded by dedicated internationalists of great intellectual ability." Several of those dedicated internationalists are here
with us this morning, and it is a privilege to salute them. The achievement of those who contributed to the Bretton Woods agreement is a continuing source of inspiration and encouragement for all of us working
to advance the cause of international economic cooperation.

Over the past 50 years, the IMF's role and activities have grown and
changed dramatically. This is not because its purposes have changed: its
statutory purposes, set out in the Articles, are the same as when they
were formulated 50 years ago. We all know them well. In fact, some of us
carry them around in our pockets! They remain equally valid today, and
in fact they have become even more relevant as growing economic interdependence among nations has increased the need for international cooperation on economic and monetary issues. But for the fulfillment of
these purposes, the IMF has had to adapt its operations to a changing
world economy and in the light of lessons learned about economic policy.

In the world economy, we have seen, for example, the emergence and
increasing role of developing countries; a trend toward greater symmetry in economic size among the industrial countries of North America,
Europe, and Asia and an associated trend toward shared leadership
among them; the emergence of a multicurrency system of reserve assets;
increasing international integration of markets, especially financial
markets; a trend toward regional integration in many parts of the
world; and the integration of the former centrally planned economies
into the world market economic system and the Fund itself. Dramatic
changes indeed! Of course, some of these changes have been assisted by
the work of the Fund and the World Bank, since by promoting an open,
multilateral system of trade and payments and policies of adjustment
and reform, the institutions have contributed to the international integration of markets, to postwar prosperity, and to the demonstrated success of market-oriented economic systems.

Then there are the lessons of five decades about economic policy: for
example, that restrictions on capital movements are less useful and
more damaging than they were viewed 50 years ago; that macroeconomic policies need to be conducted within a medium-term framework
of monetary stability and fiscal discipline, and supported by structural
policies, even for the most basic macroeconomic objectives (such as
high levels of employment) to be attained; that the institutional capacity
to design and implement policy is a major determinant of success; and

finally, that although pegged exchange rate arrangements—albeit with some flexibility—do have distinct advantages, the requirements of maintaining such arrangements are demanding.

The Fund has had to adapt to these lessons and changes. First, it has adapted its role in the exchange rate system. Following the collapse of the par value system, the right of members to choose their own exchange arrangements was recognized by the Second Amendment of the Articles in 1978. The Fund was given responsibility for overseeing the international monetary system and the policies of members in order to promote a stable system of exchange rates. Surveillance, convergence, and cooperation became the building blocks on which exchange stability and the proper functioning of the international monetary system had to be established. Fund surveillance has thus become an even more challenging task.

Second, as the industrial countries have increased their reliance on growing private capital markets for balance of payments financing and been more willing to allow their exchange rates to change, the Fund's financial assistance has become concentrated on developing countries and countries in transition. In addition, new financing facilities have been created to take account of the need for medium-term policy programs, structural reforms, concessionality for low-income countries, and special help for the economies in transition to shift to multilateral, market-based trade. These adaptations have enabled the Fund to continue providing balance of payments support as its membership has expanded and changed in composition, and as the world has evolved.

Third, technical assistance and training by the Fund in its areas of expertise began in earnest in the early 1960s with the burgeoning of newly independent developing countries and has grown dramatically in recent years, especially to help with institution building and policy implementation in the countries in transition.

These are some of the ways in which the Fund has had to adapt in order to continue serving its membership and its unchanged purposes.

I have been speaking about the past. But this conference is concerned with the future. At present, there are many black spots in the global picture, and, at times, when we see how difficult it is to put together an adequate response to new challenges, we could ask ourselves: Where is the spirit of Bretton Woods? What would our founders have said? What would our founders have said, in 1994, on seeing that unemployment in Europe is at its highest levels since the 1930s; on seeing the industrial countries' hesitation in reciprocating the dismantling of trade barriers by developing countries? I will stop this list of impertinent questions here. Yes, we face many challenges as we enter our second half century. Let me mention a few of the questions we at the Fund face—perhaps they will enter into your deliberations over the next two days:

- How can Fund surveillance be strengthened further, in order to promote greater stability in markets and ensure that the increased economic interdependence of countries is more effectively translated into a positive-sum game?
- Should the Fund pursue more keenly a return to pegged exchange arrangements among the industrial countries?
- Should the Fund encourage more actively the liberalization of capital account restrictions?
- A number of countries that have been implementing strategies of adjustment and reform have yet to see much reward in terms of faster growth: how can the growth-generating effects of our programs be speeded up?
- Do the Fund's financing facilities need to be adapted to suit the needs of the membership in our new world of globalized markets?
- How should the role of the SDR evolve, given the objective, stated in the Articles, of making it the world's principal reserve asset?

Some of these questions will doubtless be addressed by the Governors in their meetings over the next week. I shall be most interested in the views expressed by the distinguished participants in this conference on these and other issues, before offering you my thoughts and reactions at the end of our work tomorrow.

Our fiftieth anniversary is providing an extremely productive stimulus to reflection on our past and our future. This conference is a central event in our celebrations, and I am sure it will be a rewarding experience for us all.

Lewis T. Preston

I would like to thank Prime Minister Felipe González for being so generous with his time today and the Government and people of Spain for their warm hospitality. I would also like to join in welcoming all of you—many of whom have contributed so much to development—to this conference.

Importance of Flexibility

This is an occasion to praise the visionaries at Bretton Woods. Perhaps their greatest achievement was the flexibility they allowed the World Bank: to become global in its membership; to evolve into the World Bank "Group"—establishing the International Development Association (IDA), the International Finance Corporation (IFC), and the Multilateral

Investment Guarantee Agency (MIGA); to leverage about $10 billion in paid-in capital into more than $300 billion in loans and credits; and to support over 6,000 projects in over 140 countries with financing and—equally important—with objective advice.

This flexibility has enabled us to help our members respond to diverse challenges: from assisting postwar reconstruction in Europe and Japan to boosting food production in South Asia; from assisting the newly independent nations of Africa to helping Latin America overcome the debt crisis; from supporting China's integration into the global economy to assisting the transition economies in Central and Eastern Europe and the former Soviet Union.

Flexibility has been the key to the World Bank Group's effectiveness in the past. It is our most powerful asset as we think about how best to serve our members in the future.

Fifty Years of Development Experience

The delegates at Bretton Woods could not have predicted the speed or scope of development progress over the past 50 years. Life expectancy in the developing countries has improved more than during the entire previous span of human history; child mortality has been reduced by two thirds; a disease like smallpox, which was killing 5 million people a year in 1950, has been eradicated; average per capita incomes in the developing world have doubled; the GDPs of some economies have quintupled; the developing nations have become increasingly integrated into the global economy; and large numbers of people have been able to lift themselves out of poverty. In the process, the world has united as never before to support development. The Bretton Woods institutions played a major role in financing and coordinating this support.

The development effort has been a success. But it could have been even more effective had we known at the outset what we know today. Until relatively recently, there was excessive trust in the capacity of governments to manage activities that the private sector can undertake more efficiently; protectionism too often won out over competition; insufficient attention was paid to the environment; primary education was underrated; and women were not allowed enough access to development opportunities.

In the 1960s, many economists were more optimistic about sub-Saharan Africa than East Asia. Yet East Asia proved to be the "miracle" of the developing world—and sub-Saharan Africa its most daunting challenge. It is the only region where poverty is projected to increase by the end of this century. It is not, however, the only region where poverty remains pervasive. Over a billion people still struggle to survive on about a dollar a day.

Major Challenges

There are certain fundamental components that can help to achieve rapid and sustainable development. Applying these common elements across a range of increasingly diverse country circumstances is the great challenge facing us all.

First, we know that people are the means and the ends of development. Investment in human resources is linked to productivity and employment, as well as to slowing population growth rates and accelerating poverty reduction. Education is the building block. No nation has managed to take off economically with a literacy rate of less than 50 percent. Institutional strength and a country's ability to compete in a rapidly changing world depend on its trained people.

Yet too many countries still invest far too little in their people. Almost one hundred million girls in the developing countries never get the chance to go to school. Early childhood development should be given much higher priority, and we must commit ourselves to the goal of universal primary education within the next generation.

Second, good policies are crucial: macroeconomic stability; openness to trade, investment, and technology; and adequate social and physical infrastructures. The critical role of good policies is encouraging, because it implies that countries that have not so far prospered can do so. Countries like Ghana, Uganda, and others in sub-Saharan Africa that have stayed the course of reform are seeing signs of success.

Liberalizing an economy, however, brings its own set of challenges. As markets expand, a country's institutional capacities—legal, financial, and regulatory—need to keep up; safety nets must be in place to protect vulnerable groups; and the pace of reform has to be governed by a country's own view of what is practical. Mexico and Poland, for example, have shown the benefits of speed. China, however, demonstrates that a more gradual approach can also be effective. But whatever the sequencing, a country's commitment to continuous structural change is essential—as is the building of a consensus to support it.

Redefining the roles of state and market is the third challenge. Governments cannot do everything, so they must focus on what is essential. A healthy private sector reduces the burden on government; it broadens participation in the running of an economy; it attracts savings—domestic and foreign—to sound investment; and it promotes growth and jobs.

The revolution in economic management in the developing countries is well under way, but it is still far from complete. We must do more to nurture private sector growth, because that will enable more countries to become competitive and to integrate into the global economy. Experience tells us that this integration offers the best hope of prosperity. This places a premium on measures to open up world trade—particularly through speedy ratification of the Uruguay Round and by helping to bring the countries of Central and Eastern Europe and the former Soviet Union fully into the international trading system.

The fourth challenge is environmental sustainability. Two billion people in the developing world are without adequate sanitation; four million children died last year from acute respiratory diseases brought on by air pollution; almost another four million died from diarrheal diseases caused by dirty drinking water. These issues must be given priority on the environmental agenda.

We have learned that poverty reduction and environmental protection are mutually reinforcing. We must do more to act upon that knowledge.

It seems to me that another major lesson of development experience is that economics—by itself—is not enough. Good governance is imperative—accountability, transparency, and the rule of law. People must be allowed to participate in the decisions and actions that affect their lives. Resources must be allocated and used efficiently. For example, the developing countries currently spend as much on arms as they do on education. It should also be noted, of course, that the industrial countries spend ten times more on arms than they do on development assistance. This must change.

Ultimately, development can only come from within. Aid—when it is used efficiently—can help to supplement it. Twenty countries have now graduated from IDA. One of these is the Republic of Korea, extremely poor in the 1960s but today a vibrant economy, able to rely on its own savings and private capital for continued growth. This is an example of development assistance at its best. We should recognize, however, that without internal commitment neither external financing nor advice can transform economies.

Role of the World Bank

The task before the development community now is to implement what we have learned. The World Bank Group is well positioned to help. We have a long-term association with virtually every developing nation, a wealth of cross-country experience, and a service that combines finance—for public and private investment—and advice. We can tailor that service to individual country needs.

Like them, however, we too must adapt to change. Yes, the World Bank Group has been flexible in the past. But given the rapidly changing global environment—and the increasing diversity of our membership—we must be even more flexible in the future:

- To strengthen our focus, we must be more selective in the tasks we undertake;
- To enhance our impact—and that of others engaged in development—we must expand and deepen our partnerships;

• To increase our responsiveness, we must be even more cost-efficient and dedicated to excellence.

A development institution can ensure its credibility only if it is effective where it matters most: by getting results on the ground.

Conclusion

On this fiftieth anniversary of Bretton Woods, we have a tremendous opportunity to make rapid and sustainable development progress. Global links between the rich and poor countries are much stronger than they were five decades ago; policymakers have a better understanding of the options for development; and there is more agreement about what needs to be done. Now we need to do it.

Felipe González

I would like to welcome you cordially to Spain on this first opportunity I have to meet with you all. I thank you on behalf of the Spanish Government for having chosen to hold this conference in our country, and I am personally grateful for your kindness in inviting me to open this commemorative conference on 50 years after Bretton Woods.

I think that commemorative sessions are of interest when they are an opportunity to reflect on the future through past experience. The purpose of my remarks today will be to take a look at the tasks that await us and the challenges of our societies to attain, through our financial, economic, and monetary institutions, the development and well-being of our peoples.

Please allow me, both as a Spaniard and as a repository of governmental responsibility granted to me by the people, to make a brief introduction. Fifty years ago, Spain was not at the Bretton Woods conference, nor was it at the birth of the United Nations. Fifty years ago, our country was enduring the pain of profound wounds from a cruel civil confrontation and was slipping along a path of authoritarianism and isolation.

Today, Spain welcomes the meetings of the International Monetary Fund and the World Bank; today, Spain is an active, decisive member of the European Union. Today, my country participates in solidarity with United Nations peace missions and sits on the Security Council. Today, Spain is a country that is growing and developing in liberty, a country that has made democracy and the protection of human rights the basic principles of its coexistence. It has opened windows to the world in efforts to modernize its economy, becoming part of global financial and trade flows.

The Spanish people have made a tremendous effort to get this far. Fifty years ago, we were not able to collaborate. Today, we want to contribute to designing the future with the conviction that the world is increasingly interdependent and that we need to cooperate intensively.

In the last five years, political changes have decisively altered the framework of international relations, making interdependence an obvious and daily phenomenon. Today, we have common challenges that we must face in a coordinated fashion. We have shared problems that require solutions negotiated by all; above all, we have the obligation to cooperate, to the extent of our possibilities, to bring about a future worthy of the men and women of our societies.

President Franklin D. Roosevelt, a few days before the Bretton Woods conference, said that the situation of each country should be of interest to all of its neighbors, from the closest to the most remote; no country could face on its own the economic, financial, and employment problems shared by all nations.

It is not strange, therefore, to see that the spirit of interrelationship is embodied in the Articles of Agreement that were the origins of the International Monetary Fund and the World Bank. If we take a jump forward in history to the present, we see that no one would argue with the need to coordinate our actions around institutions with proven efficacy in their performance, in the context of growing international interdependence. I would like to emphasize this point further.

The experience of Fund and Bank operations offers us, in general terms, a clearly positive balance sheet. There are, of course, concrete aspects that could be improved and others that have not shown sufficient progress in favor of the international community. However, let us imagine for a moment how international economic relations would have developed had there been no institutions born at Bretton Woods.

At the risk of appearing utopic, I daresay that our conclusion would probably be that, if these institutions did not now exist, they would have to be created. The transformations that have taken place have challenged the ability of the International Monetary Fund and the World Bank to adapt to changing circumstances. Once again, we can see light and shade, but on balance, the ability to react to resolve new problems that have arisen over the years seems to me to be positive as well.

If this fiftieth anniversary had been held only a few years ago, perhaps our reflections might have been very different from today's. Perhaps at that time we might have had a debate with more ideological tones. Today, however, we can focus on how the institutions function, and we can discuss their various reforms and their capacity to adapt to a world situation very different from the one existing only seven or eight years ago.

If we take as an example the International Monetary Fund, we see that its role has been gradually evolving. It has essentially moved from being an institution fundamentally devoted to international financial order and for industrial countries to assuming a more active role with developing countries in general and with the middle-income countries in particular.

Developing countries have found in the Fund an institution able to provide and sometimes impose economic criteria that have allowed them to overcome situations, such as external debt, which until very recently overwhelmed their economies, and the Fund has helped lead them to sustainable economic growth. Other developing countries have been able to find in the Fund a guide to obtain technical advice and support in correcting patterns of behavior that are detrimental to economic stability.

All this is occurring in a framework of greater transparency and information about financial institutions, a trend that must be continued, because it can only benefit nations that are cooperating in the search for stability and development.

The industrial countries have in recent years gone through a series of economic crises from which we are evolving slowly. New flows of assistance to the most needy areas are therefore required. In recent years, in Latin America, with democracy and freedom, we have seen the growth of economic viability and the development of regional integration, which is providing stability and a sense of a future for countries that were severely criticized in the 1980s.

Both the International Monetary Fund and the World Bank have helped in this process. They have contributed substantially to this improvement. The credibility of adjustment programs designed by the Fund and agreed to with governments enabled the confidence of financial markets to be restored. On its side, the World Bank has achieved efficiency in financing projects to modernize the basic infrastructure for development.

Spectacular economic growth in numerous Asian and Pacific countries should not allow us to lose sight of the need to pay attention to the overall economic and social development of these countries. They must be included in world trade flows and must be considered in the design of generally applied trade rules and related economic policies, to achieve more homogeneous societies and sustainable development.

In other areas of the world, poverty and underdevelopment persist. Despite the efforts of the Fund and the World Bank and the cooperation of the European Union and other institutions, per capita income is not only not increasing—it is declining. We must therefore be more demanding in our work. We must contribute to creating the conditions necessary for development.

Each country, according to its own responsibility, must understand that an effort in solidarity is needed. Some countries need to point their societies and their leaders in the right direction toward joint development and not the individual wealth of a few. Others must provide these societies with the access to resources needed on the longed-for path to development.

Exactly two years ago, speculation in foreign exchange markets in a few hours brought about capital flows of such magnitudes that they endangered or even exhausted the foreign exchange reserves of many countries. Simple market forces showed that a sovereign nation in isolation does not have sufficient resources to face the pressures of a worldwide economy. This must be, no doubt, a source of reflection at this fiftieth anniversary conference. The experience of the current European Union must be part of this reflection: we have decided, as a group of industrial countries, to embark on an ambitious project, based on principles of economic convergence and harmonized behavior.

If we in the European Union are able to achieve the objective that we have set for ourselves and create an economic, monetary, and political union, this will without doubt be a fundamental element in strengthening the shared leadership that is so necessary at this time. The European Union is certainly already providing an important pillar, but its role in the future may be extraordinarily strengthened when we achieve our objectives.

Since our integration into the European Community in 1986, Spain has played an active role in all European projects. Our intention is to continue along these lines and, to the degree that we can, strengthen our constructive attitude to be among those countries at the forefront. From the European Union, and along with other associates, we must find a way to reconcile multilateralism with protection of the environment. We must make flexible labor relations—and the very necessary creation of employment—compatible with the upkeep of welfare societies. We must find ways to stimulate the initiative of private enterprise while protecting the most needy and ensure that population growth is not an obstacle to development.

In all these challenges, and in many others that could be mentioned, the role of the institutions will be decisive. Fifty years ago, it was necessary to organize the postwar period. Today, we have to organize the world that resulted from the end of the Cold War. We have the experience of these 50 years behind us; we need now to add to it the spirit of cooperation and collaboration that existed among those who started the whole process of internationalization of the economy.

At this time of economic recovery, everyone is looking toward the work that this conference will be undertaking in the coming days. Your words, your analyses, and your conclusions will be an important incentive to responsible agents in economics and in politics, and to citizens in general. In the years I have been in government, I have learned that in economics, expectations are almost more important than the data. This is why I encourage you to carry out your task in such a way that at the end of your project we may know more about economic reality. That knowledge will enable us to make the best use of recovery opportunities, and, with cooperation from all countries, we may achieve a fairer world in solidarity.

3

The IMF and the World Bank in an Evolving World

This session featured two speakers from major countries who have played active and important roles in their countries for many years. The first speaker was Manmohan Singh, the Finance Minister of India and one of the chief architects of India's recent economic reform program. He was followed by C. Fred Bergsten, the founder and Director of the Institute for International Economics and a former Assistant Secretary of the U.S. Treasury Department. After they addressed the global issues affecting the Bretton Woods institutions from their unique perspectives, the Chairman of the session—Lamberto Dini, Minister of the Treasury of Italy—offered an overview and synthesis of the suggestions presented. The speakers then responded to a number of questions and comments raised by other participants.

Manmohan Singh

When I was invited to speak at this conference, I accepted with great pleasure. Fiftieth anniversaries are festive occasions when old friends gather to relive pleasant memories, to rejoice and felicitate. I have been privileged, in various capacities in the Government of India, to deal with the Bretton Woods institutions for almost half of the 50 years we are commemorating today. I have innumerable pleasant memories and old friends associated with these institutions and it is therefore a particular pleasure to be part of this celebration.

Twoscore and ten years is not a very long time for historians, but it is time enough to reflect on the achievements of institutions and draw new blueprints for the future. The world has changed beyond recognition since the Bretton Woods conference gave birth to the Fund and the World Bank. Superpower rivalry, which was a dominant force until recently, has evaporated, and the threat of a global military conflagration is lower than it has ever been in living memory. From only a handful of developing country members at inception, the Bretton Woods institutions now have some one hundred and thirty. Instead of a world divided into market economies on the one hand and centrally planned economies on the other, we now have a truly global economy, of which all countries are a part.

The world has not just changed, it has also prospered. World output has grown faster than ever before in the half century since Bretton Woods, and world trade has grown even faster than output, increasing global interdependence. The developing world has shared in this prosperity. Some developing countries have shown spectacular performance and many others are moving confidently down the same path. Unfortunately, progress has not been even. Growth in many countries has been slow, and there is clear evidence of serious retrogression in the 1980s in sub-Saharan Africa and parts of Latin America.

These positive developments cannot be ascribed to any one cause. They are the result of several factors, economic and noneconomic, internal and external, operating differently in different countries. However, there is little doubt that one of the reasons for rising prosperity in this period has been the durable framework of multilateral cooperation in trade and international finance, supervised by the General Agreement on Tariffs and Trade (GATT) on the one hand and the Bretton Woods institutions on the other. If these institutions are to be judged solely on the basis of the postwar performance of the world economy, they can legitimately claim credit for a job well done.

In a changing world, institutions must necessarily adapt to changing circumstances and the Bretton Woods institutions are no exception to this rule. In fact, the record of the past 50 years clearly shows that these institutions have already changed considerably since their creation. It is therefore appropriate that the fiftieth anniversary should be an occasion to ask questions about the future role of the Fund and the World Bank in the light of the current world situation and emerging challenges in the future.

The challenges before us, in my view, are the following:

- If there is one single factor that explains the success of the postwar world economy, it is the sustained expansion of world trade. The international community must therefore give the highest priority to maintaining an open trading system. The world needs credible assurances that the growing trade rivalries between the United States, Europe, and Japan will not be permitted to undermine the open, multilateral, and nondiscriminatory world trading system.
- The problem of the persistent high level of unemployment in the industrial world must be addressed in a manner that promotes the growth of world output close to its underlying potential.
- The arduous programs of stabilization and structural economic reform that have been launched in dozens of developing countries over the past decade must be assisted to a successful conclusion, which calls for assured access to markets and access to finance on reasonable terms. The world economic system must provide devel-

oping countries with the economic space they need to enable them to pursue successfully outward-oriented trade and development strategies. It is an irony of our times that as developing countries are opening up their economies, the voices of protectionism, disguised in one form or another, are gaining respectability in the industrial world.

- Special efforts must be undertaken to strengthen the development process in sub-Saharan Africa and parts of South Asia, where abject poverty is most prevalent and the case for assistance is strongest.
- Ways must be found to ensure an orderly integration of the transition economies of Central and Eastern Europe into the global economic system.
- Ways must be found to reduce systemic risk in the burgeoning markets for international private capital and finance, especially in relation to portfolio flows, while strengthening private direct investment flows toward developing countries.
- International cooperation to preserve and protect the environmental heritage of our planet must be strengthened with suitable financial and technical support over the medium term.

These priorities call for concerted action by the international community on several fronts and in several different forums. They also have implications for the role of the Fund and the World Bank in the future.

Role of the IMF

There is a view that the IMF has not much relevance in a world characterized by floating exchange rates, the predominant role of the private sector in the provision of international liquidity, and the rise of such exclusive clubs as the Group of Seven for coordinating macroeconomic policies of major industrial countries. To my mind, the progressive reduction in the role of the Fund, particularly in matters involving effective surveillance of macroeconomic policies of major industrial countries, is a matter of regret, and the trend needs to be reversed.

The Fund was created to supervise the system of fixed but adjustable exchange rates and to support it as a lender of last resort. The system worked well for a while but it came under severe strain in the early 1970s and was soon abandoned as the major players moved to a system of floating exchange rates. The new system, combined with an explosive growth of private flows in global capital markets freed from exchange controls, made the Fund's role as a lender of last resort irrelevant for countries accounting for three fourths of world trade. No industrial country has borrowed from the Fund since the late 1970s, and the

Fund's lending activity has concentrated on developing countries and more recently has extended to the economies in transition.

The expectation that a regime of generalized floating exchange rates would enable countries to pursue independent macroeconomic policies in line with their domestic objectives has not materialized. In practice, exchange rates have been characterized by pronounced and prolonged deviation from the fundamentals, and there has been excessive volatility, all of which has imposed significant economic costs. Indeed, floating exchange rates make coordination of macroeconomic policies among the major countries even more important than earlier. This should have meant a strengthening of the surveillance function of the Fund, but this has not happened. The truth is that the task of coordination is not being performed as much as it should be in any forum. Attempts at coordination through the exclusive groupings of major industrial countries such as the Group of Seven, or in even smaller groupings, have achieved only limited success.

The experience with the non-system that has been in place since the mid-1970s does not inspire confidence that it represents a viable long-term arrangement. It has led to increased uncertainty in the world trading environment, growing volatility of exchange rates and capital flows, and a slowdown in the growth of world trade and output. I believe that today, more than ever before, we need a truly multilateral mechanism, above and beyond national instruments, for monetary coordination and stabilization of exchange rates. The GATT-Bretton Woods system, described as "unilateral global Keynesianism," worked well until the early 1970s largely because the United States was single-handedly prepared to direct and maintain the system. As the world became economically multipolar, the United States was neither willing nor able to perform that role. And yet there is clearly a need for effective coordination of macroeconomic policies of major developed countries for a successful and orderly functioning of a multipolar, increasingly open, and interdependent world economy.

The world community would gain by using the Fund as the principal forum for multilateral surveillance and coordination of national fiscal and monetary policies. An act of statesmanship on the part of the major industrial countries is called for, since the line between coordination and loss of sovereignty is thin. But if interdependence is to have any meaning, it should be possible to accept multilateral surveillance and discipline. We need to give the Fund a new political mandate. The developing countries have a particularly strong stake in this development, as it is only in a multilateral forum that major countries' policies are likely to be coordinated in a manner that accords due weight to the impact and implications of these policies on the rest of the world community.

Questions are also sometimes raised on whether the financing role played by the Fund should continue. I have no doubt it should. The financing role may have become irrelevant for the industrial countries, but it will undoubtedly remain highly relevant for the vast majority of developing countries and economies in transition for many years to come. It will take time before these countries are sufficiently integrated into world capital markets to be able to access the pool of liquidity available in the world, or at least to access it on reasonable terms. Until that time, they will need the assurance of the facilities provided by the Fund to correct maladjustments that may arise in their balance of payments, without resorting to measures that could be detrimental to national or international economic interests.

The growing integration of the world's money and capital markets and the inevitable increased role of private capital flows can at times greatly complicate the task of orderly economic management, particularly in developing countries with limited policy instruments at their disposal. One has to take particular note of the volatility and unpredictability of portfolio capital flows. The world needs credible international safety nets that, while preserving the freedom of capital markets, will ensure that "enterprise does not become a bubble in the whirlpool of speculation." Countries pursuing sound domestic policies ought to be able to rely on the IMF for timely help to protect the integrity of their development programs in the face of sudden outflows of private capital.

Over the years, the Fund has attempted to adjust the nature of its facilities, as well as its approach to conditionality, to improve its effectiveness as a lender for developing countries and economies in transition. It has moved away from an exclusive concern with stabilization in the design of programs to an explicit recognition of the need to protect growth. It has also recognized the need for adjustment to be stretched over a longer period. A new concern, which it must now address, is the need to design adjustment programs that avoid adverse distributional effects. In practice, this poses difficult trade-offs that may in many cases warrant a more gradual path of adjustment. These are difficult issues, and there are no ready solutions. It is to the credit of the Fund that it has shown flexibility in assisting many developing countries, my own included, at critical times. However, there is considerable scope for improvement. In the rapidly changing and uncertain world that we live in, the Fund must develop greater flexibility to respond purposefully and quickly to fast-changing economic conditions.

Role of the World Bank

Let me now turn to the role of the World Bank. The Bank too has changed over time in response to changing circumstances. It graduated very quickly from its original role of reconstruction in Europe to become the world's premier international development bank, responsible for channeling long-term loans to developing countries. The establishment of the International Development Association (IDA) in 1960 meant a significant enhancement of the World Bank Group's capacity to assist low-income countries. In the 1960s and the early 1970s, the World Bank lending program expanded rapidly, with an increase in resource transfers to developing countries. Bank flows were also a significant portion of total flows to many developing countries. The situation has changed very substantially since then. Bank lending in real terms has not increased since the early 1980s, and net resource flows have since turned negative. IDA flows have also not increased commensurate with need. Meanwhile, private flows to developing countries have expanded dramatically to swamp official and multilateral flows.

The World Bank has adjusted to these developments by altering the nature of its lending, especially by shifting from traditional project finance to policy-based lending. This shift enabled it—often in combination with the Fund—to provide quick-disbursing assistance to countries facing severe balance of payments problems in the 1980s. However, policy-based lending has posed its own problems. From the perspective of borrowers, it is often difficult to agree to wide-ranging policy conditionalities as part of a lending program even when many of these conditionalities may be in tune with the borrowers' own perceptions. Adjustment programs must be seen to be home-grown to be fully accepted. From the side of the donor countries, policy-based lending has been subjected to growing pressure to add new policy objectives that such lending must achieve. All this is made more difficult because the resources being made available to the Bank are not increasing, and tighter conditionality is therefore often seen as a device to ration scarce resources rather than as an effort to increase the effectiveness of assistance.

What should be the role of the World Bank Group in the future? First, a word about IDA, which is of particular importance for the low-income countries. In a world of massive income disparities among nations, in which fully a fourth of the world's population still lives in abject poverty, the ameliorative role of concessional multilateral development assistance, as provided by IDA, is self-evident. The issue is one of commitment. IDA has played a role in some of the major achievements of developing countries.

In India, IDA assistance was part of the effort launched by the Government of India almost 30 years ago that led to the Green Revolution and food self-sufficiency. Even today, IDA must provide critically needed finance for social infrastructure, human resource development, and the environment— all sectors that need large injections of resources in many countries and where the outcome cannot be left to market forces. However, the scale of assistance being provided by IDA is modest compared with the enormous need. If the international community is serious about the goal of eradicating the blight of poverty from our planet, there can be no better instrument than an expanded IDA commitment for the next two decades.

Turning to the World Bank itself, its role as a source of capital has been questioned in some circles on the grounds that private capital flows now amply meet the needs of developing countries. The growth of international private capital markets is undoubtedly a very important positive development for developing countries, and it is gratifying that most countries are tailoring their policies to maximize access to these flows. We must recognize, however, that the overwhelming bulk of private capital flows to the developing world are concentrated in about a score of countries. For all the other developing countries, and also the economies in transition, access to international private capital is still highly restricted or nonexistent. In all these countries, substantial lending by the World Bank will remain essential for many years to come as an assured supply of long-term capital. Indeed, with most of these countries undergoing major economic reform, it is not difficult to sketch a larger—and not a diminished—need for the World Bank Group to sustain and support investments for development, particularly in the expansion of infrastructure facilities.

I do not see any contradiction in the expansion of activity by the World Bank or the International Finance Corporation (IFC) and the expansion of private sector lending or private investment flows. On the contrary, I see these processes as complementary and mutually reinforcing. After all, the Bank and the IFC are themselves intermediaries of private capital and provide a valuable service to savers and investors in the private sector at very little public cost.

An important feature of the past decade or so is the remarkable convergence of policies followed by different developing countries all over the world. This convergence has resulted from greater knowledge of what policies have worked well in different situations. The World Bank is uniquely placed to promote greater awareness of the best practices and to disseminate this knowledge effectively to its member countries through its operations and development dialogue. As developing countries open up their economies and integrate with the world, there will be much greater need for such information as an aid to policy. The Bank can play an important role in meeting this need. However, it must also show a greater awareness of the need to keep in mind country-specific characteristics in devising appropriate strategies. Reform of economic policies has to be accompanied by institutional reforms, which, in turn, require not only legislative change, but more important, change in attitudes and mindsets, all of which take time. Impatient reformers must not forget that complex societies cannot be turned around overnight.

It is generally accepted that the World Bank Group can play a valuable part in promoting environmentally sound programs and policies in its member countries. What is not equally well recognized is that any credible effort at protecting the environment will require massive investments. The Bank should therefore be properly equipped if it is to play a significant role, and this means the ability to deploy much larger resources for environmentally sound development. It is particularly important to ensure that a concern with the environment does not take the form of obstructing development and thus letting the poor remain poor. Poverty is often the root cause of environmental damage, and poverty cannot be overcome without providing more electricity, more water, more food, and more work for the world's poor. All this requires more investments and more lending, not less. Nor should genuine concerns about the environment and the need for improving social conditions in poor countries be allowed to become vehicles for protectionism in international trade. That would cause a setback to the cause of social and environmental progress in developing nations. Environmental protection measures must also take into account the social and cultural factors, the stage of development, and the administrative capacities of developing countries. Much more work is needed to transform the Rio conference's vision of sustainable development from a mere buzzword to an operationally effective strategy of human development. The Bank is well placed to perform this task.

Finally, the World Bank of the future must return to a more focused set of priorities and activities. The past several years have witnessed a paradoxical development, in which a widening of the mandate of the Bank is sought by including new objectives to guide Bank policy even as the material resources made available to it are kept on a tight leash. A tendency has developed among industrial country shareholders to introduce new objectives under pressure from one or another domestic political constituency. Many of these concerns are in themselves unobjectionable and respond to important and legitimate interests and concerns. But when directly introduced to influence the Bank's lending priorities, they lead to a too diffused pattern of lending, whose impact on development in the recipient countries is far from certain or beneficial. The effectiveness of the World Bank as an international institution depends upon a measure of self-restraint by all shareholders to refrain from using the Bank to promote all objectives. A strengthened United Nations system would be a more appropriate forum for reaching consensus on political and social issues of general concern.

I remain a firm believer in the virtues of international cooperation. The Bretton Woods institutions can serve as vital instruments for realizing our vision of one world in which all the citizens of the world have an equal opportunity to lead productive and purposeful lives. The future is ours to make; let us prepare for it now.

C. Fred Bergsten

My view on the future role of the IMF is based on an analysis of the need to remedy the severe weaknesses of the international monetary system and the inadequate institutional underpinnings of that system.

My conclusion is that the Fund of the twenty-first century should seek to correct those weaknesses by becoming the steward of a system of currency target zones that could evolve, over time, into an effective regime of policy cooperation at least among the major industrial countries.

I will try to make the case for such a system and indicate how the Fund could thereby finally assume the global monetary role intended for it at Bretton Woods by becoming the co-manager of such a system, along with a new committee of central banks and the Group of Seven industrial countries (or a Group of Three that might succeed the Group of Seven when and if the European Union adopts economic and monetary union and hence comes to speak with a single voice on international monetary as well as trade issues). To build that case, I shall start with some revisionist history about the role of the Fund in the earlier postwar period.

The IMF at Age 50

The conventional wisdom is that the world economy and the IMF prospered together during the first quarter century of the postwar period. Global growth was rapid and widely distributed. Inflation was low. Trade was steadily liberalized and expanded rapidly. International investment and capital flows increased substantially. Payments imbalances were modest. Exchange rates were stable.

The Fund stood at the center of the international institutional structure. Countries sought convertibility and, with it, "first-class" status in the organization. The Fund was the lender of last resort, including to the largest countries in the world. Its rules for macroeconomic management were generally accepted and faithfully implemented.

Unfortunately, reality was not so rosy. Western Europe took almost 15 years to achieve convertibility. Sterling crises, systemically vital because sterling was still the world's second key currency, occurred frequently throughout the 1960s. The gold markets produced widespread disruptions. The dollar, already by far the leading currency, also came under periodic attack after 1960—leading to capital controls in the world's largest creditor nation. The inadequacies of the adjustment process were already apparent by the mid-1960s, when France sought to "dethrone the dollar" by buying gold, and U.S. policies on the balance of payments even played an important role in bringing down a German Chancellor.

On the real side of the world economy, growth of output and trade was indeed robust. But much of this was simply catchup from the devastation of the Second World War and had little to do with the new policy regime. The dominant economy of the period, the United States, grew very slowly in the late 1950s and early 1960s. By the end of the period, inflation was creeping upward almost everywhere and inter alia sowing the seeds for the oil shocks of the 1970s. Scores of developing countries—including many of the later "economic miracles"—adopted strategies of import substitution or even comprehensive socialism that produced subsequent stagnation.

Trade policy also presented a mixed picture despite the rapid expansion of trade flows. Protectionism was already on the rise, and the failure of the Bretton Woods system to correct the growing currency misalignments of the 1960s triggered an outbreak of U.S. import controls. Both key currency countries, the United States and the United Kingdom, even resorted to import surcharges—blatantly violating the rules of both the Fund and the GATT, the institutions that these same two countries had worked so hard to create barely a generation earlier.

The institutional scene was much less clear-cut than the conventional wisdom would suggest. The IMF was totally bypassed by the Marshall Plan and other intergovernmental lending in the initial reconstruction period. Its "golden age" of the 1960s in actuality relied heavily on the newly created Group of Ten for crisis management, through frequent weekend meetings to rescue sterling or the dollar; supplementary financing via the General Arrangements to Borrow and the participants' bilateral swap lines; and general systemic guidance, as in the creation of SDRs. Working Party No. 3 of the Organization for Economic Cooperation and Development, rather than the Fund, was the chief locus for discussing adjustment among the industrial countries.

Hence, neither the system nor, especially, the Fund prospered quite so dramatically. The real story, as usual in history, is much more complex and nuanced.

Contrary to the conventional wisdom, one could even argue that the Fund reached the peak of its institutional influence over the last dozen years—long after the collapse of the Bretton Woods exchange rate system and long after it had conducted its last program in a major industrial country. The IMF indisputably played a more central role in managing the Third World debt crisis of the 1980s than in managing the global monetary system of the 1960s. It is probably also playing a larger role today in managing the transformation of the former command economies.

So neither nostalgia for a past golden age nor a desire to "restore the monetary role of the Fund" can credibly motivate future reform of the international monetary system. Any such case must be made in more substantive terms: the need to remedy the severe weaknesses of the current monetary regime and its institutional underpinnings. In my view, both parts of that case can be made quite clearly and quite persuasively. In what follows, I argue that the International Monetary Fund of the twenty-first century should become the steward of a system of currency target zones that could evolve, over time, into an effective regime of macroeconomic policy coordination among at least the European Union, Japan, and the United States. In doing so, the Fund could finally assume the global monetary role intended for it at Bretton Woods by becoming the system's co-manager, along with the major countries and a new committee of central banks.

The Case for Systemic Reform

The recent report of the Bretton Woods Commission correctly concludes that "the costs of extreme exchange rate misalignment and volatility are high. When current exchange rates are misaligned, resources are misallocated; . . . . Exchange rate misalignment adds to protectionist pressures . . . in one major country after another . . ." (Bretton Woods Commission, 1994, p. A-4). "The governments of the major industrial countries should give a high priority to international monetary reforms aimed at reducing large exchange rate fluctuations and serious misalignments" (Bretton Woods Commission, 1994, p. A-1).

The most dramatic recent misalignment was, of course, the massive overvaluation of the dollar in the first half of the 1980s. The resulting decimation of U.S. competitiveness and massive trade deficits led the Reagan Administration, to quote its Secretary of the Treasury, James Baker, "to grant more import relief to U.S. industry than any of its predecessors in more than half a century" (Baker, 1987). Free traders in Congress despaired that "the Smoot-Hawley tariff itself would pass by an overwhelming majority" had it come to the House floor in the fall of 1985. The infamous Super 301 provisions of U.S. trade law, and U.S. "aggressive unilateralism" more broadly, whose implementation has come to have significant effects on the currency markets as well as on world trade, are part of the trade policy legacy of that particular currency misalignment.[1]

The most recent case of severe misalignment is Japan. The yen reached an equilibrium level (about 120:1 against the dollar, the equivalent in real terms of about 100:1 today) at the end of 1987, and, largely as a result, Japan's global current account surplus dropped to a mere \$35 billion (1.2 percent of its GDP) in 1991. But the yen was permitted to weaken by 30 percent in 1989–90, despite continued improvement in Japan's international competitive position, producing the huge renewed

---

[1]The central role of currency misalignments in fostering trade protection is demonstrated empirically in Grilli (1988).

surplus in the early 1990s that triggered sharp trade reactions elsewhere—including the "managed trade" onslaught from the United States and comprehensive automobile quotas in the European Union.

But that was only the first manifestation of this latest currency problem. The extremely rapid appreciation of the yen that inevitably followed has traumatized much of Japanese industry and, in the continuing (and inexplicable) absence of significant fiscal stimulus despite continued budget surpluses, has extended that country's recession through a record third year. Japan has thus received a double hit from this latest misalignment.

The currency misalignments that developed in Europe are even more widely recognized. The crises in the exchange rate mechanism (ERM) of 1992 and 1993, though different in nature from the dollar and yen episodes, have had equally profound (or even greater) effects on the economies of the countries involved and on the global financial system. Unemployment levels in Europe have been much higher for much longer, owing to the effort to preserve disequilibrium parities in the face of major changes in the underlying economic fundamentals, most notably German reunification but also differential inflation in Italy and elsewhere (and sterling's entry into the system at a clearly overvalued rate).

Any international monetary system that permits such large and recurrent disequilibria, with such major economic costs, is a failure. The proximate causes of the problems I have addressed were, of course, the national policies of the countries cited, not the international monetary system per se. But the system provided no help in preventing those policy errors, although a central function of any effective international monetary system is to push *national* policies in directions that are sustainable internationally and thus in the long-term interests of the countries themselves. The only relevant question is whether a better system can be constructed intellectually and implemented operationally.

Search for Stability

Both extremes have been tried. Fixed exchange rates were attempted at the global level under the original Bretton Woods system and in Europe during the second phase of the European Monetary System (EMS) after 1987. Both broke down because they became too rigid and could not accomplish needed parity changes on a timely basis.

Flexible exchange rates have existed for the past 20 years. They were implemented in nearly pure form in the first half of the 1980s and permitted the largest misalignment of all time for a major currency (and an equally large misalignment for at least one other major currency, sterling). Both "pure systems" have clearly failed.

Hence, governments have constantly sought a better regime. It is fascinating to note that much of today's discussion of international monetary reform echoes the discussion that ensued, at least outside official circles, around the time of the collapse of fixed rates in the early 1970s. Now, as then, the focus is on intermediate systems. They were then referred to as "wider bands" or "crawling pegs" or some combination of the two (see Bergsten and others, 1970). Today's proposals for "crawling target zones" are largely an amalgam of such ideas. This similarity of thinking occurs across more than two decades despite the enormous changes that have taken place in the underlying economic and political landscape—the huge increase in capital mobility, the dispersion of economic power around the world, and the end of the Cold War.

There was, of course, no agreed monetary reform in the early 1970s. But the new de facto regime of freely floating rates had a very short half-life as governments immediately revealed their preference for something better. At the regional level, Europe adopted the "snake" in the early 1970s and the EMS more recently, and now seeks full economic and monetary union (EMU).

At the global level, coordinated intervention strategies were adopted in the late 1970s and again in the middle 1980s—most dramatically, with the Plaza agreement in 1985, when the Group of Five explicitly admitted that its previous "benign neglect" and reliance on national "convergence" had failed to produce equilibrium exchange rates. Even more ambitiously, the Group of Five/Group of Seven created a system of target zones—which they called reference ranges—in the Louvre accord of 1987 (see Funabashi, 1988, for the definitive account).

The Louvre bands were too narrow, and its rates were set prematurely and, hence, did not last long because the dollar had not yet completed its needed correction. But the major industrial countries have been operating a system of de facto (or "quiet") target zones since that time:

- The trade-weighted dollar has been relatively stable since 1987, confined to a range within 10 percent on either side of its late-1987 base;
- The dollar-deutsche mark rate has fluctuated between about 1.40:1 and 1.80:1 during the past five years, with repeated intervention to preserve both ends of the range; and
- The dollar-yen rate has for most of the period ranged between about 120:1 and 160:1 (although, as indicated, the yen became significantly undervalued at that level and hence broke into a new range in 1993–94).

Moreover, the EMS responded to its crisis of 1993 not by abandoning or realigning its parities but by sharply widening the margins around them. This largest regional arrangement also thereby created a system of de facto target zones, whose record so far is quite encouraging.

Both the global and key regional monetary arrangements are thus co-alescing toward an intermediate regime. Such a regime would seek to incorporate the virtues of the two extreme systems: limitation of volatil-ity and thus greater business predictability for fixed rates, and respon-siveness to market changes for flexible rates. It would try to avoid their vices: excessive rigidity and thus periodic misalignments for fixity, and extreme misalignments and volatility under flexibility.

But the present de facto target zone system, although a decided im-provement on the failed extremes of the past, still embodies significant weaknesses. There is no orderly mechanism for adjusting the ranges to respond to changes in economic fundamentals, as revealed in the recent case of the yen. The markets are not confident that the ranges will be maintained and are constantly tempted to bet against them. Most important, implementation depends almost wholly on the indi-viduals who are in office at a given time and has no institutional locus (or even memory).[2] The present regime should thus be viewed as a tem-porary way station en route to lasting reform rather than as a satisfac-tory terminus.

Adopting Announced Target Zones

The best step would be to convert the present de facto regime into a de jure system of announced target zones among the major currencies. The zones could start at plus or minus 10 percent around notional mid-points, determined by calculating the exchange rates needed to produce and maintain sustainable current account positions—a wholly realistic objective within the prescribed margin of plus or minus 10 percent.[3] The zones would be kept under constant review, with changes in bilateral nominal rates as needed to hold real rates constant and more substantial changes in response to large external shocks (such as the sharp changes in world oil prices in the 1970s or German unification more recently).

It is nonsense for officials to reject target zones on the grounds that their limited resources do not permit them to cope with the $1 trillion of daily activity in the currency markets. The vast bulk of that flow is self-balancing, reflecting routine steps by market participants to rebalance

---

[2]Funabashi (1988) documents the rapid dissolution of the policies implanted by Baker-Miyazawa-Stoltenberg as soon as that triumvirate departed office. Even more clearly, sys-tematic rules are needed to avoid extreme and disruptive policies, such as those fostered by Beryl Sprinkel in the first half of the 1980s.

[3]This is demonstrated in the several papers reflecting the state of the art regarding such calculations in Williamson (1994). It is also noteworthy that the United States and Japan have been able to largely agree in their current framework talks on the proper current ac-count surplus for Japan (1½ percent of its GDP) despite their acrimonious conflict on vir-tually everything else.

their portfolios following normal financial transactions. Although very large sums will move if the market is convinced that the authorities are trying to defend a disequilibrium rate, net market movements for most currencies on most days are quite small.

Indeed, a credible target zone regime could convert present destabilizing private flows into stabilizing flows in the future (see Krugman, 1988). As long as the zones are set properly and defended effectively, private capital movements will help maintain rather than disrupt them. When rates approached the edges of the zones, speculators would know that they could make little money pushing further in that direction but that there was substantial scope for profit from reversing course. Governments and central banks, in their pursuit of economic and financial stability, would gain much more from these stabilizing properties of an effective monetary system than they would lose by giving up their present ability to surprise the market on occasion—and they would, of course, retain that ability for intramarginal intervention.

There is also strong empirical evidence that coordinated, announced intervention in the exchange markets can effectively defend exchange rate targets—even when the intervention is sterilized and, hence, conducted without changes in monetary policy. Dominguez and Frankel (1993), using previously unavailable German and U.S. intervention data, show that publicized intervention can be extremely potent. A study by the research staff of the Banca d'Italia, using even more extensive intervention evidence from all Group of Ten and EMS countries, reaches even stronger conclusions: that all 17 episodes of concerted intervention from 1984 to early 1992 were "definitely successful," that in no case was intervention steamrollered by the market, and that all but one major turning point in the dollar-deutsche mark and dollar-yen rates since 1985 were "exactly coincident" with episodes of concerted intervention (see Catte, Galli, and Rebecchini, forthcoming).

The combination of wide bands and effective intervention suggests that macroeconomic policy, including monetary policy, would rarely have to be devoted to external purposes under a credible target zone system. Hence, monetary and fiscal policies could largely retain their focus on domestic policy targets.

In those cases when domestic policy had to be altered, however, it would generally be in directions that are quite healthy from the long-term standpoint of the country in question (as well as the world economy as a whole). Improved *international* policy coordination could in fact promote better *domestic* policy coordination—a problem for most of the major countries despite their sophisticated policy regimes. A target zone system could on occasion reduce the short-term flexibility of macroeconomic policy in participating countries, but, in practice, it would primarily reduce their flexibility to make policy errors, as indicated in some of the most spectacular recent cases of such error:

- A target zone system, in addition to calling for intervention that would have limited the final (and totally irrational) stage of the appreciation of the dollar in 1984–85, would have pushed the United States to restrain its run-up in interest rates in the early 1980s through less fiscal expansion—surely a desirable outcome and one that many Americans now seek through far more artificial and arbitrary devices, such as balanced budget amendments and legislative procedures like Gramm-Rudman-Hollings;
- A target zone system centered on the end-1987 equilibrium rates would have sought to avoid the sharp depreciation of the yen in subsequent years, thereby pushing Japan to use fiscal rather than monetary policy to expand domestic demand and shielding it from at least the worst excesses of the "bubble economy"; and
- A target zone system would have facilitated German revaluation in the wake of reunification,[4] reducing the need for subsequent sky-high real interest rates that pushed all of Europe (especially *outside* Germany) into prolonged recession.[5]

The relationship between the monetary regime and macroeconomic policy coordination is an issue on which the Bretton Woods Commission and many other analysts make a critical error. They argue that governments should first achieve more successful coordination of their macroeconomic policies and then adopt target zones or some other better monetary regime. Unfortunately, there are no historical examples of such agreements on policy coordination. Hence, such recommendations represent pious statements of principle that are destined to remain totally nonoperational.

By contrast, there are at least two recent historical examples of monetary systems that, in turn, induced participating countries to achieve at least a degree of policy coordination. The original Bretton Woods regime of adjustable pegs produced such results to an important extent despite the caveats cited above (see Michaely, 1971). So has the EMS, most dramatically in the case of French adjustment to the disastrous ef-

---

[4]Germany was of course in the EMS at the time, but the EMS then operated as a traditional fixed rate system. Germany itself was reportedly prepared to revalue, but the system required agreement from partner countries to do so, which was not forthcoming. Under a target zone, by contrast, market forces would have pushed the deutsche mark at least to the top of the band and, hence, obtained at least some of the needed adjustment.

[5]Some argue that the breakdown of the ERM in 1992 and again in 1993 demonstrates the futility of seeking to manage exchange rates as proposed here. This is incorrect: as noted above, the ERM collapsed because, like the Bretton Woods system in the late 1960s and early 1970s, it failed to adjust its parities in the face of clear changes in the underlying economic fundamentals. The lesson is to avoid defending disequilibrium exchange rates, which, as indicated in the text, are as likely to emerge under floating rates as under fixed rates, rather than to abdicate all efforts to manage currencies.

fects of its "dash for growth" in 1982–83, but also in its evolution into a much more extensive regime of policy coordination in the 1990s and the subsequent plans for full monetary and even fiscal coordination through EMU. History suggests that the more feasible progression is from monetary accord to policy coordination rather than the reverse.[6]

There is a problem of transition in the adoption of any new monetary regime. If the starting point is fixed exchange rates, as under the original Bretton Woods system, a comprehensive realignment is required. Much of the debate in the early 1970s centered on where the new parities should be set.

If the starting point is floating rates, or even de facto target zones like today, it is much easier to launch a new system "around current levels."[7] Any need to jump to new rates could be disruptive and make institution of the new regime substantially more difficult, thus deterring governments from making the effort. Hence, governments must look for an opportune moment to launch a system of target zones (or anything more ambitious).

Fortunately, there is widespread agreement that today's exchange rates are close to long-term equilibrium levels. IMF Managing Director Michel Camdessus (1994, p. 31) has recently noted that "exchange rates among the key currencies are probably not very far from the professional consensus on the rates that are appropriate." Hence, the present moment, unlike most of the past dozen years, would permit a smooth start-up of a new regime with a dollar-yen zone centered on 100:1 and a deutsche mark-dollar zone centered on 1.60:1. Had such a regime already been in place, recent currency movements would have been viewed as well within the ranges and thus generated much less attention and concern. The opportunity should not be wasted.

Target Zones and the IMF[8]

Who would manage a system of target zones? The Group of Seven is clearly inadequate. It has no staff nor even a secretariat to keep records and produce an institutional memory. Its members frequently disagree on what they said soon after an agreement is reached. No decision-making system, let alone a procedure to resolve disputes effectively, is provided.

The only satisfactory forum within which to manage a new international monetary regime is the IMF. It is the only institution that would

---

[6]Guidelines for implementing such policy coordination can be found in Williamson and Miller (1987).

[7]As laid out in Funabashi (1988), British entry into the ERM at a clearly overvalued rate for sterling is a recent example of the perils of commencing a new regime "around current levels" when the levels are incorrect.

[8]This section draws heavily on Williamson and Henning (1994).

permit the needed integration of the decisions by participants in the regime with those of nonparticipants (for example, with respect to the selection of current account targets). Only the Fund could provide a channel for the interests of nonparticipants to be brought to bear on the decisions of the participants. It already has available the robust staff of economists, analysts, and technicians that would be needed to support the regime.[9]

At the same time, the Group of Seven industrial democracies account for a substantial majority of world economic activity and will continue to do so for some time.[10] All of the countries that are crucial to the initial success of a target zone regime are contained within that Group. They are the most likely participants in a target zone regime at its outset. They bear responsibility for systemic stability and so must play a central role in the management of any successful monetary regime.[11]

The Group of Seven finance ministers and central bank governors should therefore remain the initial locus in which implementation and administration of target zones are negotiated and discussed. They would establish the targets for the current account balances of the participants in the regime, establish the exchange rates needed to achieve and maintain those positions, and realign the target zones in response to real shocks or new evidence about the need for a payments adjustment. Decisions within the Group would continue to be taken by consensus. The ministers might meet quarterly, as they agreed at the Group of Seven summit meeting at Naples in July 1994, with their deputies meeting as often as necessary.

The finance ministers and central bank governors should, however, draw much more fully on the Fund staff by giving it responsibility, along with the staffs of the national finance ministries and central banks, for preparing discussion papers and decision memoranda for Group of Seven meetings. The Managing Director, who presently participates only in the portion of Group of Seven meetings devoted to multilateral surveillance, should be included throughout. He or she should participate in the discussion of current account targets, setting the tar-

---

[9]For an example of the Fund staff's capability to conduct the required analytical studies, see Chapter 2 of Williamson (1994).

[10]Recent suggestions that the Group of Seven share of world output has dropped to little more than 50 percent rely on unrealistically large GNP adjustments for China, India, and other developing countries to incorporate inflated estimates of purchasing power parity rather than market exchange rates.

[11]The Group of Seven should be collapsed into a Group of Three as soon as the European Union achieves economic and monetary union and can speak with a single voice on these issues. I shall henceforth refer to the Group of Seven but hope and expect that EMU will occur within the relevant future, converting it into a Group of Three and thus easing the global coordination task in the same way that creation of the original European Economic Community facilitated global trade negotiations by permitting Europe to speak with a single voice in that venue.

get zones, and pursuing any policy adjustments needed to defend them—in order to bring global systemic concerns, and those of the remaining members of the IMF, to the table.

Moreover, the Group of Seven should seek the concurrence of the appropriate bodies of the IMF before implementing any decisions that it has taken.[12] As presently constituted, however, the Fund's Executive Board would then have to pass judgment on decisions taken by officials who are much more senior than the Executive Directors themselves. Hence, it would be desirable, when making important decisions to establish and implement the new regime, to constitute the Executive Board at ministerial level.

Such a body, called the "Council," has already been provided for by the Second Amendment to the Articles of Agreement (1978) and could be activated by 85 percent of the voting power of the Fund (Article XII, Section 1; Schedule D). By involving the same finance ministers that represent their countries in the Group of Seven, the Council could consult and confer with those individuals responsible for the Group's decisions. The Interim Committee, after its 20-year "interim," should thus be converted into the Council as originally intended in the Second Amendment.[13]

To implement the new regime, and to dramatize the role that the Fund would now be playing in managing the global monetary system, the Executive Board itself should be upgraded through the appointment of ministerial deputies as Executive Directors (as proposed by Finch, 1994). Under this change, which would be implemented by each country group or "constituency" within the Fund, the Group of Seven deputies would be members of the Board that would be overseeing international monetary matters under the authority of the Council when the ministers were unable to convene (or did not need to do so). The Alternate Executive Directors, who would be appointees at roughly the same

---

[12]So should the EMS, which has largely ignored the Fund and indeed the global implications of its actions—which are substantial. However, there is no legal obligation for either the Group of Seven or the EMS to do so. The Articles of Agreement, as amended in 1978, allow groups of members to create such exchange rate regimes. Their only obligation is to notify the Fund of changes in their arrangements (Article IV, Sections 2(*a*) and 2(*b*)).

[13]Activating the Council would be a far better way to manage the new regime than relying on the existing Interim Committee or even a strengthened Interim Committee. The Interim Committee, like the proposed Council, meets at ministerial level and has the same representative configuration as the Executive Board. The Interim Committee, however, possesses no formal powers of decision making and was intended solely to provide political guidance to the work of the Executive Board. The Council, on the other hand, would have real decision-making authority within the Fund: it could approve (or reject) decisions taken within the Group of Seven with all the formal surveillance authority of the Fund, rather than relying on the Executive Board to provide formal approval indirectly.

level as the current Executive Directors, would carry on the regular business of the Fund.

The Council would then exercise the Fund's powers of surveillance over the exchange rate arrangements of its members, approving the new regime and decisions taken within it (Article IV, Sections 2(*b*) and 3(*b*)). It would examine and discuss the current account targets of both participants and nonparticipants in the regime, the target zones for the participating currencies, and policy adjustments needed to sustain them. The Council, or the Executive Board meeting under its aegis, would approve realignments, for example.

The Council and the Executive Board could be expected to accept the proposals of the Group of Seven, for whom these decisions would be far more consequential than for the nonparticipants, on most occasions. Concurrence by the Fund bodies, however, would be much more than a rubber-stamping of the decisions of that Group because:

- the Council and Board could reinforce the majority within the Group of Seven in exercising peer pressure over miscreants, adding to the prospects for prompt and constructive policy changes when needed;
- the Group of Seven would have to consult with the Council and Board throughout the process, giving them immediate notice of decisions and the right to cross-examine the representatives of the Group of Seven countries;
- the accumulation over time of a record of decisions and advice on the part of the Council and Board could contribute to both future decisions by Group of Seven countries and accession to the regime by others; and
- the Group of Seven governments do not quite command a majority of the votes within the IMF.

The actual role of the Council or Executive Board would depend on the type of Group of Seven decision being approved. General surveillance over the regime and consideration of future policy adjustments that might be required to meet regime targets, for example, could be conducted at ministerial level. A realignment of the target zones, on the other hand, would require avoidance of any substantial delay between a decision by the Group of Seven and its implementation. In this case, the Executive Board could convene on a few hours' notice at the level of the deputy ministers (or even their alternates based in Washington) to approve the decision.

The central banks, acting together in a new committee of central banks that would, in turn, confer with the Group of Seven and work within the framework of its decisions, should make all operational decisions about intervention and monetary policy adjustments (Henning, 1994). The central banks should, for example, be given authority to assign intervention responsibilities and extend credits to finance intervention.

Through their participation in the Group of Seven meetings, and through their new committee, the governors of the central banks should advise the Group on the full range of macroeconomic and monetary issues. The committee, in particular, should warn the Group of Seven when the projected fiscal policies of governments could make maintenance of the target zones impossible without provoking inflationary or deflationary changes in monetary policies in one or more participating countries. It should have the authority to propose consideration of a realignment within the Group of Seven.

The advantages of this three-part institutional infrastructure for target zones are several. It builds on existing and operating institutions: the IMF, Group of Seven, and Basel meetings of central bankers that already take place monthly. It balances the need for efficiency in decision making with the need for broader participation to enhance legitimacy. It can be implemented without any amendment of the Articles of Agreement of the Fund (or any other "constitutional" changes). It would enable the Fund to fulfill its original raison d'être of managing the international monetary regime.

Conclusions

At its recent summit in Naples, the heads of government of the Group of Seven asked, How can we adapt existing institutions and build new (international economic) institutions to ensure the future prosperity and security of our people? They inscribed the issue on the agenda for their meeting in Canada next year.

A number of changes are needed in both categories (for a comprehensive review, see Bergsten, 1994). But international monetary reform is surely the place to start. The international monetary system lies at the heart of the world economy just as national monetary policies lie at the heart of individual national economies. The present regime is clearly inadequate. A viable alternative is available. There is growing support for such reform, as indicated by the widespread and prestigious participation in the Bretton Woods Commission and the expression of personal views on the topic by the Managing Director of the Fund (Camdessus, 1994, pp. 31–32).

Yet neither the Executive Directors of the Fund, nor the Board of Governors, nor the Group of Seven have made any serious proposals in recent years to improve the system. The fiftieth anniversary of Bretton Woods would be an apt moment to begin the process of creating an effective and stable monetary regime for the years, and even decades and half century, ahead. Installation of a central monetary role for the IMF should be an integral element of any such systemic reform. There would be no more suitable time to launch the effort than at this annual meeting of the Fund.

References

Baker, James, "Remarks Before a Conference Sponsored by the Institute for International Economics," Washington, September 14, 1987.

Bergsten, C. Fred, "The Case for Reform," in *Managing the World Economy: Fifty Years After Bretton Woods*, ed. by Peter B. Kenen (Washington: Institute for International Economics, 1994).

_____, and others, *Approaches to Greater Flexibility of Exchange Rates: The Bürgenstock Papers* (Princeton, New Jersey: Princeton University Press, 1970).

Bretton Woods Commission, *Bretton Woods: Looking to the Future*, Vol. 1, Commission Report, Staff Review, and Background Papers (Washington: Bretton Woods Committee, July 1994).

Camdessus, Michel, *The IMF at Fifty: Facing the Challenges Ahead* (Washington: International Monetary Fund, October 1994).

Catte, Pietro, Giampaolo Galli, and Salvatore Rebecchini, "Concerted Intervention and the Dollar: An Analysis of Daily Data," in *The International Monetary System*, ed. by Peter B. Kenen, Fabrizio Saccomanni, and Francesco Papadia (Cambridge: Cambridge University Press, forthcoming).

Dominguez, Kathryn A., and Jeffrey A. Frankel, *Does Foreign Exchange Intervention Work?* (Washington: Institute for International Economics, 1993).

Finch, C. David, "Governance of the International Monetary Fund by Its Members," in Bretton Woods Commission, *Bretton Woods: Looking to the Future*, Vol. 1, Commission Report, Staff Review, and Background Papers (Washington: Bretton Woods Committee, July 1994).

Funabashi, Yoichi, *Managing the Dollar: From the Plaza to the Louvre* (Washington: Institute for International Economics, 1988).

Grilli, Enzo, "Macroeconomic Determinants of Trade Protection," *World Economy*, Vol. 11 (September 1988), pp. 313–26.

Henning, C. Randall, Chap. 8 in *Currencies and Politics in the United States, Germany and Japan* (Washington: Institute for International Economics, July 1994).

Krugman, Paul, "Target Zones and Exchange Rate Dynamics," NBER Working Paper 2481 (Cambridge, Massachusetts: National Bureau of Economic Research, 1988).

Michaely, Michael, *The Responsiveness of Demand Policies to Balance of Payments: Postwar Patterns* (New York: Columbia University Press, 1971).

Williamson, John, ed., *Estimating Equilibrium Exchange Rates* (Washington: Institute for International Economics, September 1994).

_____, and Marcus Miller, *Targets and Indicators: A Blueprint for the International Coordination of Economic Policy* (Washington: Institute for International Economics, 1987).

Williamson, John, and C. Randall Henning, "Managing the Monetary System," in *Managing the World Economy: Fifty Years After Bretton Woods*, ed. by Peter B. Kenen (Washington: Institute for International Economics, 1994).

Lamberto Dini

Our two speakers have presented us with inspiring thoughts on the future of the Fund and the World Bank.

In reviewing Mr. Singh's presentation, I would like to underline his firm belief—expressed also on other occasions and one that I fully share—that an open trading system is of immense value for the Third World in its fight against underemployment. A global economic environment that encourages increased flows of financial resources from developed to developing countries is also of great significance; in an increasingly interdependent world, one should not minimize the importance of an orderly and equitable management of global interdependence for fostering development. I also share his view that there is no contradiction in the expansion of World Bank activity and the expansion of private sector lending or private investment flows; on the contrary, these processes are complementary and mutually reinforcing.

On more general grounds, both speakers share the view that in today's world we need greater and more effective mechanisms for economic policy coordination. They both stressed that this task cannot be left to informal meetings of the Group of Seven; rather it should be entrusted to the IMF.

Concerning the future of the IMF, Mr. Bergsten has put forward a specific proposal that deserves serious consideration at both technical and political levels. In a nutshell, he envisages an exchange rate system based on target zones and managed by the IMF.

We all know that the search for more stability in exchange rates has gone on unabatedly over the last two decades. And so has the debate on the merits and faults of flexible exchange rates in the new environment of the world economy created by integrated capital markets that have attained unexpected dimensions and efficiency.

While I share both speakers' view that better coordination of macroeconomic policies is necessary for the prosperity of the world economy, there are a few contentious points to be considered in regard to Mr. Bergsten's proposal.

First, can we hold the collapse of the Bretton Woods regime responsible for the relatively poor macroeconomic performance of the last two decades? The correlation exists, but is it due to exchange rates or to other factors, such as the increase in energy prices, the strong labor cost-push in many countries, increased budget deficits, and declining rates of private saving and investment? The less favorable macroeconomic environment in the 1970s brought about a poorer inflation and growth performance and a change in the monetary regime. It is fair to say that floating exchange rates were the pragmatic response to problems that could not be resolved within the framework of the Bretton Woods system.

Second, it is true that protectionist pressures rose in the past Bretton Woods era. But it is difficult to correlate them with the monetary regime. In addition, progress has been made in liberalizing trade, and, on the whole, the world trade environment is much freer today than it was 30 years ago.

Third, misalignments of real exchange rates can occur both with flexible and with fixed exchange rates. Both the Bretton Woods system and the EMS show how difficult it is for the authorities to make timely adjustments to parities. Political problems, but also the fear of losing credibility in the markets, have almost invariably led authorities to excessively resist desirable exchange rate changes.

On more practical grounds, and coming back to Mr. Bergsten's proposal, I am somewhat skeptical about the prospects for a regime of target zones among the large industrial nations. The solution to the so-called *n*th country problem in fixed exchange rate regimes has always been to entrust the dominant country with the privilege (and burden) of determining the monetary policy stance for the whole area. This arrangement can work well as long as there is a dominant country and the interests of the other countries do not diverge widely from those of the former. I submit that this is hardly the situation of the world economy today. Indeed, in large democracies, it may prove extremely difficult to subordinate, at any given time, important domestic policy objectives to the pursuit of stable exchange rates.

In Mr. Bergsten's scheme, the IMF Council and the Executive Board will be entrusted with the responsibility not only for general surveillance over the exchange rate but also for consideration of future policy adjustments that may be required to meet the regime targets, as well as for realignments of target zones. Would such machinery work? Would it work any better than existing arrangements for policy coordination in today's system of flexible exchange rates among major countries?

In the present circumstances, I for one believe that we should strive to achieve better policy coordination and to reduce the variability of exchange rates; the Fund has a greater role to play in this respect. However, we should reflect further before taking the risk of committing our nations to overambitious targets!

General Discussion

Stanley Fischer, commenting on Bergsten's proposal, argued that there was nothing more dangerous in rebuilding the international financial system than proposing a system that promised more than it would deliver and that might fail. One system had already collapsed, and proposals for replacing it with one that did not work would cause more trouble than maintaining the present system, which was not prone to deep crises of the type experienced under the previous system. Indeed, one of the problems associated with reforming the present system was that it was not vulnerable to crisis; to reform it, a major crisis was needed.

The costs of the present system were currency misalignments and the related misallocation of resources. The costs of extreme misalignments were known to be large, while the costs of routine shifts and short-term volatility in exchange rates were thought to be not very large. Thus, extreme misalignments were the focus, the prime example of which since the overvaluation of the U.S. dollar in the mid-1980s.

In that context, it was useful to ask whether a target zone system would have survived the currency tensions of the mid-1980s. The evidence that Bergsten had presented on that question was actually aimed at making a different point, namely, that trade and macroeconomic policies would have been better under a target zone system. The evidence in support of that proposition was unpersuasive. In 1947, for example, there were no trade disputes that could have explained the failure to establish the proposed International Trade Organization. Moreover, the World Trade Organization would soon come into existence, despite opposition from the U.S. Congress, after a period of floating rates. Furthermore, the trade dispute between Japan and the United States was taking place at a time when, as Bergsten had noted, exchange rates among all major currencies were about right. Perhaps that dispute had its origins in the 1980s, but the evidence was not compelling. Floating rates did not seem to be the problem. Indeed, in the nineteenth century under the gold standard, commercial policy was used frequently to deal with balance of payments problems in the absence of an exchange rate option.

With respect to macroeconomic policies, there was no convincing evidence that U.S. fiscal policy would have been different in 1981 under a target zone system. Similarly, it was not clear that a system of target zones would have yielded a different outcome in 1992 and 1993 within the EMS. In fact, the crises that had emerged in the EMS centered around France's desire to keep exchange rates fixed, for reasons that had more to do with diplomacy than economic policy.

In sum, a target zone system would not have prevented the kinds of trade interventions and macroeconomic policy mistakes that had been experienced in the post-Bretton Woods era, despite the promises of its proponents. The major benefit of such a system would be in avoiding large currency misalignments, such as those that occurred in 1985; the Fund was, of course, well suited to assess the level of exchange rates. If a system of target zones were implemented, therefore, it would produce a slight improvement in the world economy.

Ariel Buira argued that the cost of the present system was not simply the incidence of currency misalignments. The macroeconomic performance of the major industrial countries had clearly been poorer since

1973. There was now a system without rules, and a system without rules meant that fiscal discipline had been relaxed. The resulting increase in government deficits in the industrial countries had a very considerable cost for the world economy. Lower saving rates in the industrial countries had not only been translated into lower rates of growth and, in turn, greater protectionism in those countries but had also meant higher interest rates and lower rates of investment in both industrial and developing countries. All developing, capital-importing countries were affected by the low rates of saving and high interest rates that had resulted from the present system. There was a clear need, therefore, for an exchange rate "system" to impose a minimum of discipline; the precise form of such a system was less important than meeting that objective.

Michael Bruno agreed with Fischer that it was important first to understand the past before discussing the future. There was no evidence that the problems experienced in the 1970s and 1980s had anything to do with the international monetary system. In fact, the system had evolved precisely because of problems such as the oil shocks and the increase in government deficits.

To take another historical example, the ERM of the EMS had worked reasonably well as long as there was a stable currency to which other members of the system fixed their exchange rates. The ERM failed with the emergence of a large fiscal, not monetary, problem, associated with the reunification of Germany. In the end, therefore, the critical issue was whether the major countries were willing to give up domestic objectives in favor of a stable world currency. Otherwise, the parallel of a national monetary policy and an international monetary policy would not work.

C. Fred Bergsten strongly disagreed with Dini and Fischer on the flaws of the present system. The views he had presented were well supported in the literature on the evolution of the trading system over the past few decades, including research by the World Bank, which clearly pointed to an enormous increase in nontariff measures, new types of protection, and the erosion of the trading system. The study by Enzo Grilli that he had cited in his presentation showed, with very robust statistical correlations, that the dominant cause of trade protection in both the United States and Europe over the past 20 years was currency misalignments. The evidence in the Grilli study was very hard to dispute.

It was true that the trade dispute between Japan and the United States coexisted with exchange rates that were broadly appropriate, but that observation only reinforced his point. That trade dispute, which had been roiling the currency markets for the past six months, in addition to potentially disrupting the entire trade system, was the legacy of misaligned currencies—first, ten years ago with the overvalued dollar, and then three or four years ago with the undervalued yen. Those were lasting systemic problems infecting the trade system, generated by currency misalignments whose very existence created problems that tended to take on lives of their own. The fact that the trade dispute could erupt in less than 48 hours with major real and financial consequences—although the bilateral exchange rate had already bounced back to equilibrium—was further evidence in support of his proposal.

The point had also been made that the present system did not lead to crises, but such a conclusion depended on a rather narrow definition of crisis. Many trade problems—the near failure of the Uruguay Round and the possible imposition of retaliatory and counter-retaliatory measures by Japan and the United States, the world's two biggest economies—could be viewed as crises. Moreover, monetary movements—even those of the past six months—that had led to sharp movements in domestic financial markets were crises of a sort. Simply because finance ministers did not occasionally have to meet on weekends to adjust parities (as they did in the 1960s) did not mean there were no crises; serious economic problems continued to emerge as a result of the operation of the present international monetary system.

To assess whether the problems he had described would have been resolved, or significantly ameliorated, under a system of target zones, it was instructive to consider two specific episodes. In the case of the EMS, the crisis had largely been generated by the effort within the ERM to maintain fixed exchange rates. If the EMS had incorporated exchange rate bands of plus or minus 10 percent at that time, a significant appreciation of the deutsche mark would have been permitted, thereby limiting the inflationary impact on the German economy of growing domestic demand pressure. Under those conditions, the extent to which the Bundesbank would have had to increase interest rates would have been reduced, which, in turn, would have minimized the recessionary implications of such a move for the rest of Europe. Thus, Europe would have been at least somewhat better off under a target zone arrangement.

The arguments supporting the proposition that U.S. fiscal policy in the early 1980s would have been better under a target zone system were strong but less definitive. If a target zone system had been in place for, say, 20 years, and if such a system had been accepted as part of the lexicon of macroeconomic policymaking, there would have been a clear set of international obligations that the United States would have been violating had it pursued the policy mix of the Reagan Administration in the early 1980s. The existence of those obligations would have provided voices within the Government, Congress, or other elements of the U.S. body politic with an important reason not to pursue the intended course of action. There was, in that respect, a strong analogy with the conduct of trade policy under the GATT: although the GATT system did not always work well, it provided a powerful line of defense against domestic protectionist pressures, as the opponents of protectionism could point to the tangible consequences of violating international trade obligations.

In short, for all their imperfections, international rules and institutions provided a defense against policy mistakes. They did not always prevail: the League of Nations did not prevent World War II, but that did not prevent the creation of the United Nations in its wake. It was certainly not true that a target zone regime, or any other international system, could have prevented the worst excesses of, say, U.S. or German fiscal policy in the early 1980s and 1990s, respectively. Such a regime would nevertheless have served to tilt the domestic debate within countries in a constructive direction. Without such a regime, therefore, the international community was denying itself the opportunity to pursue desirable policy options.

The main objective of the target zone approach was not to pinpoint precisely correct exchange rates; rather, the objective was, as Fischer had suggested, to avoid large currency misalignments. Very large imbalances in currency relationships, which reflected imbalances in domestic policies, caused significant economic distortions and major disruptions in the world trade system and, therefore, should be avoided. They did not occur often—perhaps once every five years or so—but if a monetary regime could help head off such misalignments, the world economy would be protected from enormous difficulties. Therefore, in view of the call by the Group of Seven summit in Naples for international institutions to adapt to the world of the future, it was important to take seriously the possibility of change.

Finally, the point that Dini had made about the need in a target zone system to sacrifice domestic goals to achieve international objectives was, in fact, an incorrect specification of the problem. The issue was not domestic priorities versus international priorities; rather, it was short run versus long run. A more structured monetary system would indeed reduce the short-term flexibility of policy in all countries, but that should be viewed as a positive development. If an international regime forced policymakers to think more about long-run sustainability—that is, the international compatibility of their policies—it would at least reduce the risk of repeating policy errors based on a short-term policy focus. The resulting policies would be in the longer-run interest of the countries themselves, as well as the system as a whole.

4

Establishing a Vision for
Promoting Economic Development

The first keynote speaker at the conference was A.W. Clausen, the Chairman of BankAmerica Corporation and a former President of the World Bank Group, who was asked to describe his vision of how best to promote economic development. Richard Gardner, the U.S. Ambassador to Spain, opened the session. In addition to being a seasoned diplomat, Ambassador Gardner is also one of the great scholars of the Bretton Woods conference and the world economic order that it produced.

Richard N. Gardner

I have been given a double privilege today by the organizers of this splendid conference: to say a few words about the historical origins of the Bretton Woods organizations and to introduce a most distinguished financial statesman and former World Bank President, Tom Clausen.

The victorious allies in the Second World War had a basic choice to make as they faced the task of postwar economic reconstruction. They could return to the selfish economic nationalism, currency controls, and high tariffs of the prewar period, or they could seek shared prosperity in a world of open, multilateral trade. Fortunately for all of us, they chose the latter.

The "founding fathers"—John Maynard Keynes, Harry Dexter White, and the other members of the Bretton Woods cast, some of whom are with us today—were united by a common commitment to constructive internationalism. They wanted to create permanent institutions for international cooperation on monetary, trade, and development problems. Today, we take their achievements for granted, but it is worth recalling that the Bretton Woods institutions were created in the face of powerful opposition in the United States and the United Kingdom, the two leading countries in the work of postwar reconstruction.

In the new Spanish edition of my book, *Sterling-Dollar Diplomacy: The Origins and the Future of the Bretton Woods-GATT System*, which Círculo de Lectores was good enough to publish this week, I give some examples of the British and U.S. moods at the time of Bretton Woods.

On the British side, there was profound skepticism throughout the establishment that a system based on open, multilateral trade would be in the country's interests. The Federation of British Industries and the London Chamber of Commerce were hostile. Many felt that the wave of the future was barter trade, managed markets, discriminatory arrangements, and currency controls. Many believed that the United States was destined to go into a deep depression after the war, dragging Britain into the abyss and destroying its postwar commitments to the welfare state and full employment. To these people, it seemed folly to lie down with the United States in an international system based on liberal economic principles. And, of course, there were those who wanted to make the sterling area and the system of Imperial Preference the basis for a postwar order.

Those two pillars of establishment opinion in the United Kingdom, the *Economist* and the *Times*, looked at postwar planning with deep misgivings. As the *Times* put it:

> We must reconcile ourselves once and for all to the view that the days of *laissez-faire* and the unlimited division of labor are over; that every country—including Great Britain—plans and organizes its production in the light of social and military needs; and that the regulation of this production by such "trade barriers" as tariffs, quotas, and subsidies is a necessary and integral part of this policy.

The U.S. Ambassador to Britain, John Winant, cabled Washington in 1944 that "a majority of the directors of the Bank of England are opposed to the Bretton Woods program . . . . It is argued by those in opposition that if the plan is adopted financial control will leave London and sterling exchange will be replaced by dollar exchange."

One British Member of Parliament warned that acceptance of the U.S. postwar monetary proposals "will be the end. The end of all our hopes of an expansionist policy, and of social advance. It will be the end of the Beveridge Plan, of improved education, of housing reconstruction, the end of the new Britain we are fighting to rebuild. It will lead again to world depression, to chaos, and, ultimately, to war."

The postwar economic plans had no smoother reception on the U.S. side. The *Wall Street Journal* called the Keynes plan "a machine for the regimentation of the world." The *New York Times* considered the Bretton Woods proposals unnecessary; it favored going back to the gold standard, which it considered "the most satisfactory international standard that has ever been devised." The American Bankers Association objected to the International Monetary Fund because, it said, "we should be handing over to an international body the power to determine the destination, time, and use of our money"—abandoning, without receiving anything in return, a vital part of U.S. bargaining power. The Guaranty Trust Company, progenitor of Morgan Guaranty, called both the British and U.S. plans for Bretton Woods "dangerous," on the grounds that they would "enable nations to buy merchandise without being able to pay for it." Senator Robert Taft denounced the Bretton Woods agreements, charging that the United States was "putting all the valuable money into the Fund," and would be "pouring money down a rat hole." A Senator from Utah rose in indignation on the floor of the Senate, brandished a fistful of foreign currencies, and defied any one of his colleagues to "go downtown in Washington and get his shoes shined with this whole bunch of bills."

It is in the light of such attitudes in the two countries that the creation of the postwar institutions deserves to be called a "political miracle." The miracle was only possible because it was accomplished at the end of a war, when public opinion could be mobilized in the hopeful enterprise of building a better world, and because both countries were led by men of great vision, surrounded by dedicated internationalists of outstanding ability. Today, when many people despair of undertaking necessary new initiatives because of what they see as implacable political realities, it is worth recalling how the founding fathers were able to enlarge and reshape those realities 50 years ago.

There is another political miracle that may be of interest today. We now take for granted that the world's pre-eminent institution for economic development in terms of the size of its resources and the weight of its influence is the International Bank for Reconstruction and Development. Yet in the early planning for the postwar economy, the Bank came almost as an afterthought. Virtually all the attention of the British and U.S. Governments was focused on the International Monetary Fund.

When, on the eve of Bretton Woods, the negotiators finally focused on the World Bank, they were in a conservative mood—the British did not expect to be beneficiaries, the Americans were afraid of Congress. The Bank's lending capacity was limited almost entirely to what it could raise by bonds issued on the private capital market. There was simply no conception of the vast needs of the developing countries and of the role the Bank should play in meeting them.

Indeed, the World Bank was conceived mainly as an institution for reconstruction. Incredible as it seems today, the word "development" did not even appear in Harry White's first draft circulated within the U.S. Treasury Department. So another political miracle has been the extraordinary evolution of the World Bank's development policies, assisted by the creation of its two key affiliates, the International Development Association (IDA) and the International Finance Corporation (IFC).

I close with a brief word about a third political miracle. I refer to the mutual learning process that enabled the two key actors in the world economic drama—national governments and the private banking community—to overcome their mutual hostility and work together in support of economic development in the developing world. Recall that U.S. Secretary of the Treasury Henry Morgenthau told the assembled delegates at the closing plenary session of the Bretton Woods conference that one of their major purposes was "to drive the usurious moneylenders from the temple of international finance." Two years later, when he heard that Lewis Douglas was under consideration to be the first President of the World Bank, Morgenthau (now back in private life) declared: "The idea that it is necessary to have a Wall Street financier to head the World Bank in order to sell the bank securities is quite shocking."

I wonder what Morgenthau would say today, when the "usurious moneylenders" are providing two thirds of the capital flows to developing countries (a sum of $113 billion of private capital in 1993). What would he say of the presence at the Fund and World Bank Annual Meetings of over 10,000 private bankers, or of the successive and successful Bank presidencies of bankers such as Eugene Black, George Woods, Lewis Preston, or of our distinguished speaker today, Tom Clausen?

Tom Clausen's career helps to illustrate why Henry Morgenthau was wrong. A true financial statesmen, Tom has made historic contributions as head of one of the world's major private international banking institutions, the BankAmerica Corporation, and as head of the world's principal public international banking institution, the World Bank. His long list of associations with nonprofit organizations, including important educational institutions as well as business advisory groups, testifies to his continuing contribution to the general welfare both in the United States and overseas.

A.W. Clausen

It is a great honor indeed to have been invited to address this distinguished group on such an important occasion—the celebration of the fiftieth anniversary of the Bretton Woods conference. I must confess, however, that I have arrived at a time of my life when I think of 50 years—a mere half century—as being rather young!

Despite what I perceive as the "youth" of the Bretton Woods organizations, we have come a very long way since that first conference in July 1944 in Bretton Woods, New Hampshire—and we have a record of achievement and global advancement of which we can be very proud:

- the reconstruction of economies devastated by World War II;
- successful development in East Asia;

- movement of project expertise to developing countries;
- widespread recognition of the World Bank as a repository of knowledge, experience, understanding, and research about development issues;
- development of customized structural and sector adjustment lending as a way of providing a more compatible policy framework in which development projects and programs may prosper; and, as a culmination of all these activities,
- improvements in the vital human condition by increased levels of literacy (through emphasis on basic education) and by dramatic increases in longevity and the lowering of infant mortality (through emphasis on public health programs).

Notwithstanding the substantial progress achieved in these last 50 years, however, economic progress has been very uneven across regions and between countries. More than a billion people continue to live at below poverty levels of less than one U.S. dollar a day. Sub-Saharan Africa remains the greatest regional development challenge for the future—because poverty is still on the increase and development investment is so dependent on foreign aid.

The environment is under severe attack from population growth that is far too fast for too many developing countries. Given the critical mass of the societal and economic deficiencies that still exist, sustainable development is the single largest challenge for the world to deal with in the next 50 years.

We stand today on the brink of a chasm. On one side are the economic and political realities that nations must address to achieve prosperity. On the other are the expectations of their peoples. The chasm itself might be called the "expectations gap."

The focus of the Bretton Woods organizations since their founding is to help nations build or rebuild their infrastructure and put in place sound economic and financial policies. The World Bank and the Fund have worked very hard at being apolitical in this endeavor—a sound policy that has contributed to the credibility and success of these multilateral institutions.

But the needs of many nations have changed, largely owing to the collapse of communism and the political chaos that many countries now suffer as they attempt to rebuild their economies on a free market basis. When historians or anthropologists look back on the twentieth century, they will surely view the discrediting of communism as an economic, political, and social system as one of the century's major events. In some ways, they might argue that it has been the most important and dramatic event. However, when communism disintegrated, the Cold War (which existed for most of the life of the Bretton Woods institutions) ended quite abruptly. It left the economies of many of the former republics of the U.S.S.R. in tatters.

Unfortunately, the abrupt dissolution of the old order led to the soaring of expectations of the peoples of those nations. They believed (and the free world probably played a role in that expectation) that with elections and free market economies, they would rather quickly and perhaps almost automatically enjoy the benefits that the nations of Western Europe, North America, and Asia had spent generations developing and nurturing.

This is clearly an unrealistic expectation. That is why today we may have to consider looking beyond pure economic and financial issues to help nations without a tradition of free markets to find their way through the political wilderness created when trying to establish new, market-based economies. To my mind, there is no question that—much as we would like to separate finance and economics from politics—economic development must go hand in hand with political and social development.

Here is our dilemma. While the Bretton Woods institutions stand ready to participate in economic development, we must ask who stands ready to help newly liberated nations understand the kind of political development required to provide the environment for market economies. Who will, or can, take up that challenge?

Let me make myself very clear. By no means do I suggest that we impose any mandate on nations to set up political environments emulating those in the West. However, it is very clear that many nations that understand their people's economic needs also need guidance in establishing the political environment to permit those needs to be met by market dynamics. And they need guidance on how to prepare their people for the tensions and upheavals that are inherent in the free enterprise system.

The developed nations are accustomed to the constant tension between the public and private sectors. We know that, while we may disagree strongly on the best way to achieve any given goal on any given day, we have generations of history in forging compromises that will bring the greatest good to society at large. And our success shows that so far the market approach has worked much better than any other system to unleash the most powerful force for economic development on planet earth—the power of individual entrepreneurs. In recent years, the world has turned rather dramatically toward the market principles espoused by Adam Smith more than 200 years ago.

But market economies cannot be created in a day, or in a year, or perhaps even in a decade. Even the most brilliant idea cannot be imposed on a society or a culture by mandate—it can be implemented only by a process of education, example, visible successes, and clear and continual communication. Even where there is consensus on the goals, it takes great effort and frequently excruciating pain to achieve them. There's an old saying in almost every country and every language that exclaims, "No pain—no gain!"

We say that the Bretton Woods institutions are not political institutions. They are not! Rather, they are economic and financial institutions, and their decisions are based on the economic and financial analysis of a given country, taking into consideration the complexities and dynamics of that country—all based on the pragmatic experience of the Fund and the World Bank, developed in other countries over these last 50 years.

My own experience—as a managerial executive in both the public and the private sector—is that it is so much easier—easier by factors—to make changes of emphasis and direction in the private sector than it is to do so in the public sector! I say that as a broadly based fact that not everyone realizes. The political considerations that governments must heed are at best terribly complex and interrelated with many other complicated aspects of governance, and yet the political realities are just as much a fact as the economic realities with which the Bretton Woods institutions must deal.

The nations of the world need to see role models—that is, success stories—as evidence of what can happen if appropriate government policies are adopted: policies that provide incentives for disciplined but suitable fiscal and monetary actions; policies that are conducive to sustainable development programs; and programs that reduce poverty levels in developing countries and raise the standards of living of their peoples. Fortunately, there are many examples—many success stories—for which the World Bank and the Fund deserve much recognition for their help and assistance in removing or moderating the impact of obstacles impeding economic development.

My purpose here is not to list all of the success stories or to imply that nothing more needs to be done—that the mountain of "development" has been conquered—development is never completed. But Chile and Mexico are two countries that come to mind in this connection. China is another that deserves mention, particularly in its success in raising the standard of living for approximately 100 million of its people above the poverty level in the last 15 years or so.

The Republic of Korea is indeed a success story. It was important for the 1985 Annual Meetings of the Fund and the World Bank Group to be held there so that other developing nations could see how a country that had the same per capita GDP as India in 1960 could prosper and grow faster than most other developing countries—the result of implementing appropriate policies conducive to accelerating economic growth and development. There are many other success stories. But developing countries need to have hope for the future. Solutions cannot be found if leadership of a country despairs. And success stories can raise hopes by presenting examples of what works—and what does not work!

I confess that my personal "expectations" of the time it would take to establish a Multilateral Investment Guarantee Agency (MIGA) is but one example of how difficult it is to achieve results in the public sector, and BankAmerica Corporation, on the other hand, is an example of how quickly and dramatically changes can occur in the private sector. But my experience in the public sector helped me enormously when I returned to the private sector to help a major financial institution put its house in order once again.

Similarly, the World Bank and the IMF can play an important educational and informational role in causing countries' expectations to be realistic. These institutions have both the experience and the access to help local government officials, entrepreneurs, and consumers to understand the realities of the difficult changes they are living through—and to bring expectations more closely in line with realities.

The expectations gap has led to disappointment and to disillusionment for millions of people. What is of even greater concern, the disillusionment suffered could put some countries in jeopardy of a nostalgia for those "good old days" of the managed economy, where one's most basic needs were attended to automatically. A relapse to repressive forms of government and to governments that have policies not conducive to economic growth would be tragic indeed.

Yet who is to help both the millions of citizens and their leaders come to grips with the chaos that is the immediate aftermath of the dramatic shifts to a more free and open economic and political system? The two Bretton Woods institutions are in the best position in the world to extol the virtues—in a non- "conditional" way—of the advantages of liberalizing economic regimes.

Those of us who have been involved for long periods with the Bretton Woods institutions know the elements that are critical for economic stability in nations: the creation of strong yet environmentally sensitive infrastructures; the adjustment assistance necessary to encourage developing nations to implement policies conducive to achieving the levels of sustainable economic growth necessary to raise their peoples' standards of living; sound family practice and population control policies; and serious attention to human rights and social needs, such as education, health, and the status of women.

Many, if not most of us here today—government officials, business people, financial experts, and academics—are individuals who have spent major portions of our lives focusing on the economic and financial requisites for viable nations. We know what is needed. But do we have the political will to get there? How do we begin to advise nations on how to cultivate a political climate that will promote economic development and stability in the light of a rapidly changing landscape?

Some of the finest minds in the field of international economic development will be discussing these challenges this afternoon and tomorrow, and I do not wish to pre-empt them. But I do have a few thoughts on the potential for expanding the roles of the major players who are carrying heavy responsibilities in the area of international economic development.

First, the international development institutions: the premier institutions for international economic development are, of course, the International Monetary Fund and the World Bank Group. They have been responsible for the lion's share of the development that has improved the lot of nations and their peoples over the past 50 years.

The Bretton Woods Commission issued a report in July of this year with some sound ideas for streamlining and updating the IMF and the World Bank, in order that they may adapt "to a world that has turned from public sector dominance towards private enterprise and free markets." Although I am not in total agreement with all of the Commission's recommendations, I think the report does send a clear call for the World Bank and the IMF to develop even stronger ties of cooperation in dealing with the new economic and political realities and to work more transparently and more closely with the other development bankers— the Inter-American Development Bank, the Asian Development Bank, the African Development Bank—and with Jacques de Larosière's European Bank for Reconstruction and Development.

And let us not forget the growing importance of nongovernmental organizations in many countries. I think that development needs in the future will be met more and more by the private sector and by these organizations.

The World Bank disburses huge sums of money every year, but equally important to developing nations, and in some cases even more important, is its policy advice—macro as well as micro—because I am a strong believer in "adjustment" lending—structural as well as sectoral. And that advice can only be effective when both institutions are reading from the same script. This is particularly critical if the institutions choose to lean a bit more (in a nonmandatory way) into the challenge of offering political development counsel as well as economic development counsel, and, of course, it goes without saying that close coordination on projects can maximize the effectiveness of all of these governmental development institutions.

I would submit that if we did not have an International Monetary Fund and a World Bank today, we would want to invent new institutions to fulfill their missions. Perhaps we could even create new institutions that proved to be more efficient, less bureaucratic, more flexible, and more dynamic than the ones we now have. But let us think that through just a bit. These institutions—the Fund and the Bank—are clearly not perfect! But they have adapted rather well to the changed world of today, which was *not* envisioned 50 years ago. Perfection is largely in the eye of the beholder. I think almost all of us could and would agree that it is a better world today because of the Fund and the Bank.

Why don't we resolve at this conference to work more effectively in support of our institutions—to ensure that the IFC, for example, has enough capital really to exploit the global movement toward the private sector whose momentum is increasing rather remarkably? And the same goes for the Fund as it argues for its next quota increase.

MIGA, which has just recently started to get its head above water, needs nurturing and support as it assists the development process by guaranteeing against political—noneconomic—risks in the developing countries.

The Bretton Woods report suggested that the World Bank require government performance guarantees to protect private enterprises from unpredictable changes in policy. Unfortunately, a government given to unpredictably changing its policies would probably change its policy on performance guarantees as well. I think it would be far more realistic to expand the role of MIGA, to provide insurance where development funds might be at risk.

Cynics would probably say that one who suggested in the fall of 1981 that we try once again to create a multilateral guarantee agency might well be expected to hold this view. The role of the private sector in economic development must and will grow and increase spectacularly in the decades ahead, and we should encourage the private sector to play as large a role in the future as it possibly can. Developing countries can to a large extent influence these private sector flows by making themselves more attractive. The most valuable resource in the world and in any nation is people! I believe the World Bank should devote even more attention than it has in the past to helping governments identify projects that can quickly and very visibly improve the lot of their people: hospitals, schools, housing, and a pollution-free living and working environment. And we all realize that Lew Preston and Barber Conable before him have both been giving special emphasis to this effort. More is even better!

Only by creating some visible successes can nations begin to move toward the political consensus needed to make the tough economic decisions necessary to help make steady progress toward prosperity through a market economy. National leaders must find the will and the voice to convince their populations that freedom is hard work but is well worth the prize.

We should work through the public sector wherever we can to enable the private sector to develop itself. Government alone cannot fulfill the expectations of people! Communism taught us that. But public-private partnerships can help provide the political and economic education that must underpin growth and development.

Shareholder developed nations should become more supportive of the Fund, the World Bank, and the regional development banks and develop more consistency in dealing with them. They must also be prepared to play a role in the political education of the emerging market economies.

Developed nations must get their own economic houses in order. None of our domestic populations will be willing to support economic assistance abroad if they are suffering from unemployment, poverty, and homelessness in their own backyards.

May I also suggest that the world would benefit from having stronger, more *experienced* Executive Directors appointed to both the Fund and the World Bank boards of directors. I also believe the world would benefit from having a stronger Development Committee to discuss the more substantive and new issues of development that are presenting themselves.

There has been a tendency in recent years for some developed nations to try to impose their own political agendas on the World Bank. This could be disastrous in the extreme, because the true magic of the World Bank has been its ability to be apolitical in its recommendations. It must continue to be so if it is to retain its credibility and effectiveness.

But, even while remaining apolitical in the sense of not advocating any particular political system, the Bank can do more to help educate political leaders about how best to harness the energy of their peoples to achieve realistic economic goals within a realistic period of time.

The newly industrializing economies must be encouraged to participate much more strongly in development financing. Although many of these countries belong to IDA, they must be urged to increase their support for the agency, and also to participate more fully in the international organizations that are seeking to promote world growth and stability. Because they represent recent success stories, their advice to the new market economies can have great credibility and timeliness. They should be encouraged to become role models, sharing their experience and achievements.

Finally, the IMF and the World Bank need to market their services and accomplishments more effectively to their shareholder countries, their client countries, and the citizens of those countries. In my view, the world would benefit if both institutions were to extol their virtues a bit more aggressively than their modesty currently permits! We also must extol their virtues. It is in our self interest.

We are living in perilous times, facing a future that can either bring unprecedented prosperity to the world or send large segments of its population careening back into repression and darkness. In the Bretton Woods organizations and in their memberships, we have the resources and abilities to create a better future. Let us all work positively and cooperatively in really supporting the development process in future years.

I have every expectation that even greater progress can be made in the next 50 years than has been accomplished in the first 50 years of the Bretton Woods development process. And I further expect not to be disappointed in that expectation!

5

Agendas for the Bretton Woods Institutions

This session brought together a panel of experts who had participated actively in other events analyzing the future agendas of the Bretton Woods institutions to examine the full range of issues affecting the institutions from the perspective of both industrial and developing countries. Professor Gerald K. Helleiner of the University of Toronto has served for several years as Research Coordinator for the Group of Twenty-Four Developing Countries, and he had organized the Group of Twenty-Four conference that was held in Cartagena, Colombia, in April 1994. Professor Peter B. Kenen of Princeton University had helped organize the Institute for International Economics conference held in Washington in May 1994, and he served as a member of the Commission on the Future of the Bretton Woods Institutions. Moisés Naím, Senior Associate of the Carnegie Endowment for International Peace, had been a featured speaker at both these conferences and a background contributor to the Commission's report, and brought the perspective of a former trade minister and Executive Director of the World Bank for Venezuela. Chairing the session was Abdlatif Y. Al-Hamad, the Director General and Chairman of the Board of Directors of the Arab Fund for Economic and Social Development (Kuwait), who had served as Chairman of the Boards of Governors of the World Bank and the Fund in 1982.

Introduction

Abdlatif Y. Al-Hamad remarked that, as an observer and practitioner in the field of development for more than 30 years, he wondered whether the agenda for the Bretton Woods institutions for the next 50 years would be very different from the agenda of the past 50. The emphasis might well be different, as might the clientele and the thrust of work of the institutions, but that would only be an indication of the great success of the two institutions in fulfilling the mandate set for them by their visionary founders 50 years ago. What was needed for the future, therefore, was more such success.

Having said that the Bretton Woods institutions had been very successful, it had also to be recognized that mistakes had been made. Throughout the past 50 years, both institutions had learned from their mistakes, and it might be expected that further mistakes would be made during the next 50 years, which would nevertheless be helpful in increasing the understanding of the dynamic process that leads to development. The issues that came most immediately to mind—such as poverty, population, governance, economic reform, and the environment—had been around in one form or another for many years and were likely to remain salient for many years to come.

Gerald K. Helleiner

Many of the points I shall make appear in the recently published proceedings of the Group of Twenty-Four conference in Cartagena, commemorating the fiftieth anniversary of Bretton Woods. I speak here, however, only for myself.

I shall make five points. The most important is the last.

Global Macroeconomic Management

The current system of global economic governance is unrepresentative and accident prone. It is run, de facto, by the Group or Seven or, more accurately, by the Group of Three. Neither the developing countries nor the smaller industrial countries have much confidence in its capacity to manage global economic events in the overall global interest. There is a broad global interest in the macroeconomic performance and in the macroeconomic policies of the major industrial countries and, in particular, in their steady economic growth, selection of an appropriate monetary and fiscal policy mix, maintenance of orderly foreign exchange and financial markets, full utilization of capital and labor, and their achievement of symmetry in the international adjustment process and liberal regimes for international trade. Obviously, there is also global interest in the provision of adequate liquidity, debt-relief proposals, rules for IMF behavior, and the like. The interests of the majority of the world's population are not at present seen to be well served in the decision-making processes of the industrial countries, either individually or in the Group of Seven, in these spheres.

The IMF's views carry limited weight either in the decision making of the major industrial countries or in the deliberations of the Group of Seven; effective IMF influence over economic policies is concentrated in the developing countries and the countries in transition. The Interim Committee is widely perceived as little more than a "rubber stamp" for the decisions of the Group of Seven. If the IMF is to begin to play the role originally intended by its architects 50 years ago, some way must be found both to increase significantly its role in global macroeconomic management and to "democratize" its own deliberative procedures, perhaps in conjunction with overall reform of the United Nations.

Since, for obvious reasons, the Group of Seven countries are not too interested in such change, there must be *united* efforts and pressure by nonmembers of the Group to push reform efforts in this direction. As they do so, they will find strong professional support, not only from within the IMF but also much more generally.

Volatile Private Capital Flows

In the discussions leading to the Bretton Woods conference of 1944 and at the conference itself, there was considerable debate about how best to address problems created by volatile international flows of private capital. Debate centered upon the efficacy of controls over transactions in the capital account of the balance of payments and the possibility of an IMF role in the financing of member countries experiencing outward capital flows. These discussions and debates are current once again—in a context in which the potential flows of private capital, and hence the disruption, are much greater. Many developing countries are particularly concerned at present about the implications for their stabilization and development efforts of increasing interest rates in the industrial countries.

The Managing Director of the IMF proposes that the Fund more actively encourage members to liberalize fully their capital accounts as well as (as at present) their current accounts—a step that could require an amendment to the Articles of Agreement. He sees the Bretton Woods provisions (in the existing IMF Articles) for controls over international capital flows as anomalous and counterproductive. He also suggests a new facility for the support of countries experiencing private capital outflows, an idea that originated with Peter Kenen.[1] These proposals have an old and familiar ring. Many in the developing countries and elsewhere see these proposals now, as 50 years ago, as inappropriate and the proposed facility as requiring such large sums to make the idea unworkable.

The current concerns must be addressed in a variety of ways, including the development of an agreed new regime for private international capital flows that clarifies the circumstances in which controls are appropriate and provides for greater cooperation among central banks in their application and monitoring, as well as the extension of existing swap and cooperation arrangements among central banks to include those that have not so far benefited much from them, notably the developing countries. The role and responsibilities of the IMF in international financial markets need to be clarified, and almost certainly strengthened. This

---

[1]Peter B. Kenen, "Reforming the International Monetary System: An Agenda for the Developing Countries," in *The Pursuit of Reform*, ed. by J.J. Teunissen (The Hague: Forum on Debt and Development, 1993).

review, of course, now needs to be made in conjunction with deliberations within the World Trade Organization, which has some overlapping responsibilities. The responsibility and role of the Bank for International Settlements in this context will also obviously require review.

Finance for Development

The means for the continuing provision of adequate external finance to low-income countries need rethinking. Continued reliance on official external sources of finance for these countries, sadly, is inevitable—both for liquidity and for longer-term development purposes. Consideration of these countries' needs for external finance from official sources, as well as the terms and conditions for its provision, needs to be better integrated. Bilateral sources of official development assistance, debt relief, and finance from the regional development banks and UN agencies all need to be considered as a whole and in conjunction with the contributions of the IMF and the World Bank. The needs of the low-income countries for official finance appear likely to exceed their availability—unless new sources or modalities are found.

The Development Committee, which might have been expected to play some role in this regard, is widely seen as ineffective and irrelevant. Among the issues to be addressed are the adequacy of existing sources of liquidity and contingency finance, prospective flows of official development assistance, and debt relief for low-income countries. No amount of "adjustment" will suffice for sustained development if the requisite finance is missing. In this context, there should be consideration of the appropriate utilization of IMF gold reserves and possible modalities for writing down the debt to international financial institutions in extreme circumstances. At bottom, after 50 years of sporadic funding, much greater attention needs to be paid to the possibilities for more stable and automatic sources of official global financing for development purposes.

Ownership Issues and Research

Stabilization and adjustment programs that are effective and sustainable are those that are, in appearance and in fact, locally owned. Although there is now widespread rhetorical acceptance of this fact within the international financial institutions and the donor communities, the implications are not always reflected in changing practice. There is a great deal of "hot air" and hypocrisy in donors' and international financial institutions' discussions of the need for local ownership. Conditionality should be a technical, not a political, issue. This implies a heavy hand in some cases of conditionality, although on many technical issues there is professional uncertainty.

In this connection, the credibility of the international financial institutions and donors would be greatly enhanced if they supported the significant decentralization of research and advisory services in the sphere of development policy. Both research and advice are at present inappropriately concentrated in Washington. By increasing support for, and reliance upon, local research and advisory institutions in developing countries, it is likely that there will be not only improvements in the cost-efficiency, quality, and credibility of the relevant work but also genuine increases in local ownership of programs.

Review of the Institutions and Their Roles

Most important, an overall review of the current system of international economic governance and the role of the international financial institutions therein—such as is to be undertaken within the Group of Seven—must be fully participatory and representative if it is to be effective. It is time, after 50 years, for a major intergovernmental review of the Bretton Woods institutions in the context of the overall need for global economic governance, as the Group of Seven has recognized. It is time to review the roles and responsibilities of the IMF, the World Bank, the UN agencies, the regional development banks, and the World Trade Organization in an integrated fashion. Immediately and practically, it is time to review the efficacy of the Interim Committee, the Development Committee, and the Executive Boards of the international financial institutions within the overall governance system. Any such review confined to the Group of Seven, however, will carry neither a broad sense of ownership (a term that the international financial institutions use so much) nor, therefore, much legitimacy. A review by the Group of Seven is therefore unlikely to be effective. What is required is a much more representative intergovernmental review, on the general model of the Committee of Twenty of the 1970s, of the functioning of the Bretton Woods institutions and their future role in the changing world economy.[2] The initiation of such a representative intergovernmental review should be the major outcome of these fiftieth anniversary meetings in Madrid.

Peter B. Kenen

Having reason to expect that other members of this panel will focus on the work of the International Monetary Fund and the World Bank in

---

[2]The Committee of Twenty was convened by the Board of Governors of the IMF in 1972 as a Committee of Governors. Its 20 members represented the same constituencies of member countries as the Executive Directors of the Fund. It completed its work in 1974 and was succeeded by the Interim Committee.

the developing world and the formerly planned economies, I propose to focus on the tasks that face the Fund in the developed world. How can it help to improve the quality of policies pursued by the major industrial countries? What can it do to promote exchange rate stability?

My place in the overall conference program is very appropriate for this purpose, because my position lies between the forceful stance adopted by Fred Bergsten this morning and the more cautious stance that Wendy Dobson will adopt tomorrow afternoon. My views will also echo those of the Bretton Woods Commission, which said in its report (Bretton Woods Commission, 1994, p. A-1) that the major industrial countries should take two *successive* steps: "first, strengthen their macroeconomic policies, and achieve greater economic convergence; and second, establish a more formal system of coordination to support these policy improvements and avoid excessive exchange rate misalignments and volatility." In time, the report said, "this system might include commitments to flexible exchange rate bands."

I nevertheless agree with Fred Bergsten that exchange rate commitments should come early in the process, not late. In my view, however, they cannot come before there have been significant improvements in national policies and, more important, improvements in the policymaking processes of the major industrial countries.

Means and Ends

When reading proposals for reforming exchange rate arrangements, like those recently made by Williamson and Henning (1994), I often wonder whether their authors regard exchange rate stability as an end in itself or as a way of improving national policies and promoting international policy coordination. In my view, it is both a means and an end.

Promoting Policy Coordination

In the analytical literature on policy coordination, optimal outcomes frequently involve exchange rate changes. When a first-best policy equilibrium is subjected to some shock, so that policies have to be adjusted to achieve a new equilibrium, we find that exchange rates in the new equilibrium differ from those in the old. By implication, the introduction of an exchange rate constraint will typically lead to a second-best policy equilibrium. In most cases, however, we also find that a coordinated policy outcome *with* an exchange rate constraint is distinctly superior to an uncoordinated outcome *without* an exchange rate constraint. Therefore, we may conclude that an exchange rate constraint can contribute to the improvement of national policies if it serves decisively to promote international policy coordination.

This is quite likely to be true. Tomorrow, Wendy Dobson will explain why policy coordination has become very difficult. Officials find it hard enough to do their jobs at home, in the face of domestic constraints and pressures, without taking time to engage in international policy coordination. It is indeed increasingly hard for them to coordinate their policies domestically when central banks are independent and legislatures are irresponsible, without having to coordinate them internationally. Accordingly, there is apt to be a chronic shortage of international policy coordination unless governments commit themselves firmly to the pursuit of common or collective objectives. These objectives in turn, are most readily defined in terms of common or shared variables. The exchange rate is, of course, one such shared variable. A minister or governor can properly speak of his or her own country's inflation rate, growth rate, or unemployment rate, but not of its exchange rate. By its very nature, the exchange rate belongs to a *pair* of countries.

In brief, the pursuit of exchange rate stability may be the only effective way to relieve the chronic shortage of policy coordination and thus to achieve second-best coordinated outcomes.

Two more reasons for pursuing exchange rate stability exist, however. It is a worthy end in itself. First, exchange rate uncertainty is costly in real terms. Second, large exchange rate misalignments can undermine the trading system.

The Real Costs of Exchange Rate Uncertainty

We do not have conclusive quantitative evidence that exchange rate uncertainty depresses international trade, capital formation, or economic growth, although the body of evidence is growing (see Chowdhury, 1993, and Larraín and Vergara, 1993). Most studies of the issue, however, have focused on the wrong part of the problem. They have searched for the effects of uncertainty about short-run exchange rate movements, because it is easy to measure, rather than the effects of uncertainty about long-run exchange rate trends. It is not the mere length of the "run" that matters here; firms can make five-year forward contracts to hedge against possible losses on future payments or receipts. In the long run, however, firms face an additional risk.

If a firm knows what its foreign currency payments and receipts will be five years from now, it can use forward contracts and other financial transactions to protect itself against exchange rate changes. The possibility of large exchange rate changes over a five-year horizon, however, prevents a firm from knowing what its payments and receipts will be, because they will affect the future profitability of its operations and, therefore, the sizes of its payments and receipts. It is extremely difficult, moreover, to measure this different sort of uncertainty and thus to detect its influence on trade, capital formation, or growth.

Wendy Dobson will point out tomorrow that large multinational firms hedge against this different form of uncertainty by holding diversified "portfolios" of plants. This strategy, however, is costly to the world economy. It can only work if the firms invest in spare capacity. In other words, it reduces the productivity of capital.

Exchange Rate Misalignments and the Trading System

In his remarks this morning, Fred Bergsten argued that exchange rate misalignments are a major cause of protectionist pressures, and he cited some evidence to this effect (see, for example, Williamson and Henning, 1994, and Eichengreen and Kenen, 1994). It is therefore sufficient for me to make two brief points.

When a country's macroeconomic policies cause its currency to appreciate, domestic firms that face more foreign competition find it hard to lobby for a change in the macroeconomic policy mix. In frustration, they resort to lobbying for trade policy relief. This tendency is particularly strong in countries such as the United States, where legislators represent individual states or districts and are thus sensitive to the vicissitudes of key industries in those states or districts.

When, instead, the policy mix causes the domestic currency to depreciate, foreign competitors try to preserve their export market shares by cutting their home currency export prices (so-called pricing-to-market). But this shows up as "dumping" and is, no doubt, partly responsible for the striking increase in the number of antidumping actions in recent years.

It is thus very clear that exchange rate instability is a continuing threat to a liberal trade policy regime.

Reforming Exchange Rate Arrangements

I have thus offered three reasons for endorsing the recommendation of the Bretton Woods Commission that the major industrial countries move toward more intensive exchange rate management. It is worth noting, moreover, that the same recommendation has been made by many of the other groups that have met this year to mark the fiftieth anniversary of the Bretton Woods conference. It was widely endorsed, for example, at the recent conference sponsored by the Institute for International Economics, to which Fred Bergsten referred in his remarks this morning. Let me repeat my three reasons before moving on:

- First, a commitment to greater exchange rate stability can help to overcome the shortage of policy coordination;
- Second, it can reduce the real costs of exchange rate uncertainty; and
- Third, it can contribute to the integrity of the trading system.

At this point, however, we must confront two very serious problems. First, any attempt to stabilize exchange rates will intensify the shortage of domestic policy instruments available for managing each national economy. Second, the dynamics of the game between governments and markets produces two damaging tendencies. On the one hand, regimes that are not clearly articulated, such as the "soft and quiet" target zones of the Louvre accord, tend to decay with time, partly because, as Fred Bergsten explained, the survival of these informal arrangements depends too heavily on the views and priorities of individual officials. On the other hand, regimes that *are* very clearly articulated, such as the Bretton Woods system and the European Monetary System, tend to ossify, because the durability of the regime itself becomes too closely identified with the durability of particular exchange rates.

I will devote my remaining remarks to these basic problems—relieving the shortage of domestic policy instruments and achieving short-run exchange rate stability without sacrificing long-run exchange rate flexibility.

Relieving the Shortage of Policy Instruments

In a world of very high capital mobility, official intervention by itself cannot stabilize exchange rates. It must be supported by monetary policy. Another policy instrument is therefore needed to manage the domestic economy. That is why I said at the outset that the major industrial countries must improve their policymaking processes, as well as their actual policies, before committing themselves to more intensive exchange rate management. To be specific, they must find ways of making their fiscal policies much more flexible.

Wendy Dobson is pessimistic on this score. So am I. And the attitudes of my fellow economists deepen my pessimism. Many of them are distrustful, even contemptuous, of democratic politics. They are more interested in finding ways of constraining politicians than in finding ways of helping them relax the fiscal rigidities resulting from interest group pressures.

Let there be no mistake. Fiscal consolidation must come first. We cannot afford to pile cyclical deficits on top of structural deficits—and those will continue to grow, largely for demographic reasons, unless painful adjustments are made in the size and coverage of social insurance programs. Furthermore, the adjustments can lead to serious social conflict if they are not designed carefully to achieve a new social consensus. But fiscal consolidation should not be confused with fiscal rigidity. We must impart more flexibility to fiscal policies by improving the policymaking process, as well as actual fiscal policies, before we can prudently recommend that monetary policies be redeployed to achieve exchange rate stability.

The Risk of Ossification and the Role of the Fund

My second concern, the risk of ossification, brings me at long last to the role of the International Monetary Fund in helping the major industrial countries to manage exchange rates effectively.

When governments commit themselves to this objective, as I said before, they tend in practice to defend existing exchange rates tenaciously. They are fully aware of the need for periodic exchange rate changes—for what was called in the days of the Committee of Twenty a system of "stable but adjustable exchange rates." It is nevertheless hard to make those changes in a timely fashion, and capital mobility has made it harder.

An authoritative voice is therefore needed to say, quietly but firmly, that the time has come to change exchange rates—and even to say so publicly if private warnings are ignored. That is the task of the Fund in any future attempt to achieve greater exchange rate stability.

To play that role eventually, however, the Fund and the major industrial countries should contemplate three early innovations.

First, within the Fund itself, there must be close collaboration among the relevant area departments—those concerned with the various Group of Seven countries—under the aegis of the Research Department. The Research Department, in turn, must be charged not merely with compiling the *World Economic Outlook* but with tracking current developments closely in the Group of Seven countries and in foreign exchange markets.

Second, the Managing Director and staff of the Fund must participate fully in the deliberations of the Group of Seven countries, and the deliberations must be integrated with the Article IV consultations between the Fund and the individual governments of these countries. Furthermore, the Managing Director should report regularly to the Executive Board on the deliberations of these governments, particularly on the views expressed by the Fund's participants during those deliberations. In certain circumstances, moreover, it would be entirely appropriate for the Executive Board to ask that the Managing Director convey its views to the Group of Seven governments.

Third, the Fund should have its own "Council of Economic Advisors." The members of the Council should be appointed for fixed, nonrenewable terms, to protect their independence. The Council should advise the Managing Director and the Executive Board on a continuing, confidential basis. It should also have responsibility for the preparation of the *World Economic Outlook*, each issue of which should begin with a new prescriptive chapter, in which the Council should make specific recommendations to individual governments, on its own responsibility. Finally, the Chair of the Council should serve as the Fund's Economic Counsellor, participate with the Managing Director or his representative in the deliberations of the Group of Seven governments, and have broad responsibility for the work program of the Fund's Research Department.

These are modest steps. Nevertheless, they are aimed at a large objective—restoring the Fund to an influential role in managing economic relations among the major industrial countries and moving the world decisively toward greater exchange rate stability.

References

Bretton Woods Commission, *Bretton Woods: Looking to the Future*, Vol. 1, Commission Report, Staff Review, and Background Papers (Washington: Bretton Woods Committee, July 1994).

Chowdhury, Abdur R., "Does Exchange Rate Volatility Depress Trade Flows? Evidence from Error-Correction Models,"*Review of Economics & Statistics*, Vol. 75 (November 1993), pp. 700–706.

Eichengreen, Barry, and Peter B. Kenen, "Managing the World Economy under the Bretton Woods System: An Overview," in *Managing the World Economy: Fifty Years after Bretton Woods*, ed. by Peter B. Kenen (Washington: Institute for International Economics, 1994).

Larraín, Felipe, and Rodrigo Vergara, "Investment and Macroeconomic Adjustment: The Case of East Asia," in *Striving for Growth after Adjustment: The Role of Capital Formation*, ed. by Luis Servén and Andrés Solimano (Washington: World Bank, 1993), Chap. 11, p. 25.

Williamson, John, and C. Randall Henning, "Managing the Monetary System," in *Managing the World Economy: Fifty Years After Bretton Woods*, ed. by Peter B. Kenen (Washington: Institute for International Economics, 1994).

Moisés Naím

Most of the analyses and proposals prompted by this fiftieth anniversary of the Bretton Woods institutions center on large systemic issues of global governance, on the need to respond to new economic and political realities, or on the impact of the policies of the Fund and the World Bank. From the search for mechanisms to dampen exchange rate volatility to proposals to merge the Fund and the Bank, or even to close them down, to the effects of structural adjustment, the anniversary has stimulated a wide debate on many important issues. Yet surprisingly little attention has been given to the factors that shape the internal behavior of the Bretton Woods institutions. The way in which these institutions are governed, the mechanisms and processes through which their priorities are chosen and their strategies defined, and the incentives and values that drive their internal culture have received scant attention. In fact, these are generally perceived as minor, even bureaucratic, details that can easily be dismissed. The attractive challenges for most officials and analysts are either to get the policy prescriptions right or to activate the political process that would lead to the adoption of the systemic changes they favor.

It is indeed possible that as a result of the debates spurred by the anniversary we will see some major adaptations of the Bretton Woods institutions to the economic, political, and technological circumstances of the world. Unfortunately, policy-induced changes in global governance require the agreement of a large number of countries that often have sharply differing views and priorities. Therefore, regardless of the quality and merit of proposals to alter radically the way in which the international economy is currently governed, the probability that sweeping changes will be adopted is not very high. The mid-1990s finds the world without a country that can effectively serve as a rallier of nations and capable of assembling the international coalitions needed to induce the systemic reforms called for by the changes in the international economy that have occurred since the Bretton Woods conference 50 years ago. Such adaptations, therefore, have to be made within the context of the existing institutional framework. From this perspective, gaining a deeper understanding of how the institutions really work and of the factors that influence their performance can provide useful insights into their ability to adapt to the new challenges. It is therefore useful to highlight some of these issues that are often overlooked but that deserve more attention when discussing proposals to reform the world economy. Let me start with the mission and the strategic orientation of these institutions.

Most of the conferences leading up to this meeting concerning the Bretton Woods anniversary and the status of the institutions and the reviews of the Fund, the World Bank, or the regional development banks have concluded that they suffer from the lack of a precisely defined mission. Changes in the international financial system have eroded the mission of the Fund while the adoption of an ever-expanding definition of the determinants of underdevelopment has led to an increasing portfolio of goals that the development banks are expected to address. In recent years, the need to assist countries emerging from decades of communism has also added to the diversification of the goals of the Fund and the Bank. Paradoxically, the lack of a precise mission has allowed the institutions to adapt quite effectively to changes in their environment.

Since their creation, the World Bank and the Fund have reinvented themselves several times in response to new challenges that their founders had not contemplated. The downside of this flexibility is, of course, a significant dose of strategic ambiguity. The combination of a blurred mission, a drastically changing external environment, constantly growing demands, and a problematic governance structure has led to a rapid accumulation of goals. The excessive number of priorities breeds not only goal congestion but strategic confusion. Obviously, such conditions would impair effectiveness and efficiency in any organization. Goal congestion is most visible in the development banks, with portfolios of goals that range from the role of women in development to the regulation of telephone companies. But it has also plagued the operations and organizational effectiveness of the Fund. Goal congestion derives not only from a blurred, changing mission. It is also the result of the very different expectations of influential constituencies regarding the fundamental role of these institutions. No doubt, ambiguity of mission, goal congestion, and strategic volatility in the Bretton Woods institutions are largely the consequence of their external environment. But they are also undoubtedly the consequences of how decision making at the top of these institutions is organized. In general, once an objective is incorporated as part of the agenda, it becomes almost impossible to remove it. Political factors, organizational inertia, and the governance of these institutions make it very difficult to shed goals, at least formally.

It is fair to recognize, however, that the existing governance system of the World Bank and the Fund has worked fairly well. It has not replicated some of the sorry experiences of other multilateral institutions. It has also proved capable of responding to new demands imposed by the international political and economic environment. In effect, one can argue that it is almost a miracle that the Bank and Fund are still—as is recognized even by some of their harshest critics—technically competent organizations. To their credit, over the years they have been able to attract and retain a respected pool of highly talented and skilled professionals. As a general rule, in the Bank and Fund, staff recruitment and promotion are determined more by merit than by politics. In many areas, the reports produced in the institutions become indispensable references in any relevant discussion. Furthermore, at a time when the world's capacity for effective multilateral action seems to have been impaired by the end of the Cold War, the Bretton Woods institutions continue to offer a conduit through which international collective action can be reliably channeled. Such unique strengths and values therefore counsel caution in any attempt to reform the institutions. Experience has repeatedly shown that even the most resilient and sturdy of institutions is extremely vulnerable to mistakes made in the course of well-meaning reforms. This caveat notwithstanding, the Fund and the Bank, and even more so the regional development banks, like all institutions, constantly need organizational repair and maintenance.

The governance system of a multilateral financial institution typically has a board of governors composed of ministers or central bank presidents or governors who delegate responsibility to a full-time board of directors. Management responsibility falls on a strong president or chief executive officer, and the authority to adopt new strategic initiatives usually rests with the president and the top management, even though in some cases such initiatives are taken as a result of the pressures of influential external constituencies. In fact, in recent years, legislatures, nongovernmental organizations, and the media have substantially increased their capacity to shape the agenda and even the strategy of the multilateral financial institutions. The Bretton Woods institutions are more often than not found on the defensive in terms of public affairs and media attention.

An important element of the governance system is the board of Executive Directors of each Bretton Woods institution. As a consequence of an agreement made early on in the life of the World Bank and the Fund—not as a requirement of their Articles of Agreement—these boards are full-time resident bodies. Although the formal role of the board is quite clear, in practice it is quite complex and ambiguous. The board represents the interests of the shareholders and has almost total authority over the affairs of the institutions. Executive Directors, however, do not have any management responsibility and are not individually accountable for any specific decision made by the institution. Although the board has to approve every transaction and policy initiative, such initiatives are usually launched by management. Also, while Executive Directors do not have any day-to-day responsibilities, they work full-time in the institution, and although they are representatives of the governments that appoint them, they are, in fact, employees paid by the institution.

In all organizations, tension exists between shareholders (or their representatives, the board of directors) and management. This is true not just of private sector organizations but whenever an overseeing body has authority over the group of people who are responsible for daily management. Management tends to want to maximize growth, autonomy, and scope for its operations, whereas the board seeks to minimize risk, exposure, and the need for capital increases. This tension in the relationship can, in fact, be very productive. But if it is excessive, management is usually stifled, and an atmosphere of distrust, resentment, and inefficiency ensues. If, on the other hand, this tension is too weak, organizations tend to develop an operational bias toward the priorities favored by management, sometimes at the expense of shareholders' interests. Striking a healthy balance in the tension between board and management is an important precondition for the long-term institutional survival of any organization.

In the Bretton Woods institutions, the balance between shareholders and management is particularly fragile. Governors tend to be ministers who already have such a full agenda that they cannot devote enough of their time, effort, and attention to the supervision and overall management of the institutions. In fact, the issues relating to the institutions typically come to the governors' attention only when they pertain to their own countries or when there is a major crisis. Partly out of necessity, the governors delegate the monitoring, oversight, and the provisioning of the sense of direction of the institutions to the middle-level staff in their ministries and to the board of Executive Directors. The board, in turn, is fraught with conflicts of interest and other structural deficiencies that limit its effectiveness.

First, some Executive Directors represent borrowing countries, others represent donor countries, and still others represent both borrowing and donor countries. Second, whereas management is typically composed of specialists with many years of experience in the institution, Executive Directors are political appointees who rarely spend more than three years in the job. Third, paradoxically, even if they are political appointees, Executive Directors tend to have less access to the higher echelons of their governments than do the top management of the World Bank or the IMF. Fourth, with the growing complexity and diversity of the institution's agenda, it becomes very difficult for Executive Directors to exercise effective oversight over all the issues on which they are supposed to make decisions. Very often, this leads to a highly ritualized and symbolic decision-making process in which management receives very little strategic direction from the board.

Reforming the way in which Executive Directors are recruited and prepared for the job, together with a concerted effort to upgrade the way in which the boards of directors of the Bretton Woods institutions operate, may have more beneficial effects than many of the good ideas about global reform that unfortunately have little chance of being implemented. High turnover rates in the boards of the Bretton Woods institutions impair the effectiveness of the boards, but high turnover is also an important factor in their general functioning.

As I have noted, Executive Directors stay for too short a time, and when they are becoming more effective they have to leave the institution. But turnover is also a factor in its top management. Take the President of the World Bank, for example. I know that the last three former presidents, and even the current one, are the first to recognize that it takes at least two or three years to develop a detailed knowledge of the intricacies of the institution and its work. By then, their term is almost over. Only after several years is it possible to grasp the essence of the problems faced by borrowing countries. Five years is too short for anybody to develop the command needed to ensure that good ideas or good intentions are, in effect, implemented and transformed into good outcomes. This is even more so if in their previous careers those appointed to the presidency of the World Bank were not exposed over a substantial period of time to the bewildering dilemmas of development or to the many specificities of the World Bank as an organization.

In the coming years, the World Bank will have to cope with major changes in its external environment, some of which have been and will be discussed here. Not often discussed, however, are the many internal changes that the Bank will experience in the future, especially in the turnover of its top management. Essentially, an unavoidable—and not always positive—generational change at the top levels of the Bank is going to coincide with substantial changes outside the Bank. Coping with both will be an enormous challenge, which, as with all challenges, will present unique opportunities to the governors and the shareholders, and to the management of the institution.

Transforming this challenge into a positive opportunity requires those who are part of the governance system of the Bretton Woods institutions to change their ways. In the coming years, nothing threatens more the stability and the effectiveness of these institutions than the possibility that their shareholders continue to behave as absentee owners, becoming interested in their collective property only when they realize that it is in great and evident danger. As we know, when danger is imminent, it is often too late to act and to be effective.

General Discussion

Ismael Serageldin asked Naím to elaborate on the emergence of the so-called civil society and the role of other external groups advocating single or multiple issues, the links among those groups, governments, the Executive Directors, and the media, and how greater openness and change in the international community would need to be reflected in the governance of the two institutions.

Naím replied that the issues that Serageldin had raised were becoming increasingly important. In an earlier paper, he had noted that the World Bank was an inward-looking institution, and he had examined the internal incentives and modalities that had led to that organizational culture.[3] As a consequence of that culture, the Bank's relationship with the external environment had never been given high priority.

The World Bank and the Fund appeared increasingly defensive and reactive. In recent years, the globalization of the media, the growing democratization in the world, the increased competition that the Bank was facing, and the growing influence of legislatures were having an ever-increasing role in shaping the behavior of the Bretton Woods institution. Many nongovernmental organizations had found a way, through their parliaments, to affect the agenda and the strategy of the Bank, for example. Those developments called for a more proactive, integrated strat-

---

[3]Moisés Naím, "The World Bank: Its Role, Governance, and Organizational Culture," in Bretton Woods Commission, *Bretton Woods: Looking to the Future*, Background Papers (Washington: Bretton Woods Committee, July 1994).

egy for communicating with a fragmented and volatile external environment, which would impose unprecedented constraints on the Bank.

The overhaul of the governance system of the World Bank and the Fund was an important goal for the future. It was unfair to leave the Bank shouldering alone responsibilities that had actually been imposed on it by its Governors. Indeed, many of the policies for which the Bank was criticized came from other sources, although it was also true that internally generated policies had also drawn criticism. A better organized, more intelligent governance system should be able to respond better to the new realities of the world.

Wendy Dobson asked Kenen whether he could elaborate on the key point that he had made, namely, that there had to be more flexibility in domestic policy processes, particularly with regard to fiscal policy. Although she agreed with Kenen on that point, she also agreed that such a change was a huge challenge.

Kenen replied that it would be easy to dismiss Dobson's question by merely pointing out that more flexibility would not be possible until there had been more fiscal consolidation. It would not be possible to introduce flexibility around excessively large deficits, for example, which some countries still maintained. To further the discussion, however, he would assume away that problem and confront the issue of flexibility itself.

Some years ago, he had suggested that it should be possible, although politically difficult, to devise a fast-track procedure in the United States for tax changes of a temporary duration that would allow much greater flexibility.[4] One of the major problems in the United States, of course, is that any proposed change in taxes becomes an opportunity for interest group pressure to emerge on matters extraneous to the principal fiscal issues. In his view, the U.S. President should be given the power to propose, subject to approval by an up-or-down vote in both houses of Congress, a temporary income tax surcharge—nothing as complex or sophisticated as an investment tax credit, but something very straightforward and simple that would allow some variation in the fiscal stance. The problem, as he understood it, was quite different in Japan and in some other parliamentary democracies, but he was concerned that without that kind of flexibility, monetary policy would continue to be overburdened.

Jo Marie Griesgraber noted that Helleiner had described his fifth and final point—on reviewing the current systems of international economic governance and the role of the international financial institutions—as the most important. Helleiner had alluded to the work of the Committee of Twenty in the 1970s as a prototype for such a review, and she

---

[4] "Beyond Recovery," in *The Global Repercussions of U.S. Monetary and Fiscal Policy,* ed. by S.A. Hewlett, Henry Kaufman, and Peter B. Kenen (Cambridge: Ballinger, 1984).

asked him to elaborate on what such a committee should be asked to do in the current circumstances, what its agenda should be, and how it should be constituted.

Helleiner, observing that a number of participants in the work of the Committee of Twenty were in the audience, noted that the details of that work were less important now than the principle that had been established: the review should be undertaken by a representative intergovernmental body that was external to the organizations. The terms of reference of such a committee should be established in a representative fashion and should be related to the governance issues raised by Naím and to the substantive issues that had occupied much of the debate during 1994 on the role of the Fund and the World Bank. At a minimum, a review should cover such issues as the relationship between the Bretton Woods institutions and the regional development banks, the United Nations agencies, and the World Trade Organization.

One way to begin the process was simply to agree to constitute such a body, and perhaps even to establish its terms of reference, which might not, at least on the monetary side, be that different from those agreed for the Committee of Twenty in 1972. Many observers were concerned that, following the very rich exchange of views over the course of the year on critically important matters of global economic governance and the functioning of the Fund and the Bank, nothing very much would be achieved. To achieve something substantive, therefore, it was necessary first to establish a process that made it possible for outcomes to emerge.

As articulated in the Cartagena conference, the issues of particular concern to developing countries that would need to be addressed included provision of adequate liquidity, mechanisms for appropriate macroeconomic governance, appropriate provisions for longer-term development finance, procedures to be employed for the exchange rate regime, and provisions governing the liberalized and vastly increased flows of private portfolio capital. Although some countries might highlight other issues, such as Fund surveillance, the essential point was that the terms of reference for such a review needed to be broadly agreed and not handled within the Group of Seven, which was unrepresentative of the world economy as a whole and in which the rest of the world did not at present repose sufficient trust. The terms of reference should be set within the framework of the World Bank and the Fund.

Kenen commented that no one, including those who had brought the Group of Seven together, had ever thought of it as an executive committee for managing the world economy. The Group of Seven process had originated when countries with similar concerns and problems, and a similar stake in the international institutions, had begun to consult one another about their positions and interests in the system. If the Group were abolished tomorrow, it would recreate itself the next day, because those countries would want to concert their positions on key issues.

The Group of Seven as an arrangement for exchange rate management or macroeconomic consultation was a little different, but its role in the governance of the system arose from the role of the countries concerned in the system, their leverage, their influence, the size of their financial support, and their common concerns. Thus, he wondered whether Helleiner, in calling for the Group's reform, was suggesting a reduction in the weight of those countries in the voting power and formal governance of the institutions. Helleiner's suggestion might be interpreted to mean further democratization of the institutions in the sense of reducing the decision-making influence of that oligarchy, or no further consultation among the Group of Seven countries. If the Group of Seven were given less weight in decision making, it was not clear how the willingness of those countries to support the institutions financially could be sustained.

Helleiner noted that no one was recommending the abolition of the Group of Seven. It had every right to handle the matters of greatest concern to it in any way that it deemed appropriate. Apparently, one such issue was the need for a review of the international financial institutions and the appropriateness of the existing multilateral machinery for the twenty-first century. If such a review were to take place, clearly the rest of the world would have an interest in the process; the rest of the world had a voice and needed to be consulted on the key issues. In the end, if there were no way of pursuing in a more cooperative fashion the review called for by the Group of Seven, the rest of the world might have to conduct its own review.

He was not entirely sure how the issue of democratization and the oligarchic structure of the international financial institutions would evolve. Clearly, some system through which countries with the greatest economic power contributing most to the institutions were given a greater voice was appropriate and inevitable. Difficulties were likely to arise, however, particularly for the World Bank, which prided itself in many of its publications on being a development institution as opposed to a bank, although views within the World Bank on this point no doubt varied. The Bank's literature relating to development institutions did not disagree on the absolute need for participation, involvement, and ownership by those who were the object of development. If the role, governance, and procedures of the World Bank were to be reviewed— given that the Bank was probably the single most important development institution—all affected parties must be involved. The result of such a review could, of course, be that the World Bank's decision-making procedures would not be altered all that much because of the factors noted by Kenen. But it was important to bear in mind that under pressure for increased transparency, openness, and participation, the Bank had already initiated new operating methods. There was, therefore, room for maneuver in many of those areas.

One of the suggestions that had arisen in a review of the Bretton Woods system that he had chaired for Commonwealth Finance Ministers some ten years earlier[5] was that technical issues considered within the Executive Board (such as the details of adjustment programs or projects) should not be governed in the same way as issues of finance and control. On purely technical issues, a larger weight should not be assigned to the arguments of those making the largest financial contribution to the institution; indeed, on such issues, a system of weighting was probably inappropriate. Without discussing the interaction of the Bretton Woods institutions with the United Nations system, the problems associated with their voting procedures, and the ways of achieving appropriate representation, he would simply note that the issue was likely to be raised during the 1994 Annual Meetings. Some way must be found to return to the degree of acceptance of the global economic machinery that had existed when the United Nations had been founded in 1945. The large degree of acceptance of that machinery had somehow been lost along the way as the center of influence and power on those issues had shifted to Washington.

In concluding the session, *Al-Hamad* remarked that it would be difficult to bring harmony to the many rich and conflicting ideas raised during the discussion. He would note only that the debate over issues of governance was just beginning and would continue for a long time. In his view, the issue went beyond the operation of the international financial system and the Bretton Woods institutions and included governance within individual nations and societies. All countries would need to be aware of the issues involved and to contribute to the debate in their own way.

---

[5]Gerald K. Helleiner, and others, *Towards a New Bretton Woods: Challenges for the World Financial and Trading System: Report by a Commonwealth Study Group* (London: The Commonwealth Secretariat, 1983).

6

The Challenge and Experience
of Economic Liberalization and Reform

This session focused on the challenges that the Bretton Woods institutions face in helping member countries make the transition from central planning to a market economy. The first speaker was Liu Zhongli, the Minister of Finance of the People's Republic of China, who spoke about China's approach to reform. He was followed by Richard Portes, who, as Director of the Centre for Economic Policy Research, has undertaken an extensive program of research on these issues. He discussed the experience of Eastern Europe in economic liberalization. The session was chaired by Viktor Gerashchenko, the Chairman of the Central Bank of the Russian Federation.

Liu Zhongli

I am very pleased to address this session focusing on economic reform, because China itself has been undertaking broad and deep reforms. Over the past 15 years, China has prominently emerged on the path to reform, demonstrating its special characteristics—the reform path that we have chosen to take in the context of the actual situation of our country. At present, we are moving toward the goal of building a socialist market economy. I would like to take this opportunity to provide you with information about China's reform, our perception of it, and our practice.

The Chinese people initiated the reform program on their own volition. A strong state and a prosperous nation is what the Chinese people have been striving for generation after generation. Ever since the founding of the People's Republic of China, the Chinese people have been ambitious about reconstructing and developing their country as fast as possible by relying on their own efforts, thereby lifting themselves out of poverty and backwardness. Confronted with the then international environment and the country's circumstances, China embarked on the road of development based on a highly centrally planned economy.

In the early stages of development in the new China, the economic system of highly centralized planning played an historic role; however, with time and changing circumstances, this traditional system turned out to be increasingly ill-suited to meet the needs of the Chinese economy and was hindering the further improvement of productivity. A development model of self-imposed isolation from the outside world will not enable China to modernize. Faced with a rapidly changing world, the Chinese Government and the people reached a consensus: only through reform will China be prosperous and only by opening up will it keep pace with the outside world.

Unlike other pioneering countries undertaking market-oriented reforms, China was faced at the outset with a unique situation: first, as a low-income, populous developing country, it was characterized by a rural community accounting for 80 percent of the population, regional disparity in development, a generally low level of productivity, and serious poverty problems; and second, China had a system of a highly centrally planned economy with an egalitarian distribution of income and, as a result, had forged an interest structure that suffered from a lack of incentive and discipline.

The restraints of the traditional economic system and the fragility of the low-income economy constituted dual constraints to reform. Reform is a profound transition, which will inevitably break down the traditional interest structure. However, with low incomes and a large population, economic growth has to be the precondition for readjustment of this structure. Only by making a larger cake will it be possible to adjust the way it is shared with the support of the overwhelming majority of the population. China's reform program has to be implemented in the context of economic growth, and the phasing in of the new economic system must take place alongside the phasing out of the old one. Therefore, a gradualist approach has been adopted to ensure the success of reform under the conditions of the dual constraints. The reform program has been implemented with a balanced combination of short-term and long-term objectives and with proper emphasis on the linkage between reform, development, and stability to ensure the irreversible trend of reform.

Indeed, the reform program aimed at both short- and long-term objectives reflects a strategy to harmonize desirability and practicality. To avert an earthshaking impact on the national economy, the reform program in China did not completely crush the old system overnight. Instead, it advanced from the periphery to the center and from individual parts to the complete whole in order to achieve a range of realistic short-term objectives in succession—as stepping-stones to attain long-term objectives.

In China, reform, development, and stability are interlaced and interdependent. Reform is the engine of development. As development is the groundwork for social stability and national prosperity, it is both the ultimate goal of reform and a necessary condition for its smooth implementation. Stability is a sine qua non of reform and development. We make a point of maintaining stability in order to keep our balance in moving ahead faster than would otherwise be possible. Therefore, it follows that Chinese reform takes the gradualist approach, which has become its distinct feature. This approach has proved effective in China.

Over the past 15 years, the program of reform and opening up has unleashed productive forces and raised the overall strength of the national economy. In 1978–93, China's GNP grew at an average annual rate of 9 percent, and per capita income of the rural and urban inhabitants, adjusted for inflation, at 6 percent and 8 percent, respectively. Having reaped visible and tangible benefits, the Chinese people, 1.2 billion strong, have embraced the program with the greatest enthusiasm and with unqualified support. They are deeply convinced that they have a significant stake in the far-reaching reform program.

The goal of China's reform is to establish a socialist market economy. And the reform has continuously evolved in theory and in practice.

Development in theoretical exploration for the reform has focused on how the issue of planning versus market should be addressed. Ranging from the idea of a "dominant planned economy supplemented by market regulation," which was proposed in 1979 at the early stage of reforms, to that of building a planned socialist commodity economy, as announced in 1984, and then to the goal of building a socialist market economy set by the Party's Fourteenth Congress in 1992, this process of conceptualization reflects the progress of our understanding of the issue of planning and market.

In practice, the reform program has advanced chronologically in three phases, reflecting the gradual process of the intensifying reform.

In the first phase of about six years, reform efforts were concentrated in rural areas, providing incentives to farmers to produce agricultural products for the market by setting up various forms of the household contract responsibility system. In urban areas, enterprise reforms intended to extend autonomy were initiated on a trial basis. Meanwhile, special economic zones were established, and 14 port cities were opened to the outside. By launching the reform program in rural areas, which had remained peripheral to the Chinese system of a planned economy, China managed to set reform in motion at the lowest possible cost. For such a large agrarian country, the instant success of the rural reforms was the first critical step in addressing agriculture as a fundamental problem in the Chinese economy, thereby laying a solid foundation for reforms to be developed in a comprehensive way. A remarkable feature of the rural reforms was the mushrooming of township and village enterprises, which injected the vitality of a new mechanism into the Chinese economic system, serving as an instructive prelude to enterprise reform in urban areas.

The second phase covered seven years. During this period, reform efforts shifted to urban areas, with emphasis on revitalizing enterprises. Efforts were made to increase the autonomy of enterprises by delinking them from the government and to transform their operating mechanisms. Meanwhile, moves were also gradually initiated to develop markets and to implement price reform and reform in macroeconomic management. Broad reforms were evolving in both urban and rural areas, in science and technology, education, and the political system. The coastal areas in southern and eastern China were further opened up. Reforms at this stage began to make inroads into the core of the system of the planned economy. Prominent features were the implementation of individual packages and special regional emphasis in a bid to achieve breakthroughs up front in unraveling the old system in certain areas and regions. Price reform was the area that achieved the most outstanding success, with the market beginning to replace planning step by step in price determination.

The third phase started in 1992 when China's reform entered the era of building a socialist market economy. The essence of the reform at this stage was to create a modern enterprise mechanism, supplemented by sweeping reforms that encompass planning, fiscal policy and taxation, and pricing, labor, and wage systems, as well as the financial, commercial, and trade sectors. Emphasis began to shift from breaking through the old systems to establishing new ones; from readjusting policy to building up a new institutional and regulatory framework; from individual reform packages to integrated reforms; and from prioritization to advancement on all fronts, reinforced by special focuses. Opening up to the outside intensified and broadened on an unprecedented scale.

The 15 years of reforms have led to a sea change in the Chinese economic system and its operating mechanism. The market is beginning to play a dominant role in resource allocation. Nevertheless, China remains in transition from the old to the new system. The flawed traditional system, deficient in discipline and economic incentives, still exists, while the market mechanism of resource allocation is still being developed. Conflict and friction between the two systems have spawned uncertainties in economic activities. The resolution of certain problems has made structural problems even more acute. For instance, questions remain on how to strengthen the basic agriculture sector and overall rural economic development; how to transform the operating mechanisms of enterprises and improve their efficiency; how to narrow regional development disparities between east and west and reduce poverty; and how to develop social equity and establish a social security system without compromising efficiency.

For these issues to be resolved in a fundamental way, the reform process must be accelerated, and a full-fledged socialist market economy established. At present, our basic policy is to seize the opportunity, intensify reform, open up further, promote development, and maintain stability. The priorities are to establish modern enterprise systems and speed up the reform of macroeconomic management systems in fiscal, taxation, financial, and investment areas, to be supplemented with reforms in related areas. A legal framework for a modern market economy is to be established to govern the new systems with laws and regulations. Substantive measures must now be taken to strengthen and improve macroeconomic management, control inflation, strike a proper balance between reform, development, and stability, and ensure the smooth implementation of reforms. We envisage that by the end of the 1990s a socialist market economy will largely have been established, which will further develop into a mature and stable system in another 20 years or so.

Opening up to the outside world constitutes an integral component of our reform program, and China is committed to more extensive exchanges with the international community in this process. Chinese history contains a humiliating chapter of being coerced to open her doors. Today, full of national confidence, the Chinese people have taken the initiative to open up to the outside. Like a vast ocean willingly absorbing water from all sources, the nation is now opening its arms to the fruits of civilization of the entire human race, including the physical and nonphysical fruits of civilization created by capitalism over the centuries. Opening up to the outside world has substantially contributed to the reform process in China, integrating its economic development with that of the rest of the world.

While mainly relying on our own efforts to implement reform, we have also benefited from broad international support and drawn on valuable cross-country experience. We shall continue to strengthen such international cooperation. It is our consistent view that national situations—economic, cultural, etc.—vary from country to country and that there is no such thing as a universally applicable reform model. China's reform program has to fit into the actual situation of the country, and the principle governing its implementation is to follow whatever is sound and feasible.

Permit me to say a few words about our cooperation with the World Bank and the IMF in the field of promoting reform. The direct support of these two institutions for our reform is mainly reflected in two areas: at the macro level—providing advisory services for the formulation of policies and strategies—and at the micro level, so far as the Bank is concerned—supporting the actual implementation of the reform program through investment projects charged with reform objectives. Obviously, our cooperation in this way has been very successful, and we expect to enhance our efforts further in this respect. We feel that advisory services and financial support are mutually reinforcing and that therefore neither should be neglected. We feel that the two institutions can play a positive role in supporting the reforms of member countries, as long as they respect member countries' decision making and take into account their actual situations and their needs.

On the occasion of the fiftieth anniversary of the Bretton Woods institutions, we welcome the continued efforts of the World Bank and Fund to support the undertaking of reform in developing member countries. We think that the institutions should give increasing attention to the special difficulties of low-income countries under reform while addressing the generic issues in developing countries and the common issues of economies in transition. In our view, support for reform and assistance for development are mutually complementary. Reform is aimed at promoting development, which, in turn, will create the necessary material conditions for its further enhancement. This is particularly true in low-income countries where the growth of social wealth is instrumental in the readjustment of the interest structure affecting different groups of people. Following this rationale in stressing their assistance for reform, the Bank and the Fund should not overlook the strategic implications of development for reform. Furthermore, the two institutions should give consideration to the relationship between efficiency and equity. Reform should not only improve the efficiency of economic activities and promote growth but also bring benefits to the majority of people, to ensure the sustainability of reforms. Indeed, this is the ultimate objective of reform.

We appreciate the principle of client orientation recently proposed by the World Bank. We find that low-income countries have a special need for infrastructure development, poverty alleviation, human resource development, and institution building. The Bank's support in all these areas will bring about favorable economic and social conditions to facilitate reform in these countries.

It is crucial for such a low-income developing country with one fifth of the world's population as China to set up a socialist market economy. There are still many twists and turns on the road to accomplishing this complex and daunting task. It is our strong belief, however, that China's reform is in the fundamental interests of this nation and that it also contributes to world peace, stability, and development. Bracing ourselves for future challenges, we will unswervingly move along the path we ourselves have chosen. We are fully confident that we shall be able to attain our objectives!

Richard Portes

Purpose, Procedure, and Principles

We have not seen a reversion to communism or central planning in Eastern Europe and most of the former Soviet Union, and west of

Ukraine, the recovery from the depression of the early 1990s has begun. But the economic transformation of Eastern Europe has proved much slower, more difficult, and more costly than we all expected five years ago.

Where incipient hyperinflation was stopped, inflation still remains stubborn in the 25–60 percent per annum range, and some stabilizations have failed. The initial fall in output was far deeper than projected and in some countries still has not been reversed. Liberalization of prices and elimination of central allocation did create functioning markets rapidly, but the accompanying redistribution of income has strained social cohesion. Often the corruption engendered by bureaucratic allocation has given way to more overt criminal activity in unregulated markets. Even giving away state enterprises to private owners takes time (finishing only now in the Czech Republic), and "large privatization" has in most cases gone very slowly. In both state-owned and privatized firms, there has been significant "defensive" restructuring, but the forward-looking, strategic action that changes industrial structure requires both domestic and foreign investment, which has so far been lacking.

Some participants with major stakes or political ambitions maintain that there was no (better) alternative to the policies followed, and they claim vindication in the first signs of recovery. They finally see the light at the end of the tunnel under the vale of tears—not before time, though many had claimed to see it much earlier. Politics is unforgiving, and doubtless one cannot afford the luxury of admitting error. Nevertheless, there is a striking lack of detachment in some of the ex post rationalizations that appear not just in the press but also in the professional literature.

I shall not examine a particular country's experience, but there is no space for a comprehensive survey. So I shall take a selective, critical view. I shall take most of the "good news" as known—it is natural for policymakers to dwell on their achievements, and this paper is directed toward the policy community. It will therefore focus primarily on errors in the design of the transformation so far, giving some attention to further dangers on the path ahead. The experience of the vanguard should be instructive for the next wave,despite the specificity of individual countries. Evidently, this exercise benefits enormously from the perspective of hindsight. I shall devote special attention to the role in policymaking of the international financial institutions, especially the IMF.

I shall not be so ambitious as to hand down "commandments" to guide the transition or to expose "fallacies" in the positions of other commentators. Both the professional literature and the events of the past five years suggest humility, as well as skepticism toward political rhetoric: the most ardent proponent of "radical shock therapy" or free market ideologist may choose not to raise rents or energy prices to market levels immediately in a single step, to hold back on enforcement of bankruptcy laws, and in other ways to manage the transformation pragmatically—and successfully.

We should therefore avoid labels: not even "radicals" and "gradualists." It is no more helpful to divide the field among neo- (or any other kind of) liberals, Keynesians, planners, institutionalists, or evolutionists. Economic analysis can get us beyond these clashing categories and the misleading metaphors often used to support them.

We are frequently reminded that we have no general theory of the transformation, no optimal paths or well-defined end points. That is neither surprising nor cause for concern. We do have a wide range of useful tools. As always, we can get quite far with supply and demand embedded in a suitable general equilibrium framework. For macro, we have revealing models of hyperinflation, different approaches to stabilization, and the roles of nominal and real anchors. The political equilibrium literature helps us with credibility and sequencing. Trade theory, economic geography, and gravity models can illuminate trade and investment policy choices. Recent work on incentives, regulation, corporate governance, and financial repression, as well as tax-benefit models all have extensive applications to the issues that arise in transformation.

There are nevertheless key differences between the economic transformation of Eastern Europe and two common analogies: postwar reconstruction; and stabilization, liberalization, and adjustment in middle-income developing countries. I would stress three features that require intellectual and policy innovation:

- The unprecedented need to move from comprehensive central planning and state ownership simultaneously to markets and private ownership;
- The underdevelopment of market economy institutions side by side with overdevelopment of industry; and
- The exceptional degree and extent of distortions in prices, technology, capital stock, and behavior (of managers, workers, and households).

These distinctive characteristics of the transformation were not always properly addressed by our existing tools, and mistakes were made. Before turning to the lessons to be learned, we should note that although these features did not appear in postwar Europe, nor in Latin America, they were—all three—present in China when it began its economic reforms. That is why there are, in fact, many ways in which the East European experience of economic transformation is relevant to China, and conversely.

The Big Issues

Radical/Shock Versus Gradualism/Sequencing Versus Minimum Bang

This issue does not bear lengthy discussion: it is another example of slogans displacing analysis. There is confused, misleading argument over whether Russia did or did not try shock therapy; over whether so-called Polish radicalism has been more successful than so-called Hungarian gradualism, with no attention paid to the initial conditions in each country. This rhetoric is understandable when it comes from politicians, inexcusable from economists.

Here, I have not abandoned my early view that a "robust sequence" should follow a "credible regime change." The opening package of measures must be sufficient to make the regime change credible, but it is administratively impossible and economically unwise to try to do everything at once. The legal, institutional, economic, and behavioral infrastructure of the capitalist market economy cannot be installed quickly and by fiat, except possibly by a government as authoritarian as the worst of those overthrown in the revolutions of 1989. Thus, policymakers *must* choose a sequence. It is better to design that sequence consciously, insofar as possible, rather than just to follow the political winds.

This position may well be "gradualism," but that is widely (often intentionally) misinterpreted: a gradualist program for a sequence of policy measures is just the opposite of the uncoordinated improvisation of which gradualism is often accused; if it really is drift, then it is not deliberate policy. On the other hand, avoiding drift in a gradualist program does require some ability to precommit, as well as to retain some credibility when political imperatives or exogenous shocks force reoptimization. That is hard, so trying to do everything at once may actually seem easier. It is not, nor is it feasible.

We should therefore beware of those who take the conventional refuge of the extremist ideologue in claiming that the program has not failed, it has just not been implemented fully and consistently. That is a hypothesis that is in principle not testable, because it will *always* be possible to find a "key" element of the program that could not be applied.

In any case, the range of sensible strategies is limited, and there may be little margin for choice. Some elements of stabilization and liberalization make sense only when done simultaneously. The range observed across countries is in fact surprisingly limited and is mainly a function of initial conditions. Foresight, sequencing, implementation, and political support are the key differences and potential weaknesses. And no country fits particularly well the stereotype that the ideologues assign to it: "gradualist" Hungary was much more "radical" than Poland in its implementation of bankruptcy legislation, and Czechoslovakia was more "radical" than either with its voucher privatization program.

The choices posed by sequencing are not merely sources of academic dispute. There are serious, major decisions: about the priority to be given to privatization of large state-owned enterprises relative to other institutional changes and demonopolization; the urgency of creating a healthy structure of financial intermediation; and many others. These choices are conditioned by political feasibility, but for an economic policy program, the political considerations fall under tactics rather than strategy—and as our models demonstrate, political feasibility is endogenous.

Country Specificities

The range of countries that can now be classed as "in transformation" is vast: Hungary, the Czech Republic, Poland, and Slovakia (the "Central European" or "Visegrád" four); with Bulgaria and Romania, we have the "core six"; adding Slovenia and the Baltic states, we arrive at the likely full list for European Union association agreements (the "Europe agreements")—the medium-run candidates for accession to the Union; Albania and the rest of the former Yugoslavia complete "Eastern Europe"; farther east, we have Russia, Ukraine, the rest of the former Soviet Union, Mongolia, China, and Viet Nam. Most of my observations will be drawn from the experience of the "core six," but we want the conclusions to have more general relevance. Is that possible?

Comparisons are undermined by differences in initial conditions. Time series are still short, and we cannot rerun history, so it is especially tempting to compare the experiences of different countries. But they (their policymakers) all think they are quite specific and cannot learn much from each other, much less from countries not undergoing this particular form of transformation.

There are indeed significant differences in initial conditions (see Islam and Mandelbaum, 1993): foreign debt, the history of workers' power in enterprise management, industrial history, agricultural institutions, the sectoral structure of output and employment, macroeconomic imbalance, natural resources, trade structure, political culture and institutions, previous duration of communism and central planning, previous "reform" efforts, and doubtless much more. There are equally significant differences in the policies these countries have followed.

Politicians and policymakers understandably stress the specificity of their own countries—their circumstances, needs, and achievements. Every country is of course different. But economics aspires to generality, and noting specific successes and failures here and there is little help unless we can interpret what they imply. It is unhelpful to select only the comparisons and generalizations that suit one's prejudices: for example, those who do see important lessons from the Chinese case for

Eastern Europe often reject any analogies with Latin American countries, whereas those relying on the general features of stabilization in Latin America find such strongly specific characteristics in China as to make it irrelevant for Eastern Europe.

Our models and methods help us to make allowances for the clearly relevant differences, and cross-country comparisons are our only hope of constructing counterfactuals. In any case, it is certainly not my purpose here to evaluate various countries' policies and their relative success—that is hard enough even when the initial conditions are much more similar than they were in Eastern Europe in 1989—but rather to look for generalizations (a representative sample of comparisons and generalizations in the literature might include European Commission, 1991; Portes, 1993; Blanchard and others, 1994; and European Bank for Reconstruction and Development, 1994).

The Importance of Rents

In a fundamental sense, transformation is all about economic rents and income distribution. That is in good part why it is transformation, rather than a smooth transition. Distortions create rents, which in turn create rigidities, resistance to change. In these conditions, economic agents do not so much seek rents but rather seek to protect those rents they have. That is a major source of inertia. It is hard to identify the rents; but if one could, and then proceed to eliminate them all, the government would fall immediately. And such a wrenching redistribution would doubtless be highly inequitable, too.

More concretely, some claim that the initial capital stock in Eastern Europe, both physical and human, was almost entirely unusable or wrongly allocated but not transferable. Experience has shown that this is false. At the same time, however, clear losers are emerging, such as the many who are forced to retire prematurely or simply to withdraw from the labor force when their jobs disappear, because they cannot be moved or retrained. This, in turn, gives some justification, not merely on political but also on equity grounds, for not trying to reduce pension entitlements too drastically even though they are an immense and growing burden on state budgets. The older generation suffered longer under communism, may have lost their savings in a burst of "corrective" inflation, and will have less time to enjoy the fruits of a protracted transformation.

Good News and Bad News

Initial Successes

Considerable progress has been achieved, even in Russia. Farther west, the relative stability of transformation-oriented economic policies through elections and major political swings testifies to credible regime changes in several countries besides the Central European four. Liberalization has been a considerable success, though some of its distributional consequences have been drastic and unfortunate. Price adjustment has been remarkably rapid, except for the remaining controlled prices; in general, goods prices are more flexible than we might have thought and are more likely to adjust to international relative prices quickly. This may be partly a result of the comprehensiveness of the liberalization and the concomitant substantial increases in the overall price level. Stabilization has also succeeded in most of the cases in which it was necessary and feasible, following fairly similar "heterodox" approaches with multiple anchors.

Opening up to market-oriented trade, with relatively liberal trade policies, has brought a successful reorientation of trade flows to the West, especially the European Union. Current account convertibility has proved sustainable where it has been introduced. And correspondingly, policymakers in these countries have been able to conduct a constructive dialogue with the Bretton Woods institutions. There is more good news, including substantial institutional change—but that is not what this paper is about.

Initial Errors

Why were the transformation programs not more successful, more quickly? Two reasons stand out: some of their architects thought it would be easy; and the specificities of these economies were not fully understood, nor their implications appreciated, even by domestic policymakers. Here, I mean not so much the country-specific differences in initial conditions, but rather the differences between economic transformation and either postwar reconstruction or the experience of developing countries.

What were the consequences? First, all forecasts and projections were way off the mark: they underestimated the size of the initial price level shock ("corrective" inflation), the extent of the fall in output and its persistence, and the initial improvement but subsequent deterioration of the fiscal balance and the current account; and they overestimated the amount of foreign investment and aid and, overall, the speed of the transformation process (especially privatization). From precise estimates to broad assessments, almost all these projections were quite overoptimistic. The major exception to that generalization is perhaps the general political stability and progressive character of political development, which are superior to expectations and remarkably restrained in the light of the economic results. Yet the errors were considerable and had political consequences, as shown by the recent Polish and Hungarian elections. Nor can we associate these mistaken expectations with variables overshooting their long-run equilibrium values, whatever those might have been—these were just bad judgments.

The policy errors were closely related to the forecast errors and their causes. Evidently—and fortunately—not all can be observed in any given country, but several appear frequently. Again, they are not features of policies imposed from the outside, by the IMF or anyone else; in most cases, whatever the sources of the arguments that influenced them, the domestic policymakers themselves did want these policies.

Here, it is most convenient just to list the major policy errors briefly before elaborating on them:

- Programs of *restitution* of physical property—both real estate and plant and equipment—to pre-nationalization owners, which created great uncertainty and discouraged investment;
- Overemphasis on *macro*economic relative to *micro*economic policies;
- Excessively tight monetary policies (overestimating the importance of the "monetary overhang" and having to control the exaggerated price shock caused by excessive devaluation);
- Excessive devaluation and inadequately specified exchange rate policy;
- Misunderstanding of the capacities and behavior of the state-owned enterprises (and many who thought these enterprises would collapse quickly also thought the private sector could easily step in to compensate for their absence);
- Overly complex and ambitious plans to privatize state-owned enterprises, which lacked incentives for stakeholders;
- Sequencing errors—especially the delay in dealing with undercapitalized and technically backward banks and the overhang of bad debt of state-owned enterprises, as well as the initial overemphasis on the potential role of stock markets;
- Deliberate early dissolution of the Council for Mutual Economic Assistance (CMEA), which contributed to the dramatic fall in interregional trade;
- Overly ambitious and hasty elimination of tariff protection and rejection of *any* kind of "industrial policies"; and
- Inadequate emphasis on debt reduction (except Poland) for those countries that required it, and excessive delay in all cases—an error committed by not only domestic policymakers (as in Hungary) but also the international financial institutions and the banks.

The Fall in Output

Rationalizations of the steep fall in output throughout the region are often contradictory. Some apologists admit that the data do not grossly distort the depth of the depression. But they argue that it was inevitable and necessary, indeed desirable, insofar as it represented the abandoning of unwanted or inferior or uneconomic production. Others, on the contrary, claim it is much overstated by the official statistics and has had little impact on "welfare," especially in view of the elimination of queues. Some find that as the decline has been roughly the same everywhere, it must be due to factors exogenous to domestic policies. Others maintain that as there is significantly less cumulative loss of output in the countries that have chosen radical stabilization, the depression must be due to gradualist policies.

For the majority who regard the fall in output as real, of surprising duration, and on the whole undesirable (for example, Kornai, 1993; the full range of views is reflected in Blejer and others, 1993), there are many plausible explanations. It is difficult to distinguish in the data between demand and supply shocks. The fall in CMEA trade is big enough to account for a lot, but that was partly endogenous, and exports to the West from most countries rose immediately and by almost as much. The military-industrial complex is not big enough, even in Russia, to account for a substantial share of the lost production. My own preferred story is a combination, the weights differing among countries, of excessive monetary contraction (beyond that needed for stabilization, at least if devaluation had not overshot) and the inadequacy of supply response (itself caused by inadequate microfoundations) in the face of shifts in demand that required reallocation.

This story would explain why we do not observe the short-run boost to output that is normal in exchange-rate-based stabilization programs and would thus suggest that the Latin American model is in this respect inappropriate. It does not explain the similar depth of the depression in all the countries of the region; here, we really must go back to country specificities—for example, in Hungary, the (self-inflicted) wave of bankruptcies and the debt-service burden, with its ramifications throughout domestic policy.

Evaluation of Policies

Macroeconomic Policies

We could say monetary policy was too tight here, fiscal policy too loose there, and go into further detail. The main error, however, was simply the overemphasis on macroeconomic policy itself. This is not merely because some countries did not need to stabilize or would not have done so if they had not devalued excessively (for example, Czechoslovakia). The preoccupation with stabilization may be partly a reflection of the leading role of the IMF and its macroeconomic conditionality. This was reinforced by advisors who believed in the endemic macroeconomic disequilibrium of socialist economies and saw hyperinflation around every corner. It was accepted voluntarily by politicians who needed external support and in any case often found IMF policies wholly convincing.

I believe this was a serious strategic error. It was right for the Fund to focus on short-run macroeconomic policies, internal and external balance—that is its mission, if not its *déformation professionnelle*—but it was wrong to make all other aid conditional on agreement to a stabilization program with the Fund and thereby to put its priorities at the top of policymakers' agendas. The Fund could not devote much effort to the microfoundations of the macro policies; and until lately, its performance criteria were put entirely in terms of macroeconomic indicators (while the recently imposed conditions on structural reforms appear not to have been enforced—see Gomulka, forthcoming).

The initial conditions described above should have indicated, however, that mere liberalization would not create the microeconomic, institutional basis for the macroeconomic policies appropriate to a market economy. Policymakers have limited time, administrative resources, and political capital. For too long, they devoted an excessive share to only one dimension of the transformation process, and too little to anticipating and dealing with the many other obstacles that would impede it.

That might nevertheless have been justified if macroeconomic stabilization were a necessary condition for microeconomic, structural reforms and for opening the economy to trade. There is ample evidence, however, that this is not so. Recent work on Latin America suggests that this aspect of the conventional wisdom on sequencing has been ignored by several countries, with considerable success (Edwards, 1994). Similarly, in Eastern Europe itself, it has proved possible to implement substantial structural change in high-inflation environments.

Of course it would be better still if there was stabilization, and there may be no medium-run trade-off between stabilization and either output or the speed of transformation. The issue then is feasibility. If immediate stabilization is not feasible (see the "war of attrition" models), there may still be very useful things that can be done, which, by constructing parts of the microfoundations, may also make stabilization that much easier when it does come onto the political agenda.

Fiscal Policy

The initial fiscal deficits in Eastern Europe were not huge by Western European standards, but they were much more difficult to finance in a noninflationary manner. It was relatively easy to cut expenditure in the short run, mainly because price liberalization automatically eliminates large subsidies. Revenue then drops, partly because of recession, partly because of the difficulty of taxing private firms. In the medium run, the basic problem is expenditure—subsidies fall, but social spending rises, especially pensions (early retirement) and unemployment benefits. Unless fast growth finally arrives, the long-run problem will be servicing domestic debt, with large deficits and growth rates below real interest rates.

External Policy

Here, the mistake was not early convertibility or fixed nominal exchange rates, where these were implemented. The big errors were overdevaluation and insufficient precision and clarity regarding the exchange rate regime. The danger of serious overshooting with the initial devaluation arises because there is no reliable indicator of an equilibrium rate, so policymakers take too seriously the preliberalization "free market" rate, which is always deeply undervalued. And even the "equilibrium" rate suggested by purely monetary considerations is likely to be significantly undervalued. The fall in exports to CMEA partners releases resources for export elsewhere, the fall in output reduces the demand for imports, the rationalization of distortions raises the efficiency of trade, and the required expansion of the nontraded services sector should be led by an increase in the relative price of services—hence, a real exchange rate appreciation.

The macroeconomic costs of serious overshooting are an excessive initial price shock, requiring, in turn, excessive monetary stringency to stop it from setting off rapid inflation at the outset and, hence, a strong negative demand shock, coupled with a negative supply shock to import-dependent firms; and, in due course, because the initial real wage is unsustainably low and domestic firms still have significant market power, a catch-up, cost-push inflationary process with real appreciation is required. In Czechoslovakia, the excessive initial devaluation may have actually fostered a shift to lower value-added production, inimical to competitiveness in the medium run.

The trade-off between a fixed and a crawling peg is well understood: a nominal anchor for monetary stability versus a real exchange rate target to maintain competitiveness. Initially the needs of stabilization are paramount and accentuated by the role of a fixed nominal rate in anchoring the price structure, which is shifting radically. Subsequent real appreciation is inevitable and desirable, however, so it is best to announce at the outset that the crawl will begin when the authorities judge that the real rate is in an appropriate longer-run range, which itself is likely to shift gradually.

Current account convertibility frequently has come early in the sequencing of the transformation process—and rightly, at least for the smaller economies with relatively high trade participation and some initial access to international reserves. It is more important in the formerly planned economies than elsewhere because it can play such a key role in creating markets and helping them to function properly. It eliminates bureaucratic influence on the allocation of foreign exchange. And early convertibility, if it can be sustained, is popular and highly visible, so it greatly enhances the credibility of policymakers. Payments union proposals (and their surrogates, like the "Interstate Bank") were never an appropriate substitute for convertibility, either for Central Europe or the former Soviet Union.

These countries should not, however, suddenly open up their capital accounts, and in general they have not. There are dangers in uncontrolled capital inflows, as well as outflows. Capital account inconvertibility need not discourage foreign direct investment as long as current account convertibility guarantees the freedom to remit profits. Opening up successfully to capital account transactions requires positive real interest rates, a realistic exchange rate, and some depth in domestic financial markets.

Although the postwar European experience was not fully relevant for the Central and Eastern European countries, the Marshall Plan did demonstrate the importance of external assistance and debt consolidation in economic transformation and recovery. Several Eastern European countries, including Poland, Hungary, Bulgaria, and Russia, had serious external debt problems at the outset of the transformation. Given these debt burdens, it has been regrettable that the major western countries' severe budgetary constraints have made large-scale grants unrealistic; debt relief, which might have been an adequate substitute, has been quite insufficient.

Poland simply did not pay and eventually—in a deal finalized almost five years after the revolutions of 1989—achieved substantial debt reduction. Bulgaria, too, has finally reached a deal; it has meanwhile suffered considerably from the constraints on its external transactions. Hungary presents the most interesting case: walking into the trap, springing it, and struggling valiantly without (yet) crying out.

The initial Hungarian story was that exports were growing so fast that there was no difficulty in financing debt service. This was true until 1993, but only for external finance. The domestic fiscal burden of debt service is crushing, and investment is severely depressed by the impact on financial markets. Fiscal reforms that would imply austerity (in pensions, etc.) are much more difficult, given the austerity already imposed by debt service: debt relief is complementary to, not substitutable for, the "tough policies" needed to put the Hungarian fiscal house in order.

The denouement was foreseeable, and it is partly the fault of the West. The Fund claims unconvincingly that the high proportion of Hungarian debt in bonds would limit the benefit to Hungary of debt reduction relative to the cost of impaired capital market access. But debt consolidation can take many forms, and history suggests a solution could be found if Hungary wanted it and the international institutions offered help rather than opposition. If Mexico deserved and could benefit greatly from debt reduction—and gained rather than lost capital inflows—so also could Hungary. Perhaps policymakers inside and outside Hungary will learn something from the recent announcement that J.P. Morgan expects to receive the "highly prized" mandate for Poland's forthcoming $500 million Euromarket issue and to offer significantly finer terms than Hungary could get (*Financial Times*, December 1, 1994). So much for the "elephantine memory" of capital markets and the rewards for "good behavior"!

The external constraint is likely to bite soon and may prematurely inhibit expansion in those economies where recovery is finally beginning. The initial trade balance successes were temporary, the result of special factors: abnormally depressed domestic demand, temporary undervaluation, excess stocks to liquidate, the opening of European Union markets, and the need of state-owned enterprises to maintain cash flows in the face of monetary tightness. Trade balances already deteriorated in 1993, on both exports and imports (except for the Czech Republic and Russia). The good outcome assumed in the early writing on transformation would involve much larger foreign capital inflows to support the imports of investment goods that these countries need. So far, however, foreign direct investment has been disappointingly low. Portfolio capital inflows may pose (familiar) problems in a few countries, including undesired upward pressure on the exchange rate; and in more normal circumstances, Russia's natural resources might present it with a Dutch disease. These problems of success would be welcome.

Household Behavior

Here, there were no mistaken perceptions: households in these economies have behaved rationally and adapted quickly. Moreover, some problems that were expected have not been significant. Household saving has in most countries held up well, as precautionary motives appear to have dominated life-cycle considerations (even there, while permanent incomes should have risen, the perceived need to provide privately for retirement might also have risen). Migration was a potential vicious circle, insofar as departure of the best and brightest would reduce the attractiveness of investment and, hence, reduce the growth of output and real incomes and stimulate further outflows. For those trying to get the West to increase aid to the East, this specter was a useful lever; but so far, the flows have not been large.

The serious problem arising from household behavior is widespread and strong consumer preference for imports, with little regard to the price differential. That is due partly to long-standing conditioning and the attractions of the previously unattainable, but it is proving remarkably persistent.

State-Owned Enterprises

The role and prospects of these enterprises were underestimated—often with colorful images of dinosaurs producing obsolete goods for the region's bloated industrial sectors, in particular their rapidly contracting defense establishment. There was no coherent policy toward them, except to privatize as rapidly as possible or simply to make them fold by cutting off finance, so little thought went into trying consciously to modify their behavior before privatization. The result was "state desertion," sometimes going further to involve explicit tax and other discrimination against state-owned enterprises vis-à-vis private firms.

Recent research suggests that many of the state-owned enterprises can in fact adapt, at least enough to warrant reconsidering policies that explicitly seek to starve them quickly. For example, after an initial lag, they are in most countries reducing employment in advance of privatization, so productivity is beginning to recover. The key is to stop open-ended subsidies and to create incentives with the prospect of ultimate privatization that will not necessarily involve sacking all the managers. Fiscal pressures can actually be useful here, in convincing managers that there is no money so they cannot expect any. Then they must discover that they cannot get it from the banks (see below).

Very severe financial tightening at the aggregate level can have mixed effects through state-owned enterprises on the development of the private sector. The limited credit available tends to go to these enterprises, but it is not enough, and they respond by releasing both labor and capital stock to the private sector. Nevertheless, an excessively severe demand shock weakens the ability of these enterprises to respond, and the shortage of credit hampers restructuring. The pressure can go too far, as it demonstrably has in many cases.

Continuous pressure must be maintained, however, perhaps for a long time to come, because in most countries comprehensive privatization of state-owned enterprises is still not in prospect, and the examples of rapid privatization in Czechoslovakia and Russia are at best problematic. It is much too early to evaluate the results of the Czech voucher privatization scheme, except to applaud the efficiency and determination with which it was executed. It does appear, however, to have created an extraordinary system of corporate governance. The firms are owned by the investment privatization companies to which most individuals entrusted their vouchers. Most of these are managed by the large banks, of which the state still owns (on average) 40 percent, and to which the former state-owned enterprises are heavily indebted.

The banks are naturally reticent to call in their loans, even when they look bad, and the authorities have pursued a conscious anti-bankruptcy policy through the activities of the National Property Fund and the Consolidation Bank. The Russian case is simpler, in that in most firms control seems to have gone to insiders; but, again, it is too soon to judge.

Thus the delay in privatization of large state-owned enterprises may not have been as unfortunate as most of us thought, or at least not disastrous, given the constraints and the alternatives. There is still time to do some of the restructuring necessary to make privatization successful.

Financial Intermediation

It now seems to be commonly accepted that the single most important error in sequencing, at least in the core six countries, was not to have implemented urgently a financial cleanout: recapitalizing the banks, canceling debts of state-owned enterprises at the time of privatization, and instituting cash-limited fiscal subsidies to them meanwhile, so that the banks would not have to extend them new loans or capitalize their arrears. Capitalism cannot function without capital markets; stock markets were and are clearly not going to be a major mechanism for financial intermediation or corporate control for many years to come. The banks had to take on the task, and they were too weak to do so. Investment and the growth of new private firms have thereby suffered. Both monetary tightness and the need to maintain high bank intermediation margins to build up a capital base, in the absence of recapitalization, have contributed to high real interest rates, and thus to low investment.

This extremely serious problem was avoidable, but not widely foreseen or understood. The exercise could have been done quickly and comprehensively, and hence better than the partial and repeated efforts that have followed in several countries and that have created considerable moral hazard. It need not have impaired the credibility of the authorities—suggesting they were "soft" financially—if the debt cancellation had been tied explicitly to the one-off event of privatization. The fiscal impact, looking at the accounts of the consolidated public sector, is zero. As long as both banks and firms are state-owned enterprises, the public sector borrowing requirement remains unchanged. For some time, however, the IMF cautioned against the supposed effect on the deficit, and even now one sees warnings against the "high fiscal cost" in World Bank publications. This is nonsense, as the Fund is now willing to state publicly.

Alone among Eastern European countries, Hungary sprang the bankruptcy trap. Any firm unable to meet payments to any creditor had to file for bankruptcy, and a financial restructuring required unanimous consent by creditors. The system could not cope with the resulting 17,000 cases filed for financial restructuring or liquidation in 1992 and early 1993. Those who have been calling for vigorous enforcement of bankruptcy to force true restructuring should examine the Hungarian case and tell us whether any positive longer-run consequences will outweigh the negative short-run effects. In contrast, the Czech Republic has assiduously sought to avoid bankruptcies and the consequent restructuring, at least as long as voucher privatization was still incomplete. There, one can only conjecture how the complex, financially unsound structure of indebtedness and corporate control will unwind.

Labor Markets

In view of the lag in adjustment, unemployment will not control inflation in the early phase of the transformation, so incomes policies are necessary. In the macroeconomics of central planning, incomes policies played the role of nonexistent monetary policies, and until monetary policy can develop its full role as a macroeconomic policy instrument, it will need that help. Most of the initial stabilization programs satisfied this requirement with some version of the "tax on wage increases" first introduced in Hungary in the late 1960s. The inefficiencies created by such a tax may not be too damaging, since there is a case for maintaining a constraint on relative wages (an effect of most versions of this tax), and a perception that wage-setting decisions in state-owned enterprises may be interpreted simply as allocating rents.

Despite real wage moderation, unemployment began to rise. Contrary to some conjectures, the registered unemployed in Eastern Europe really are unemployed, and there are more, according to labor force surveys. Benefits rules are no longer generous. In most countries, there are small inflows into the pool of unemployed, but very small outflows. Hence the long-run problem: the creation of a pool of long-term unemployed, having no moderating influence on wage pressure but constituting a growing fiscal burden, which, in turn, brings restrictive measures that tend to increase unemployment. Starting from extremely high levels, participation rates have already fallen below the norms for industrial countries; that is a social as well as a fiscal burden.

What can be done to promote job creation? Not much in the state-owned enterprises or newly privatized larger firms, and after the first wave, job creation in small and medium-sized enterprises will require investment and, hence, functioning capital markets. Active labor market policies have succeeded in the Czech Republic, and public works offer a more direct alternative: public investment has been abnormally depressed, while infrastructure and public services (health, education, etc.) have deteriorated drastically, bringing a significant perceived decline in welfare. The fiscal burden of paying wages rather than unemployment or other social benefits may not be so great.

Trade and Industrial Policies

The first trap here opened with the deliberate destruction of the CMEA (Csaba, 1994, p. 15, refers to "their [the Visegrád countries'] thrust to get rid of Comecon from late 1989 onwards") and the disintegration of the former Soviet Union. Eastern Europe compensated, however, by raising exports to the West, mainly the European Union, and especially Germany before its recession took hold.

The next step was to negotiate agreements with the European Union on a bilateral basis. The resulting hub-and-spoke pattern of trade relations marginalizes the individual Eastern countries, artificially discourages economic relations among them, and favors investment in Germany or Austria to supply the East rather than in the East itself. Meanwhile, accession to membership in the Union is likely to take much longer than hopeful early proposals (including my own) had suggested: these countries are too poor, too agricultural, and too populous for the European Union budget to accommodate under anything like present rules. Yet the economic advantages to the Union of opening up to the East are considerable (Faini and Portes, 1995). And if these countries do not have clear prospects for accession to the Union, there is the danger of another vicious circle of low investment, slow growth, and indefinitely receding prospects of membership.

All this argues for mapping out a clearer path to accession that would multilateralize the Europe agreements to create a comprehensive free trade area, then deepen integration in an approach to something like the planned "European Economic Area" comprising the European Union and the European Free Trade Association (Baldwin, 1994). This would be attractive to foreign investors, would promote institutional transformation, and would help to raise intraregional trade further toward the potential levels that gravity models suggest.

Two other policy orientations in this domain testify to exaggerated rejection of governmental action: the rush not only to discard import quotas and other nontariff barriers but also to lower tariffs to negligible levels; and the explicit avoidance of any policies that might possibly be labeled "industrial policies," no matter how market-friendly, nonselective, nondiscretionary, and transparent they might be. A moderate tariff can yield useful revenue while temporarily protecting "senile" industries, as the demand-shift explanation of output decline would suggest is desirable. The initial overshooting weakened these countries' negotiating position vis-à-vis the European Union, and it led in any case to irresistible pressures to re-establish various forms of protection.

Nonselective export promotion services and partial state guarantees for credits to small and medium-sized enterprises are examples of industrial policies that might be helpful and not lend themselves to abuse. Anything that helps to create markets or to deal with market failures systematically is surely to be welcomed. The financial cleanout and active labor market policies recommended above are equally examples of such structural policies. It is economic illiteracy or misplaced ideological purity to equate microeconomic policies with detailed state intervention in economic decision making.

Conclusion

The early analyses of the economic opening up and transformation of the East stressed growth: catch-up and convergence. The depression that came unexpectedly in the first years of transformation now requires a "rubber band" response, an equally swift and strong recovery to the trend convergence path. In many countries, the conditions are there, and now that the initial policy errors have been recognized, it should be easier not to repeat them. There will continue to be argument about how much time and output has been avoidably lost, how much physical and human capital rendered unnecessarily obsolete or prematurely scrapped. There will be reform fatigue in an environment of "normal politics." We may hope, however, that fatigue will not long delay the time when these economies become "normal economies."

The IMF is implicated in some of the policy errors, and the World Bank, too, especially where it has deferred to the Fund. But this was often the consequence of the mandate given to the Fund. The IMF has played an important role in encouraging liberalization, stabilization, and opening up these economies to the rest of the world; and it is becoming increasingly interested in microeconomic, structural reforms, even where those are not included in its performance criteria. That role must continue and mature.

References

Baldwin, Richard E., *Towards an Integrated Europe* (London: Centre for Economic Policy Research, 1994).

Blanchard, Olivier, Kenneth Froot, and Jeffrey Sachs, eds., *The Transition in Eastern Europe*, vols. 1 and 2 (Chicago and London: University of Chicago Press, 1994).

Blejer, Mario I., and others, eds., *Eastern Europe in Transition: From Recession to Growth* (Washington: World Bank, 1993).

Csaba, Laszlo, "The EU and Eastern Europe: A Post-Transformation Perspective," Kopint-Datorg Discussion Paper No. 25 (Budapest: Kopint-Datorg Foundation for Economic Research, 1994).

Edwards, Sebastian, "Macroeconomic Stabilization in Latin America: Recent Experience and Some Sequencing Issues," NBER Working Paper 4697 (Cambridge, Massachusetts: National Bureau of Economic Research, April 1994).

European Bank for Reconstruction and Development, *Transition Report* (London: European Bank for Reconstruction and Development, 1994).

European Commission, *The Path of Reform in Central and Eastern Europe,* Special Issue No. 2 of *European Economy* (Luxembourg: European Commission, 1991).

Faini, Riccardo, and Richard Portes, *European Union Trade with Eastern Europe: Adjustment and Opportunities* (London: Centre for Economic Policy Research, 1995).

Gomulka, Stanislaw, "The Role of International Financial Institutions: The Polish and Russian Experiences 1989–94," *Journal of Comparative Economics* (forthcoming, 1995).

Islam, Shafiqul, and Michael Mandelbaum, eds., *Making Markets* (New York: Council on Foreign Relations, 1993).

Kornai, Janos, "Transformational Recession," Collegium Budapest, Institute for Advanced Studies, Discussion Paper 1 (1993).

Portes, Richard, ed., *Economic Transformation in Central Europe: A Progress Report* (London: Centre for Economic Policy Research; Luxembourg: European Commission, 1993).

Chairman's Remarks

Viktor Gerashchenko agreed with Portes that the countries in transition had made mistakes. Nevertheless, they were trying to learn from their mistakes and the mistakes of others. Russia was currently working on the policy statement of the Government and the Central Bank in close cooperation with the staff of the Fund, a process that was constantly improving. Russia's initial mistakes were clearly connected with rather abrupt changes that had taken place in 1991; the Government that had come to power in 1992 had been compelled to deal very quickly with the problems that had emerged throughout that huge country. He also agreed with the point made by Portes that the banking system in many transition countries, especially Russia, was still underdeveloped. While some banks had been developing quite well in Russia, they were involved in providing credit not only for short-term finance but also for the industrial sector. Those banks needed, and indeed were demanding from the Government, clear-cut economic priorities.

The Central Bank of Russia was trying to use the instruments at its disposal. For the time being, those instruments were limited to reserve requirements and interest rates, which were closely connected to the interbank market. At the same time, the Central Bank was very much tied up with the problem of financing the budget deficit, because the attitude of the population, companies, and banks was changing only gradually toward a willingness to buy treasury bills. He hoped that the treasury bill market would be developed more actively in 1995. It was by now generally recognized within Russia that the country's main problem was the budget deficit.

General Discussion

Peter Bod noted that Portes had suggested that mistakes had led to the sharp fall in output—unprecedented in peacetime—among the Visegrád countries. Indeed, according to the official statistics, the output decline of that group amounted to 20–30 percent of GDP. Looking at the social development of those countries—particularly the absence of civil war and mass poverty—it was tempting to conclude that the region was blessed with brilliant politicians and very bad economists. As a central bank governor, lying somewhere between a politician and an economist, he did not agree with that view—and the voters did not seem to agree either. He was not convinced that the approach that Portes had decried as involving a focus on macroeconomic policies at the expense of attention to microeconomic policies, such as excessively tight monetary policy and overambitious trade liberalization, had, in fact, been a mistake. If it was, however, a certain degree of self-criticism would be in order, inasmuch as decision makers in the Visegrád countries had acted under pressure from their colleagues in the West and from international agencies.

In his view, the problem lay mainly in the supply conditions, such as limited access to foreign markets. In the case of the Visegrád countries, the main problem was access to the market of the European Union, especially in the so-called sensitive sectors—agriculture, steel, and textiles—in which the Visegrád countries were competitive. Another problem was the lack of a clear-cut strategy for integrating the countries of Eastern Europe into the European Union, which, together with a lack of pre-accession funding, was discouraging foreign direct investment in the region. Clearly, those countries would need a lot of fresh money for infrastructure.

The reference by Portes to Hungary in the context of debt relief was misplaced. The underlying problem in Hungary was not debt service: in 1993, the interest burden had amounted to 3–4 percent of GDP, while the inflow of foreign capital in the form of foreign direct investment had amounted to 7 percent of GDP. Moreover, any discussion of the need for debt relief would be very risky indeed, possibly endangering the inflow of foreign direct investment.

In sum, the transition countries needed both improved supply conditions—access to markets and to foreign direct investment—as well as strong demand management, which called for macroeconomic stabilization. Thus, his reading of history differed somewhat from that of Portes, although only future economic historians would be able to judge which approach was correct and how far the transition countries had gone toward becoming fully fledged market economies.

Salvatore Zecchini recalled that Liu had clearly stated that the aim of the third phase of economic reform in China was to create a socialist market economy. That aim contrasted very much with the efforts of the former centrally planned economies to move toward a market economy and with the system that was in place in most industrial economies. He asked Liu whether he could elaborate on the difference between a market system and a socialist market system and, in particular, what the qualifier "socialist" added to a market system: it could not be the gradualism to which the minister had referred, as gradualism was a question of timing, not of objective; and it was not a question of sequencing, as Portes had suggested.

Liu replied that in September 1993 China had announced a detailed plan setting out the steps it would follow to achieve the objective of a socialist market economy. Such an economy differed from a purely market economy in two respects: a socialist market economy was based on the dominance of public ownership, supplemented by a variety of different forms of ownership; and it was grounded in a distribution of income based on labor—incomes would not all rise at the same rate. The ultimate goal, however, was to reach common prosperity.

Burke Dillon remarked that Portes and many other academics envisioned a banking system in Russia in which the necessary actions were taken to save the existing system—by canceling debts, for example—in order to move ahead and take over the functions of the new system. In practice, Russia seemed to be following a policy that was more akin to letting 2,000 flowers bloom and allowing only the fittest to survive, a very market-oriented philosophy. She would be interested in Gerashchenko's reaction to the model envisioned by Portes, and the comments of Portes on the evolution of the banks in Russia.

Gerashchenko replied that the number of banks in Russia was not excessive. Throughout the former Soviet Union, there had been about 6,500 banking enterprises, most of which had been branches of the State Bank of the U.S.S.R., the main commercial banking institution, and approximately 1,000 branches of the Investment Bank. As of September 1, 1994, however, one third of Russia's 2,400 licensed banking institutions were concentrated in Moscow, which was developing as a financial center; some regions of the country were still without a bank of any type, which was why clearing centers were compelled to serve a small number of clients.

The quality of banking institutions in Russia was also different. He would not go as far as Dillon, however, in suggesting that Russia was allowing all the flowers to bloom before weeding out those that could not survive on their own. Eventually, there would be a period of stabilization in the banking sector, with the liquidation of a number of banks and the successful takeover of others.

As was well known, the Central Bank of Russia had already increased the minimum capital requirements for banks on two occasions. Initially, the decision to increase those requirements had been widely criticized, but it was now accepted by the banking community. It was hoped that toward the beginning of 1999 Russia's minimum capital requirements would be similar to those prevailing in Western Europe. The Central Bank was also trying to improve dramatically its banking supervision role; the hope was that revised legislation on banks and banking activity, which was expected to have its second reading in parliament in November 1994, would provide the Central Bank with more clearly defined rights in that respect. He could certainly agree with Portes that some of the banks in Russia were not adequately prepared for the task that they would need to play in a changing economy.

Portes remarked that, while he was not familiar with the banking system of Russia, the Central European experience provided some useful insight. First, it was not possible simply to let the fittest banks survive, because they were almost all unfit ex ante. If such a policy were to be pursued, it would be necessary first to try to rehabilitate the banks. It was unlikely that new, smaller banks would at the outset be able to take over the role of the existing banks with respect to the savings bank network, on the one hand, and their questionable assets, on the other. Therefore, a solution had to be found to the problems of the existing banks.

A second lesson from the Central European experience was that the sorts of operations he had suggested could not be implemented until and unless serious budget constraints were imposed on state-owned enterprises through the budget, in the form of cash-limited fiscal subsidies, rather than trying to impose discipline through the banking system. The Central European countries had been prepared to take that step very early on in the reform process, although it was unfortunate that they had not immediately conducted the kind of financial cleanout that he had suggested. In any event, it was not clear that the ground had been prepared for such an approach in Russia.

Referring to the earlier comments of Peter Bod, Portes agreed that it was reasonable to ask whether the absence of civil war and mass poverty in Central and Eastern Europe implied that the politicians in the region were very good, and the economists bad. In certain cases, of course, politicians had been thrown out of office, which might be part of the answer. More generally, however, the social development of those countries was testimony to the remarkable degree of political maturity and stability, and to the ethos underlying economic transformation itself coming out of the revolutions of 1989. He also sympathized with the problems of the decision makers. Indeed, those who were merely observers should be humble.

In answer to the question posed by Bod, Portes viewed the mistakes that had been made as the shared responsibility of everyone involved. With that in mind, it was useful to ask how a better result could have been achieved. As far as the European Union was concerned, Bod had raised some important and very topical issues. He had great sympathy for the view that the market access offered by the European Union in its association agreements with the countries of Eastern Europe was inadequate; access had been improved somewhat, but it was still inadequate. He agreed that there was a lack of a clear-cut strategy for integrating those countries into the European Union, which was partly the fault of the European Union, and that the absence of such a strategy was holding back foreign direct investment. Nevertheless, Eastern Europe had succeeded—despite the limits on sensitive exports and the impact of the Common Agricultural Policy—in expanding exports to the European Union very rapidly. Moreover, the absence of an integration strategy also stemmed from the inability of the Eastern European countries themselves, and the Visegrád countries in particular, to cooperate with each other to any significant extent. The inability to come to joint positions in negotiating with the European Union, for example, had not helped. Finally, he accepted the point made by Bod with respect to the judgment of economic historians, and he realized that his own attempt to draw some tentative conclusions from the experience of Eastern Europe was somewhat presumptuous. Nevertheless, his remarks about Hungary were themselves informed by his work on sovereign borrowing and debt in the 1920s and 1930s.

Portes could not accept the view expressed by Bod about the burden of servicing debt. As he had stated explicitly in his formal presentation, the external debt burden was financeable. The real issue was the internal consequences of the debt burden: for an economy like Hungary, in which domestic financial markets were still inadequately developed, the issuance of government paper to deal with the fiscal deficit had pushed up domestic real interest rates to an intolerable level. It was true, of course, that the interest burden had been only 3–4 percent of GDP in 1993, somewhat lower than the year before, and that foreign direct investment had been strong. The essential question, however, was how to deal with the fiscal burden of servicing debt, an issue that had been clarified by the Latin American experience. The consequences of servicing debt had been extremely unfortunate in Hungary, and he was somewhat surprised that Bod did not seem to consider the issue to be one of Hungary's biggest problems.

7

Responding to Transformations
in the Developing World

The first day of the conference concluded with a dinner at the Castillo de Viñuelas outside Madrid. In that historic setting, Pedro Aspe Armella, the Secretary of Finance and Public Credit of Mexico, presented the second keynote address on the implications for the Bretton Woods institutions of the transformations under way in Mexico and many other developing countries. Mr. Aspe's speech was introduced by Wim Duisenberg, the President of De Nederlandsche Bank and of the Bank for International Settlements. Mr. Duisenberg's remarks focused on the importance for the IMF of maintaining its monetary character as it responds to a changing world economy.

Wim Duisenberg

Although the Articles of Agreement still bear considerable resemblance to the first issue of 1944, the Fund has clearly changed over the years, focusing its activities on those areas in which they have been most needed. Yet its fiftieth anniversary calls for reflection on whether the IMF train is still running in the proper direction. Tonight's keynote speaker is planning to take up the role of the Fund in Latin America. To provide some counterweight, I would like to make a few observations on the monetary role of the Fund.

In this respect, two somewhat extreme views can be distinguished. One is that the industrial countries no longer need the Fund either as a provider of financial assistance or as a forum for multilateral surveillance. The first function is now taken care of by the international capital markets. The second is not really taken care of, or perhaps one could argue that the caretaker is the nonsystem of floating exchange rates. The upshot of this view is that the Fund should focus its activities on the developing countries and the transforming economies in Central and Eastern Europe and the former Soviet Union. The other view, essentially taken by the Bretton Woods Commission, is that the Fund should return to its original key monetary tasks—giving guidance to the international monetary system and keeping substantial distance from financing developing and transition countries. ‹

I have a lot of sympathy for those who say the Fund should focus more on its middle initial. But I would hesitate to draw the conclusion that the Fund should consequently reduce its advisory role in developing countries and in the transition process for several reasons, one of which I will specify. The reforms undertaken in the eastern part of Europe are of vital importance for the international community, on economic as well as on political grounds. It is crucial that this process is adequately supported. The Fund has done a valuable job there, through its policy advice, technical assistance, and financial support. Of course, in this area, too, the IMF should live up to its guiding principle that only sound programs deserve strong financial support. Sound programs form the basis permitting private capital flows to play an increasingly important role in closing balance of payments financing gaps.

Despite my support for the role of the Fund in nonindustrial countries, greater focus by the IMF on its middle initial is desirable because it is important that the world have an effective multilateral forum for policy coordination. Why is it important? In the international monetary system, a key question is whether exchange rates should be left to float freely, or whether we should try to influence them by some kind of mutually agreed rules. In principle, I would prefer a system providing an incentive for stability, but not stability in the sense that exchange rates should be fixed. Rigidity is not synonymous with stability. Fixed rates based on imbalanced fundamentals will certainly prove unsustainable. What I would like to see is stability in the sense that the system disciplines domestic budgetary and monetary policies. The notion that no coordination is necessary because exchange rates will remain stable and sustainable if everyone puts his own house in order is probably an illusion. First, because not everyone's house is in order. Second, different countries have different views on what "in order"actually means. Does it imply a budget deficit of 4 percent of GDP or a balanced budget? Does it mean an inflation rate of 3 percent or zero percent to 2 percent? As long as such different perceptions prevail, exchange rates will stay adrift. A free float is asking too much of the self-restraint of governments. Misalignments and undue volatility will come along with it.

You might expect, having heard this, that I would be a proponent of target zones. I am not—not at present. Financial markets would be all too eager to test the resolve of the authorities as soon as the boundaries of the zones came into sight. Any halfhearted attempt to defend prevailing exchange rates would prove to be a failure, as the amounts of capital that fund managers can nowadays provide are no doubt larger than central banks could mobilize. Thus, a determined, fierce defense of a target zone would require adjustment of interest rates, even if such an adjustment were not seen necessary from a domestic point of view. And that, in turn, would require a strong commitment by the authorities. Only then might target zones be beneficial. But if such a commitment is nonexistent, as it is currently, introduction of target zones will prove counterproductive.

Therefore, I would argue for a middle road where the members of the Fund frankly ask themselves a number of incisive questions. Are we fully aware of the external implications of domestic policy decisions, and do we take these external consequences seriously into account? If exchange rate movements signal diverging policy stances, it may be concluded that the policies pursued are nonetheless appropriate. Yet if the conclusion is that policies might have to be adjusted, to replace action with words is no solution. Markets cannot be fooled. And the crucial question is, Is our own house in order? Do we agree on what this means? Is vacuum cleaning enough, or should the furniture be polished as well? And, mind you, it is not the housekeeper who will take care of this; we have to do it ourselves!

The Fund could do valuable work here. Until now, it has tried to come up with several initiatives to influence international discussions in the exchange rate field. Success has been limited, perhaps partly because the Fund did not always express an unambiguous view on exchange rate issues. Some Fund documents show more appreciation for efforts to stabilize exchange rates, for example in Europe, than others. It would perhaps be more effective if the Fund simply accepted, explicitly, the choice of a country's exchange rate regime—as long as it does not hurt others!—also among the major countries. And from that starting point, the Fund could act as a neutral, high-quality advisor on economic, monetary, and exchange rate issues. It could show in its Article IV reports and on other occasions when these understandings are apparently misunderstood how certain policy measures affect other countries and how they should be judged.

We could go one step further. Would it not be appropriate to publish the Fund's analyses made in Article IV reports? So far, the policy not to do so has always had my support because confidentiality enhances the frankness and thus the quality of the discussions. Yet it is increasingly disturbing that these thorough analyses hardly seem to play a role in the policy discussions in the industrial world. Publication would probably change this, but it would also risk watering down the analyses when a country is averse to a critical assessment of its policies. Therefore, carefully designed rules to prevent such a situation would be necessary. I believe we should seriously consider whether such a policy can be made effective, and whether the conditions could be created under which the staff would be in a position to put the real issues on the—public—table.

Not at all afraid of a critical assessment is our next speaker. His face is extremely familiar in the Fund. A representative of the very country that shocked the international community in 1982, he delighted the same community later on, making Mexico the showpiece of the debt strategy. As Minister of Finance since 1988, he has made a crucial contribution to the economic revival of Mexico. He may rightly be considered a personification of stability, but stability based on sound fundamentals.

Pedro Aspe Armella

It is a great honor to address such a distinguished audience on the fiftieth anniversary of the Bretton Woods conference. I am sure that the proposals that will result from the working sessions that are taking place during this commemoration will produce concrete results for the benefit of our nations.

Five decades ago, leaders of 44 nations gathered at Bretton Woods to set the basis for a new international economic and financial order. During this half century, the world has experienced profound transformations. The Berlin Wall was raised and later demolished. Eastern European countries transited into socialism and out of it and are now striving to rejoin the international community. Apartheid and numerous dictatorships have disappeared. Closed economies and societies have proved their unfeasibility.

Competition, but also poverty and inequality, have increased. National and international actors, as well as rules and objectives, have acquired new weights and dimensions. The end of the Cold War has brought with it new opportunities but has also revealed or exacerbated challenges such as regionalism, ethnic and religious conflicts, inequalities between and within nations, and increased migration flows.

In the light of these events, the world at the end of the century is moving from the postwar order, which is giving way to new forms of integration and cooperation whose rules and structures are gradually emerging. From a bipolar logic, we have moved to a multipolar one, marked by economic globalization and national interdependence. The international community is constructing new agreements and consensus and, at the same time, is removing old processes and structures.

In this flow of change, consumption patterns and cultural spheres are now globalized, and a new consensus for social and political action has been designed, including most notably on human rights, environmental protection, economic growth, the fight against extreme poverty, and the consolidation of democracy. These important contemporary issues, jointly with each country's own requirements, have forced nations to undertake transformations of their own structures.

Mexico's response to these internal and external challenges ha
the Reform of the State. It was imperative for my country to formulate a
viable development model, to open new opportunities for society as a
whole, and to be able to respond to the challenges of the new international order. We had to leave behind us the closed economy and society
in order to construct an open system. Modernization has touched practically all aspects of our economic, social, and political life. We openly
face and welcome the challenge of increased international competition,
convinced of our capacity to change and to work constructively and
productively.

Let me comment on some of the main aspects of Mexico's transformation that have enabled the conciliation of economic stability with improving living standards in a competitive political system.

At the end of the 1980s, Mexico was going through particularly difficult economic circumstances: high inflation of close to 160 percent annually, a public sector deficit of 16 percent of GDP, a large external debt
representing almost half of GDP, low growth rates, and a lack of competitiveness in the country's productive plant.

Starting from a global approach that recognized the need for integral
reform with the participation of all social sectors, an economic reform
program was formulated with three fundamental aspects: macroeconomic stabilization, structural change, and the fight against extreme
poverty.

Under these three aspects, the program included actions in the following areas: a macroeconomic stabilization program; tax reform; budget reform; privatization of publicly owned enterprises; the fight
against extreme poverty; trade reform and economic deregulation; and
financial sector liberalization. Let me briefly analyze these main elements of the Mexican economic transformation.

The program and actions that came about as a result of the reform implemented since 1987 have been achieved through an intense process of
social agreements and a constant effort to obtain a fairer distribution of
the benefits of development.

Designed as a mechanism to overcome stagnation and to achieve stable and sustainable growth, the main social actors in Mexico seven
years ago signed a pact, nowadays called the Pact for Stability, Growth,
and the Improvement of Living Standards, which defines the basic pattern of agreement between urban and rural workers, and between entrepreneurs and the Government. This mechanism has generated a
more just distribution of the costs of adjustment, facilitating the coordination of actions among the participant sectors and therefore reducing
the negative impacts of stabilization.

The Pact complemented the orthodox stabilization measures—such as
fiscal deficit reduction and control of domestic credit growth—with an
unceasing search for consensus. New consensus-reaching mechanisms

were implemented to establish guidelines for determining wages and other leader prices in the economy, based on expected future inflation and not on past inflation. Furthermore, an exchange rate policy that promotes stability and competitiveness was announced, with enough anticipation to give certainty to economic agents about the future evolution of this variable.

Inflation has been reduced from 160 percent in 1987 to 8.1 percent in 1993 and to 6.7 percent this year, which is the lowest inflation rate in the last 21 years. It is also the lowest that over half of all Mexicans have seen during their lifetimes, and it was achieved with practically a complete supply of goods and services—showing that the reduction in inflation has not been artificial and that it is founded on a structurally sounder economy. This reduction in inflation was achieved while maintaining economic growth. Between 1989 and 1994, GDP has grown annually at an average rate of 2.9 percent in real terms; this rate is favorable, considering the significant reduction in inflation and the intense structural change experienced in the country's industrial base.

The permanence of macroeconomic stability is based on the structural correction of the public sector deficit and on the autonomy of the central bank decreed in 1993. Before the central bank could be made autonomous, the structural correction of the public deficit had to be consolidated. Without this prerequisite, autonomy would not have been feasible. Today, the Constitution establishes the achievement of price stability as the bank's primary objective. No authority can force the bank to provide financing, and the members of the bank's governing body can be removed only in case of grave faults. The autonomy of the bank will protect future generations from the damaging effects that inflation can have all over the basic social fabric.

An essential condition for moderating inflation was the elimination of the external debt overhang. Before the debt renegotiation, Mexico's transfers to the rest of the world had been greater than those demanded from the defeated nations in the aftermath of the First World War. The excessive burden of these transfers nullified the effectiveness of any measure to reduce inflation and re-establish growth.

As you are aware, the renegotiation process was a difficult and complex task. The solid economic reform program undertaken by Mexico, the support of the international financial institutions, in particular the International Monetary Fund and the World Bank, the design of an imaginative package with various options for commercial banks, and the support of most governments of the industrial nations were the basic elements for obtaining a favorable agreement.

Mexico was the pioneer in achieving a multiannual renegotiation package that implied a definitive solution to the debt problem. Mexico was the first to do it, and, fortunately, other countries have followed. The agreement generated a reduction of over $7 billion in debt principal and an annual average reduction in transfers to the rest of the world, from 1990 to 1994, of more than $4 billion a year, owing to the reduction in interest payments, fresh resources, and the rescheduling of amortization payments. With this agreement, Mexico regained access to voluntary capital markets, and, most important, it was able to leave behind the external debt issue to pursue other economic reforms.

The structural correction of public finances in Mexico stands out among the most profound in the world. The adjustment generated a shift from a deficit of 16 percent of GDP in 1987 to complete equilibrium in 1992, 1993, and 1994, excluding all the proceeds obtained from the privatization process. The reduction of fiscal deficits is always an arduous task. However, the truly difficult part was to carry out the adjustment permanently and so that tax rates and the number of taxes were reduced while social expenditure and public investment increased in a sustainable manner. The structural and permanent correction of the deficit prevents the recurrence of any future inflationary pressure and frees resources that can be applied to social programs and to infrastructure projects.

The main elements of the tax reform were the reduction in the number of taxes and in tax rates, the widening of the taxpayer base, and the strict enforcement of fiscal laws to fight fiscal evasion. In 1988, there were 19 federal taxes; today there are less than half that number. The corporate income tax rate was reduced from 39.2 percent in 1988 to 34 percent in 1994. This tax rate is lower than the U.S. federal corporate income tax rate of 35 percent. In addition, local corporate taxes in the United States increase the total tax rate to an average of 39.5 percent. In Mexico, the tax base is also smaller, owing to adjustments for inflation and the elimination of the tax on dividends.

The value-added tax rate has been reduced from a dual rate of 20 percent and 15 percent in 1988 to a single one of 10 percent in 1994, and the maximum rate for personal income tax was reduced from 50 percent to 35 percent. Workers on the lower end of the income tax schedule receive an income tax credit that implies a positive transfer from the Government. For workers who receive one minimum wage, the income tax credit implies an increase of 13 percent in their disposable income.

The changes I have just mentioned constitute the easy part of the tax reform: fewer taxes and lower rates. The difficult part—but inseparable from the first—consists of increasing the number of taxpayers and rigorously enforcing the tax law. Excluding salaried workers whose taxes are withheld in their workplaces, the taxpayer base increased from 1.7 million taxpayers in 1988 to 5.5 million in 1993. Between 1917 and 1988, only two indictments were issued for fiscal evasion. Between 1989 and 1994, more than 500 cases were presented. As a result, notwithstanding the reduction in tax rates, tax revenues increased by 35 percent in real terms, while GDP has increased by 18.8 percent in the same period.

An important element of the structural reform in public finances was the privatization of government-owned enterprises. In 1982, the public sector participated in almost all economic sectors and owned 1,155 public enterprises. By the end of 1994, the number of public enterprises has been reduced by more than 80 percent.

The privatization process yields once-and-for-all revenues. Therefore, they have not been used to finance current spending but have been applied to cancel public debt. These proceeds, together with the renegotiation of the external debt and the increase in tax revenues, have allowed a reduction in the consolidated public debt from about 64 percent of GDP in 1988 to 22 percent in 1994, which is one of the lowest among nations of the Organization for Economic Cooperation and Development (OECD).

Interest payments on the public debt have been reduced from 18 percent of GDP in 1988 to only 2.5 percent in 1994; in terms of the public budget, they have declined from 44 percent of total government spending in 1988 to 10 percent at present.

The lower interest payments, the smaller transfers to money-losing public enterprises, and the increased tax revenues have permitted a permanent and noninflationary increase in social spending. Public expenditures on education, health, housing, and environmental protection have increased from 6.3 percent of GDP in 1988 to 10.2 percent in 1994. As a share of government programmable expenditures, they have risen from 33 percent in 1988 to 54 percent in 1994. These expenditures represent the highest levels in Mexican history.

The Mexican Government now spends more resources on its people and less on interest payments. The increase in the resources channeled to social expenditure implies that, during this Administration, 14 million more Mexicans have drinking water, 12 million more have sewage service, and 20 million more have electricity.

This process brings out another important lesson for Mexico: equality of opportunities and better distribution of the benefits from development are essential conditions for achieving a more just society. We Mexicans are very proud of these accomplishments, but we recognize that much still needs to be done for all Mexican families to have acceptable living standards.

To promote efficiency and to gain access to a wider variety of consumer goods and production inputs, as well as to advanced technologies, Mexico has implemented a profound trade liberalization process and an economic deregulation program.

During President Salinas's Administration, various deregulation actions have been initiated that must be intensified in the future. The reforms have begun in the financial, communications, transportation, industrial, commercial, and agricultural sectors. As a result, these reforms have reduced barriers to entry in several industries and have opened more opportunities for productive private investment. During the last five years, physical private investment had an accumulated growth of 60 percent in real terms.

The trade-liberalizing process dismantled an excessively protectionist regime and has provided the right incentives to modernize the productive plant and to gain greater access to foreign markets.

Mexico has moved from a closed economy to one of the most open economies in the world; as a result, our industry has become more competitive and has achieved price and quality standards that make it possible for a wide range of exports to have a significant presence in international markets.

Our economy, and especially our external trade, are today less dependent on oil. In 1982, oil represented about 80 percent of total exports while manufacturing exports were only 14 percent. At present, the situation has been reversed. During 1993, manufacturing exports represented about 80 percent of total exports and oil exports were only 14 percent.

Through the signing of free trade agreements with the United States and Canada, Chile, Venezuela, Colombia, and Costa Rica, and by joining international economic cooperation organizations such as the OECD, the General Agreement on Tariffs and Trade (GATT), and the Asia Pacific Economic Cooperation (APEC) forum, Mexico has institutionalized its trade liberalization process. Allow me to point out that the North American Free Trade Agreement (NAFTA) is already stimulating trade flows in the region. During the first semester of this year, Mexican exports to the United States increased by more than 20 percent, while exports from the United States to Mexico rose by 16 percent.

Mexico's financial relations with the rest of the world have also been transformed. Mexico has shifted from a situation of transferring considerable amounts of resources to the rest of the world to being a net recipient of foreign capital. Last year, the capital account surplus reached $30.9 billion. These results have had as a natural counterpart an increase in the current account deficit and a significant accumulation of foreign reserves. There has also been an important change in the composition of capital inflows. During the early 1980s, most of the foreign resources were commercial bank loans to the public sector. In 1993, 95 percent of capital account inflows were in the form of direct and portfolio foreign investment.

The modernization of the financial system had two main objectives: first, to increase financial savings in the economy and allocate resources toward the most productive investment projects; and second, to provide access to financial services for a larger share of the population. To achieve these objectives, a process of liberalization was implemented through a more competitive and sound financial structure. New financial legislation was passed, and commercial banks, which were owned by the public sector, were privatized.

Among the most important changes were the introduction of universal banking; the participation of foreign capital in domestic institutions; the establishment of capitalization requirements in accordance with internationally accepted standards; central bank autonomy; and the creation of new financial groups. Furthermore, many new financial intermediaries have been authorized. In particular, the number of commercial banks has increased from 19 in 1988 to 36 at present.

Owing to the reforms, Mexico has a more competitive and stable financial system, in which the number of intermediaries has doubled. In accordance with international agreements and domestic legislation, we received last July 102 applications from international financial institutions that want to open subsidiaries in Mexico. The capital of these institutions amounts to $2.7 billion. In October, the first authorizations will be granted. This increase in competition has been accompanied by more strict regulation to guarantee that intermediaries act in strict accordance with the law.

Those of us who have had the privilege of participating in some of the decisions and reforms in our countries know that, at the dawn of the twenty-first century, the competitive position of a country does not depend on its natural resources but on its capacity to innovate and to be more productive. This microeconomic reform is a necessary condition for the construction of a market economy. Only in this way can we increase efficiency and avoid overexploitation of our natural resources.

The guiding principles of the microeconomic reform have been to increase productivity levels, reduce costs, widen employment opportunities, transform labor and business practices, and develop a competitive and flexible industrial structure.

Our world, at the end of the century, is radically different from the one in which the founders of the Bretton Woods institutions lived. No single country, to a greater or a lesser extent, has escaped from the dynamics of a more integrated world economy. In Mexico, we are facing the new challenges through the Reform of the State. Allow me to share with you seven reflections that follow from Mexico's experience with economic transformation and that may be useful guidelines for the future evolution of the Bretton Woods institutions.

First, institutional reforms are essential for the success of economic reform programs. On the macroeconomic front, stabilization does not only require austerity in public finances and a restrictive monetary policy; it is also essential to carry out structural and permanent transformations. This is the main challenge.

In the Mexican case, the Pact has allowed actions to be coordinated between sectors to distribute the costs of the adjustment fairly and to unify efforts. The reduction in the public deficit has been accompanied by a profound tax reform, a rationalization of budgetary expenses, and a prudent monetary policy that is guaranteed by the autonomy of the central bank.

These same principles apply to microeconomic reform. Regarding trade liberalization, it is not enough to lower tariffs and to reduce quantitative restrictions. Investors, and society in general, need assurance as to the permanence of the liberalization and its specifics. By joining GATT and the OECD, and by signing NAFTA, together with other bilateral and regional trade agreements, Mexico has precisely established the modalities of its integration into the international economy for decades to come.

A fundamental aspect of institutional reform is the strengthening of property rights. Not only does this policy promote economic efficiency but it also generates a better distribution of income and wealth. In Mexico, for instance, with the objective of promoting rural development, the Constitution was reformed to strengthen peasants' property rights over their land. Also, to increase domestic savings and to achieve dignified standards of living for senior citizens, we have implemented a structural and operational reform of our pension system.

Second, efforts must be concentrated in social programs and the protection of the environment must be promoted. The crucial factor for development in any country is the motivation and the skills of its men and women, whose welfare, in turn, is the ultimate objective of economic progress. Elements such as capital, technology, and intermediate inputs are very important for economic activity, but, in the contemporary world, they are extremely mobile between countries. Even though today we observe substantial migration flows, labor mobility is significantly lower than that of the other factors of production.

Therefore, the promotion of education, worker training programs, and health care projects is a necessary condition for increasing productivity and improving living standards. These types of programs generate a better distribution of opportunities, which is the most effective policy for increasing social mobility and promoting a more just income distribution.

Sustained development requires special attention to the environment to ensure that the rising levels of production do not further damage our habitat and also to attempt to recover what has been lost.

In Mexico, we have redirected government efforts toward attaining the priority of social needs. As I mentioned before, public expenditures in health, education, environmental protection, and housing are at their highest levels in our history. Our National Program of Solidarity channels important amounts of resources toward the neediest groups in society through an innovative scheme in which citizens themselves participate in the design and evaluation of the projects undertaken.

In this sense, the World Bank should intensify its support for social programs. Technical assistance projects must increase in number and improve in quality to ensure that, with close cooperation from the governments of each country, resources actually reach the poorest social groups and are applied efficiently.

Third, sustainable economic growth should be actively promoted. In terms of economic development, middle- and low-income countries have to catch up with industrial nations. Therefore, it is not sufficient just to take measures that guarantee macroeconomic stability. Governments have to assume an active role in the promotion of growth. The guiding principle must be to complement markets or to create them when they do not exist.

Governments, with the firm support of the Bretton Woods institutions, should undertake sound policies to promote and to open opportunities for private investment. The continuous globalization of all types of economic transactions implies the need for a tighter integration of the economies that participate in the Bretton Woods institutions.

Fourth, increased financing to the private sector is necessary. Governments must set the basis for and promote economic development. Nevertheless, the main engine of growth has to be the private sector. To encourage it, the first premise is that governments must not absorb the resources generated by society. Therefore, healthy public finances are imperative.

When governments establish adequate incentives and permit the orderly operation of markets, creativity and the initiative of individuals and groups will translate into socially productive projects. In most cases, the main restriction is access to adequate financing. This problem is particularly troublesome for small and medium-sized enterprises, which have great potential for innovation and for job creation.

The resources of the Bretton Woods institutions must not replace the financial flows of private intermediaries. On the contrary, they must complement them. The emphasis must be centered on covering those risks for which no market instruments exist. Furthermore, the institutions must support the internationalization of emerging markets, as well as collaborate with developing nations' authorities in developing their domestic financial markets, such as stock exchanges, pension funds, mortgage markets, and venture capital funds.

Fifth, the internal operation of the institutions should be improved. Most developing nations that have so far undertaken successful economic reform programs have improved the internal operation and evaluation systems of their governmental agencies. They have simplified structures and have improved the technical capacity and moral quality of their public servants.

In the Mexican case, the Pact has been an effective instrument for executing the economic reform program because the worker unions and the business and peasant organizations that participate in it are well organized and highly representative of their members. This participation permits meaningful consensus and a high degree of effectiveness to be reached. Furthermore, institutional restrictions have been established to prevent undesirable deviations from the agreed economic policy. The best example is the autonomy of the central bank, which not only guarantees a prudent monetary policy but also guarantees its independence in providing domestic credit. In practice, this implies a limit to fiscal deficits, since they would have to be financed exclusively through capital markets with a consequent increase in interest rates.

In this same vein, the Bretton Woods institutions face a double task. First, they should start at home and modernize their administrative apparatus. Second, they must promote among all member countries the implementation of new structures and processes with enough freedom of action to respond adequately to society's demands but also with firm controls to prevent them from deviations or corruption.

Sixth, the International Monetary Fund and the World Bank must complement each other. To promote efficiency and to avoid an excessive concentration of tasks and resources in one institution, there should be some specialization of functions between the Fund and the Bank. The Fund must concentrate its financial resources and its analytical capabilities on short-term macroeconomic situations. The Bank must concentrate its efforts on promoting and supporting long-term structural transformations.

However, both institutions must work in close coordination. In most cases, macroeconomic imbalances are the result of long-term structural problems. For example, chronic inflation is generally a result of large fiscal deficits caused by obsolete tax systems, excessive public expenditures, or inefficient public enterprises. The correction of these imbalances requires the application of both macroeconomic and microeconomic measures, and, therefore, participation and coordination between the Fund and the World Bank.

Seventh, a long-term perspective must be maintained. The undeniable sign of our times is accelerated change, not only in the technological and economic arenas but also in the political and social settings. Half a century ago, leaders of various countries had the vision to set the foundations for a new system of international coordination and cooperation on economic issues. From the Bretton Woods agreements, institutions such as the Fund and the World Bank emerged, both having served well the interests of the international financial community. It is time again to look to the future, and to do so in a permanent way. Today, more than ever, the Bretton Woods institutions must be alert to finding new opportunities that benefit member countries as they work to prevent possible future crises.

To detect risks and opportunities, the institutions must carefully evaluate the economic performance of both developed and developing economies. Their recommendations and proposals must follow homogenous criteria and must be applied uniformly, without granting any privileges to developed economies. I must say that in the past a double standard has been used. Substantial imbalances in developed nations have seemed to go unnoticed by the institutions, whereas the disequilibria in developing nations have promptly been sharply criticized, and little flexibility shown in the provision of financial resources.

It is the responsibility of member countries, more than that of its Directors, who are known to conduct themselves with technical and professional excellence, to provide the Bretton Woods institutions with a clear mandate and sufficient autonomy to act objectively, based on technical parameters that are independent of the degree of development or the political weight of the country in question.

The institutions must take the initiative in facing new challenges. We must act—countries and institutions together—with the creativity and close collaboration that characterized the renegotiation of Mexico's external debt. At that time, the schemes prevailing to alleviate the debt-overhang problem had already shown their ineffectiveness. Meanwhile, indebted nations, including Mexico, were suffering the effects of increasing transfers to the rest of the world.

In this context, the Mexican Government, the U.S. financial authorities, and the Executive Directors of the Fund and the World Bank—and here I want to publicly acknowledge the support of Michel Camdessus, Barber Conable, and Lewis Preston—worked together and designed an innovative and imaginative mechanism to achieve a permanent solution to the debt problem. The scheme was new and not without risks; nevertheless, the concerted efforts and determination to surmount the problem led to success. The mechanism has proved useful not only for Mexico but for other nations as well.

The main lesson from the Mexican debt-renegotiation experience is that it reveals the great potential for joint and creative work between governments and multilateral institutions. The Fund and the World Bank must provide the leadership needed to create and take advantage of all kinds of new opportunities for the benefit of all member countries.

The last decade has been one of profound economic, political, and social reform in Mexico. Much has been done, but we still have vast challenges to overcome. These have been years of sustained effort by Mexico's society and Government. We have learned much. In my own personal experiences, I have been able to perceive vividly the enthusiasm and courage of the Mexican people; I have seen how national unity and the desire for shared prosperity have been stronger than economic crises, overcoming any intent to make us deviate from our national project. I have also had the privilege to work together with an outstanding team of public servants, led by the great vision and firm compromise of President Carlos Salinas de Gortari.

As a public servant, I have learned that true leadership is shown in times of adversity. It is then that one must decide promptly and correctly among different courses of action and, through agreement, negotiation, and hope, convince society to act together in the chosen direction. Short-term sacrifices are frequently required, and it is the leader's task to convince the parties with the truth and with a vision of the better future that is to come.

If I had to sum up the main lesson that I have learned during my years as a public servant, it would be that true development must embrace all facets of the human dimension. It is not enough to achieve sustained economic growth. Its fruits must be distributed justly among society. Individuals and groups must act with complete freedom in an environment that promotes creativity and personal initiative. Development must also include increased openness and participation in the political, social, and cultural spheres. Democratic participation, free expression of ideas, and personal enrichment through culture, tradition, and history are crucial elements that must be the essence of any nation's development.

The particular case of economic reform cannot be implemented alone; it must be accompanied by political and social openness to be permanent. The best guarantee for the continuity of an economic program lies in a society that is convinced about the chosen route, and where this consensus is expressed through its political participation and everyday activities.

In Mexico, we have undertaken a profound Reform of the State in order to improve economic efficiency, generate more political participation, and achieve more equity and freedom in the social arena. To reach the twenty-first century in the best possible conditions of strength and viability, Mexico is fostering individual and community development, a market economy and social justice, liberty and equality, sovereignty and globalization, and stability and democracy.

Mexico is a country with an extensive diversity of ideas and with increasing political participation. Last August, we held the most clear and transparent presidential elections in our history, which were even praised by the international community. Voter turnout was an outstanding 77 percent of registered voters. This process reveals the will of Mexicans to continue advancing through political openness and democracy.

To attain the future that our nations deserve, societies and governments must work together and share costs and benefits justly among groups and individuals. The will and the participation of society are the main factors of change, which account for the permanence of the successes achieved. Honest, capable, and committed leaders, who project their societies' goals and guide them to their achievement, are also needed. Multilateral organizations must provide this type of leadership in the international arena.

The Bretton Woods institutions face a new international environment. Disparities between and within nations have increased. The challenge of human development is more present than ever before. It would be difficult for any country to overcome these challenges in isolation. International cooperation, through the coordination of policies and the allocation of resources, will be the key to promoting global development.

With the end of the Cold War, the role of the Bretton Woods institutions has become more prominent. Military alliances are no longer the main keepers of national security and sovereignty. Economic development is the new pillar and the new objective for world stability. This is the great challenge for the Bretton Woods institutions. Mexico, as I am sure is true for all member nations, will participate with enthusiasm and a spirit of compromise in strengthening the Bretton Woods institutions for the benefit of the international community as a whole.

8

Adjustment and Economic Growth

The second day of the conference opened with a session on ways to ensure that adjustment programs contribute effectively to economic growth in developing countries. The first speaker was Tony Killick, Senior Research Fellow and former Director of the Overseas Development Institute, who spoke on conditionality and the connection between adjustment and development. He has published numerous studies analyzing the effectiveness of adjustment programs. He was followed by Alassane Ouattara, who has dealt with the linkages between adjustment and growth both in his former capacities as Governor of the Central Bank of the West African States and as Prime Minister of Côte d'Ivoire and in his present capacity as Deputy Managing Director of the IMF. The Governor of the Central Bank of Spain, Luis Angel Rojo, chaired the session and moderated the discussion that followed the formal presentations.

Tony Killick

Good Policies, Weak Results

I start with a paradox: the thrust of the policies favored by the Bretton Woods institutions has had demonstrably beneficial effects on the economic progress of many countries but the results of their structural adjustment programs—which embody the institutions' policy recommendations—have been patchy, at best. In broad terms, the institutions' approach to policy improvement in developing countries can be boiled down to three fundamentals:

- avoiding large macroeconomic imbalances;
- working in cooperation with, and in support of, the private sector, and through market signals rather than in opposition to them; and
- taking maximum advantage of opportunities in foreign trade and for the attraction of foreign investment.

There is substantial cross-country evidence that this type of policy strategy produces economic results superior both to what has gone before and to available alternatives. In addition to the results of academic investigations, an appeal to the recent histories of major countries and regions appears to demonstrate the strategy's efficacy. The remarkable response of the Chinese people to the rolling back of central planning, the encouragement of private enterprise, and the gradual liberalization and opening up of the economy is a case in point. Of longer standing are the extraordinary results achieved by the East Asian "miracle" countries—countries that departed in important ways from the standard model favored by the Bretton Woods institutions but that nonetheless observed the three fundamentals spelled out above. Less dramatically and with the help of large but undependable capital inflows, Latin American countries that a few years ago appeared hopelessly mired in the debt morass have also achieved an economic turnaround on the basis of similar policy changes. India, too, shows signs of shrugging off its economic lethargy in response to a like package of policy changes.

In each of the cases cited above, the positive connection between adjustment and development is palpable. Even in troubled sub-Saharan Africa, there is supporting evidence, as the World Bank's (1994) study, *Adjustment in Africa*, assembles fairly persuasive evidence linking improvements in policies and performance.

However—and here is the paradox—the evidence on the economic consequences of structural adjustment programs, which incorporate the same policy strategy, does not point to strong results. Assessment of the impact of structural adjustment programs is fraught with difficulty, particularly because we can only guess at what would have happened without a program. However, enough expertise has developed, and enough evidence accumulated, to provide some firm indicators. The following generalizations are among the principal results of the empirical literature on the consequences of adjustment programs supported by the Bretton Woods institutions.[1]

- *Programs have limited revealed ability to achieve their own objectives.* Although there is consistent evidence for both Bretton Woods insti-

---

[1]There is an extensive empirical literature on the effects of Bank and Fund programs. Khan (1990) offers a valuable discussion of the methodological problems and surveys the literature on the effects of IMF programs. Killick (1993 and forthcoming, 1995) offers a more recent survey and additional evidence of his own. The IMF (Schadler and others, 1993) review of experiences with ESAF programs should also be consulted, although see Killick (forthcoming, 1995) for a critique. The best independent source on the effects of World Bank structural adjustment programs is Mosley, Harrigan, and Toye (1991); see also Corbo and Rojas (1991). Substantial in-house Bank evaluations are provided in World Bank (1992a and 1992b). Results in Africa are presented in World Bank (1994) and Elbadawi, Ghura, and Uwujaren (1992). I am also drawing upon as yet unpublished results from ongoing research.

tutions that programs are associated with improvements in export performance and other balance of payments indicators, programs do not make much difference to economic growth or inflation. In the case of the IMF, most tests indicate no significant correlation between programs and changes in GDP growth. Evidence on World Bank programs is more mixed: some tests show a similar absence of significant association; others indicate more positive results. The recent Bank report on Africa shows as many adjusting countries slipping back as those accelerating their growth. One reason for the poor growth results is that structural adjustment programs are associated with reduced investment levels, a joint result of reduced public investment levels and sluggish private sector responses to program measures. Evidence on inflation is similarly indeterminate, with price-reducing and price-raising influences tending to offset each other.

- *Programs have high mortality or interruption rates.* Over half (53 percent) of all IMF stand-by, extended Fund facility, and structural adjustment facility (SAF) programs were discontinued before the end of their intended life in 1980–93; 61 percent were discontinued in 1991–93. As of April 1993, only 5 of a total of 26 programs under the enhanced structural adjustment facility (ESAF) had been completed within their planned period, and 8 had apparently broken down altogether. Three fourths of World Bank adjustment loans had installment tranche releases delayed because of nonimplementation of policy conditions in 1980–88, the latest period for which data are publicly available. By no means do all of these departures from the plan represent "failures," but enough of them do for the two institutions to be concerned.

- *There is little evidence of a strong connection between structural adjustment programs and implementation of policy reforms.* In the case of the IMF, even balance of payments improvements are not strongly connected with program implementation;[2] the Bank's *Adjustment in Africa* (1994, p. 216) similarly reports an absence of correlation between macroeconomic policy improvements and adjustment lending.

---

[2]See Killick (forthcoming, 1995, Table 4 and p. 596) for a comparison of outcomes between completed and uncompleted programs. The results for the external current account were of equal significance for both groups, although quantitatively larger for countries with completed programs. The paper suggests, however, that this finding was due to the more adverse terms of trade experiences of noncompleters and shows that in the overall balance of payments changes were both larger and more significant for this group than for completers.

- *Structural adjustment programs seek to achieve improved economic performance by raising the quality of domestic policies and strengthening institutions.* However, the evidence reveals that programs have only modest impact on key policy variables and even less on institutions. There is little evidence that programs exert restraint on the core IMF program component of domestic credit,[3] or of strong influence by the Bretton Woods institutions on budget deficits, with much slippage in the implementation of fiscal conditionality. The institutions' conditionality does, however, exert a decisive and sustained influence on the exchange rate. There is also quite a strong association with reform of other price variables, such as interest rates, agricultural producer prices, and the deregulation of consumer prices. However, they have far greater difficulty in influencing institutional change, for example, in financial sector reforms and privatization programs. The World Bank's *Adjustment in Africa* (1994) judges that only 6 out of 29 *adjusting* countries had achieved decisive improvements in macroeconomic policies (the most important of which, Nigeria, has since jumped off this pedestal), and that about one third of "adjusting" African countries still combine poor macroeconomic policies with extensive interventionism.
- *Even the above limited claims probably overstate the degree of program influence, because some of the changes would have been introduced in any case.* Moreover, many of the reforms are not sustained, and some governments regress, reverting to old practices or introducing equivalent interventions through the back door.

In the light of this evidence, it seems justified to describe the effectiveness of structural adjustment programs as patchy, at best. Given the strongly positive results achieved by others that have followed the three-pronged policy strategy described earlier, the puzzle is to understand why structural adjustment programs have such limited revealed potency. The remainder of this paper tries to explain this paradox.

We should note here that the explanation is unlikely to lie with the influence of exogenous shocks, as the success-story countries identified earlier also experienced shocks but overcame them.

---

[3]Killick (forthcoming, 1995, Table 4) shows that, although there is some tendency for the growth of domestic credit to decline, absolutely and relative to GDP, the relative decline is nonsignificant and there is no significant difference between the results obtained by countries that did and did not complete their programs. He also shows there is no significant reduction in the share of credit going to the central government relative to the private sector. Schadler and others (1993, Table 2) do show substantial reductions in the increase in domestic credit by comparison with the pre-program situation, but unfortunately these data are not related to program implementation, nor is any statistical testing attempted.

Various other possible explanations suggest themselves. The problem might lie with weaknesses in the detailed design and sequencing of structural adjustment programs (as distinct from their broad thrust). The Bretton Woods institutions themselves are apt to point to frequent and major deficiencies in what they call governments' "political will," or with what might more fruitfully be thought of as the internal political conditions bearing upon program execution.

I shall return to these explanations later but in what follows will concentrate on two additional clusters of explanations, to argue that structural adjustment programs (a) would be strengthened if they were based on a more satisfactory appreciation of the linkage between medium-term adjustment and long-run development; and (b) are far too reliant on a mode of trying to achieve change (conditionality) of very limited proven effectiveness.

The Adjustment-Development Link

Adjustment as Catharsis

At some risk of oversimplification, the Bretton Woods institutions' positions on this can be characterized as viewing adjustment as a preliminary to the resumption of sustainable growth and development. The Fund, for example, often describes its programs as "laying the foundations" for resumed economic growth. The World Bank has similarly tended to view its 1980s shift into adjustment lending as transitional, a response to the particularly severe disruptions caused by the second oil shock, the associated world economic downturn, and then the breaking of the debt crisis. It initially thought adjustment could be completed quite quickly, and, although it now accepts that adjustment often takes a long time, it still appears to regard the task as a preliminary to a resumption of development (and a return by the Bank to its traditional project-lending and sector-lending focus).

Two further considerations reinforce this view of adjustment as catharsis. First, the Bretton Woods institutions (and the wider creditor community) have tended to define the solution of the debt problems of middle-income developing countries in terms of the restoration of creditworthiness: the language of transition again. Second, as the structural adjustment movement developed, increased emphasis was placed on the need to rectify past interventionist policy mistakes, the implication being that once the policy framework had been corrected, the adjustment task was essentially accomplished. On this view, then, structural adjustment is a phenomenon of the late twentieth century.

Of course, no one believes there is any stark dichotomy between adjustment and development, and the institutions have never, to my knowledge, articulated any definitive view of how they see the connection. That may be part of the problem. I nevertheless think it is fair to characterize their view in terms of adjustment as catharsis.

Adjustment as Continuous Adaptation[4]

An alternative view sees a permanent need for economies to adapt to changing circumstances, and this adaptation as intrinsic to development. All economies are constantly in a state of flux, buffeted by developments in the rest of the world, by shifts in the composition of demand, and by technological change. There is thus an ever-present need to respond to—and take advantage of—such changes in the economic environment. The imperative to do so has been intensified in recent decades as economic interdependence has increased, with the rise of trade and international capital movements relative to domestic economic activity, and as the pace of technological change has accelerated. There are rich rewards for those who find ways of leading this expansion; increasingly, none can afford to be left out.

Economies' responses to these stimuli will result in long-term changes in their productive and institutional structures, of the type studied by such writers as Kuznets, Chenery, and Syrquin. Inflexible economies can expect retarded development, with disjunctures between demand and supply creating bottlenecks, foreign exchange shortages, inflationary pressures, and other dislocations.

Various contemporary examples can be cited of the evident importance of flexibility for economic development:

- The well-known success of the newly industrializing countries of East and Southeast Asia in taking advantage of opportunities in world markets for manufactured goods. This region has been characterized by the speed with which it has been able to accommodate rapid adjustment and structural change and the apparently low social costs incurred in the process.
- The starkly contrasting failures of the former Soviet Union and other former communist countries of Eastern Europe to keep abreast of modern industrial technologies, trading opportunities, and changing consumer preferences, attributable in part to the rigidities of central planning.

---

[4]The next few paragraphs are based on Chapter 12 of Killick (1995). See also Killick (1993), Chaps. 2 and 3.

- The great difficulties created for many of the economies of Africa by their failure to diversify their export bases in response to trend declines in world real prices for their traditional commodity exports.
- Concerns about the long-term growth-retarding effects of "eurosclerosis," seen as eroding Northern Europe's ability to remain internationally competitive, and about a perceived general loss of flexibility among mature industrial economies, for example, as articulated in Olson (1982).

Adjustment can, in the adjustment-as-continuous-adaptation view, be thought of as induced or planned adaptation, with adjustment policies as the instruments deployed to achieve the desired adaptations and to enhance the economy's flexibility. Structural adjustment can then be viewed as measures targeted at structural variables, particularly the productive system and the human, physical, and institutional infrastructure.

There is a good deal of congruence in the policy implications of these two views of adjustment. There is agreement that adjustment *can* be consciously promoted and that the policy environment makes a crucial difference to the responsiveness of an economy. There is also agreement about the potentially heavy costs of deferred adjustment. If governments decline to act or seek to avert change, the economy will still be forced to respond to outside pressures, but it will be able to do so only by imposing heavy, avoidable costs on its citizens. There is also much in the characteristic policy content of programs supported by the Bretton Woods institutions that is congruent with the needs of long-term adaptation: the importance of prudent, well-designed macroeconomic management, of measures to raise the efficiency of markets, and of improving incentives for structural adaptation, of which the exchange rate is a price signal of exceptional importance.

In these ways and others, structural adjustment programs typically seek to move the institutional and policy environment in directions that enhance economy-wide flexibility. However, there are also important ways in which the policy implications of the two views of the adjustment-development connection diverge.

The adjustment-as-continuous-adaptation view focuses attention on the factors impacting on the long-term flexibility of an economy, and these tend to go well beyond the main thrust of structural adjustment programs supported by the Bretton Woods institutions. In all developing countries, this focus draws special attention to the importance of institutional development, which is crucial to economic adaptation and for reducing transactions costs in the face of increasing structural complexity (North, 1990). In low-income countries, the improvement of education and other investments in human skills is also crucial, together with other measures that can increase economies' technological capabilities. So too is industrialization, which in various ways adds to economies' capacity to adjust.

In other words, structural adjustment programs can be seen as too narrow, neglecting important aspects of the task of raising economies' flexibility. Sometimes, indeed, structural adjustment program policies may get in the way. For example, adjustment programs supported by the Bretton Woods institutions rarely contain much by way of an industrial policy apart from the liberalization of trade and investment regimes, but in low-income countries industrial firms often do not have the managerial and technical capacity to be able to withstand, let alone take advantage of, heightened competition from imports and greater openness.

In other respects, too, the concentration in most structural adjustment programs on moving away from interventionist policy stances and on "getting prices right" is too narrow. It is important to attend to a wider range of factors bearing upon technological capabilities, institutional development, information flows, skill creation, the adequacy of the infrastructure, and the provision of other public goods. Indeed, to the extent that programs supported by the Bretton Woods institutions are associated—as they are—with reductions in public sector services and investments, they may make it harder for economies to adapt.

There is also the matter of time perspectives. Under adjustment as catharsis, the idea that the World Bank (but not the Fund, whose *permanent* responsibility is to offer support for countries needing to strengthen their balances of payments) should revert to its traditional project-lending focus after a transitional period of structural adjustment lending has some plausibility. It has none if we see the need for economies to adapt, and for international assistance with that task, as an indefinite requirement, intrinsic to the long-run development that is the Bank's remit, and not merely a phenomenon of the late twentieth century.

A further respect in which the approaches of the Bretton Woods institutions may get in the way of long-term adaptation brings us to the second line of explanation of the relative ineffectiveness of structural adjustment programs, which relates to the processes through which change can be effected.

Conditionality and the Processes of Reform

The perspective of adjustment as continuous adaptation views the adjustment movement of the last 15 years as simply the latest episode in a history of economic adaptation at least as old as the invention of money and trade, although the circumstances of the early 1980s meant that it was an unusually intense episode. What was truly unique about it, however, was the extent to which the intellectual and policy impulse for change came from outside the affected countries. In many countries the Bretton Woods institutions played a lead role, a tendency greatly enhanced by the move of the World Bank into structural adjustment lending and the initiation by the IMF of its two structural adjustment facilities. The last decade and a half have seen a veritable explosion of conditionality-related policy changes in developing countries.

Table 1 shows the rapid growth in adjustment lending by the World Bank since the early 1980s, with the number of new loans increasing fivefold over the period. The trend is less clear in the case of the Fund, but by the last period shown it was making an unprecedented large number of high-conditionality (excluding SAF) structural adjustment loans.

In addition to the growing number of governments entering into structural adjustment arrangements with the Bretton Woods institutions, the number of policy stipulations per credit has also been increasing. Conditionality in World Bank structural adjustment programs has always been wide-ranging, and its staff's tendency to be overambitious in program design has been a recurring source of concern in internal Bank evaluations of its adjustment lending. This self-criticism has not, however, prevented further proliferation of policy conditions (see Table 2).

A specific but not unusual illustration of this conditionality is provided by an unpublished World Bank report on Uganda, a country still trying to rebuild its public administration after the ravages of prolonged civil war. This report sets out a total of 86 specific policy commitments for 1991/92–1993/94, of which 79 should have been undertaken or initiated in fiscal year 1991/92 alone.

Table 1. Adjustment Lending by the IMF and the World Bank
(Average new credits and commitments per annum)

	IMF				World Bank	
	All credits		Structural adjustment[1]			
	Number	Value[2]	Number	Value[2]	Number	Value
1980–82	28	8.24	7	4.64	7	0.81
1983–85	27	7.24	2	2.92	17	2.18
1986–88	27	3.51	9	0.86	28	4.48
1989–93[4]	24	6.79	10	3.48	35	5.77

Sources: World Bank (1992b), Annex 1; World Bank, *Annual Report, 1993*, p. 13; and IMF, *Annual Report, 1993*, Table II.1.

[1]Includes extended Fund facility, SAF, and ESAF credits.
[2]In billions of SDRs.
[3]In billions of U.S. dollars.
[4]Latest IMF data to April 30, 1993; latest World Bank data to June 30, 1993.

Table 2. Average Number of Bank
Conditions per Adjustment Loan

	1980–88	1989–91
Preconditions (prior actions)	9	18
Legal requirements[1]	12	17
Other policy commitments	18	21
Total	39	56

Source: World Bank (1992b), Table A2.3.

[1]In the sense that their observance is required if a loan tranche is to be released, and thus similar in status to IMF performance criteria.

In the IMF, the tendency toward proliferation is most obvious with its ESAF programs. The range of policy conditions in these is considerably wider than in traditional stand-by arrangements. Preconditions have been extensively used, but the starkest evidence on proliferation was provided by Polak (1991, p. 14), who noted that the number of performance criteria rose from less than 6 in the period 1968–77 to 7 (1979–84) and then to $9\frac{1}{2}$ (1984–87). A principal reason for this proliferation is that Fund conditionality now goes beyond its traditional demand-management concentration to stipulate supply-side measures, for example, as regards trade liberalization, pricing policies, or privatization, but these extensions are additional to its traditional demand-management stipulations. Under pressure from some members of its Board, the Fund has also begun to take a more active interest in the impact of its programs on vulnerable groups, including spending on social welfare programs.

There have also been important changes in the Fund's thinking on fiscal conditionality (Tanzi, 1989), which have further increased the intrusiveness of Fund conditionality. Internal staff papers now write disparagingly of the past tendency of programs to go for "quick fixes" and to overconcentrate on aggregate spending ceilings. Detailed attention is now paid to improving the content of government expenditures, as well as to tax reforms and other revenue-raising measures, to raise the "quality" of fiscal adjustment.

Where the Bretton Woods institutions have led the way, bilateral donors have, in varying degrees, followed (Hewitt and Killick, forthcoming, 1995). It is increasingly common for the granting or disbursement of bilateral aid to be made conditional on continued compliance with the institutions' conditionality, but several donors have not stopped there. There have been a number of well-known cases where donors have stipulated *political* reforms in the directions of improved observance of human rights, reduced military spending, accountability, and democratization. A number of donors have also widened the net of policy conditionality, going beyond the Bretton Woods institutions to insist on measures for environmental protection, poverty reduction, enhancement of the role of women, and private enterprise development. Some have further attached conditions to the ways in which governments use counterpart funds generated by program support.

This proliferation tends to undermine the development of indigenous policymaking capacity. Relatedly, conditionality can give the impression that programs are being imposed upon a reluctant government even when that is not so. Such public perceptions may undermine the legitimacy of a program and hence the likelihood that it will be implemented and sustained. Even where that does not occur, external determination of program content will weaken what the World Bank calls the government's sense of "ownership" of the program, which may well be the most important determinant of its success.

It is surprising that little attention has been paid to the findings of a report by the World Bank (1992a), which provided substantial, statistically highly significant evidence on the importance of this factor. This report assessed program ownership by the extent to which the initiative for the program's policies was local or external, the level of intellectual conviction in the appropriateness of its measures, the extent of support from the top political leadership, and efforts toward consensus-building among the wider public, and tested for correlation between this variable and its assessment of the satisfactory outcomes of programs. The result was that the extent of government ownership predicted the satisfactory outcomes of adjustment programs in three fourths (73 percent) of all cases, with most outliers explained by exogenous shocks. Ownership was high in most programs achieving good outcomes and low in most unsatisfactory programs. In the absence of ownership, governments evade commitments and regress when opportunities arise.

Unfortunately, conditionality, being essentially coercive, undermines ownership.[5] Its imposed nature can result in resentments by the ministers and officials who must implement the measures—and live with their consequences. In the more extreme cases, public perceptions of imposition can undermine the legitimacy of programs and strengthen opposition to reform. (For this reason, the Bretton Woods institutions' complaints of "weakness of political will" by governments that were mentioned earlier are often unhelpful.) Berg (1991, pp. 217 and 219) has put the point trenchantly:

---

[5]I anticipate objections to a description of conditionality as coercive. But conditionality requires governments to take measures that they otherwise would not choose (if not, it is redundant) against the threat of the withholding of financial help. This is *not* the same as saying that relationships between governments and the Bretton Woods institutions are coercive, which is the exception rather than the rule.

> Explicit conditionality coexists uneasily and indeed may be incompat-
> ible with the notion of local "ownership" of adjustment programs . . . .
> [It] gives the impression of being imposed from outside, even when it
> is not. It causes liberalization ideas and policies to be identified with
> outsiders. Local critics attack the "World Bank's austerity program"
> or the "World Bank's liberalization scheme"; foreign reporters write
> about it in the same way . . . . The overall effect is to discourage the
> growth of local "ownership," discredit the policy ideas at issue, and
> delay the growth of political responsibility.

The Bretton Woods institutions deny that conditionality is coercive or
that programs are imposed, but the degree of imposition is more common than they are willing to admit. This is strongly confirmed by evidence in the World Bank report just cited (1992a) showing that government ownership was regarded *by Bank staff* as "low" or "very low" in
half of the programs (40/81), and "very high" in only one fifth (16/81).

There is no equivalent information on the Fund, but there is a strong
presumption that similar considerations apply with at least equal force,
not least because many of the World Bank structural adjustment programs analyzed were accompanied by Fund programs. That the Fund
has been unforthcoming on this subject is not, I suspect, because it
thinks ownership is unimportant, but because it has particular difficulties in dealing with this subject. Many of these difficulties arise from the
crisis conditions in which governments often turn to it, the intense pressure of work under which its country staff commonly operate, the speed
with which its programs are prepared, and their relatively short-term
nature. In such circumstances, with negotiating missions commonly
lasting two or three weeks, its staff does not have time to ensure that the
government is fully "on board," just as the government often will not
have time (even when it has the inclination) to undertake the consultations and public information necessary for consensus building.

However, the Fund's modalities of operation compound these intrinsic difficulties. Its key document is the "letter of intent," in which the
borrowing government formally presents the policies it will undertake
to promote program objectives. Herein, it might be said, lies program
"ownership." However, these letters, although ostensibly from the government, are still almost invariably drafted in Washington, with the government left trying to negotiate variations in a draft presented to them. It
is difficult to imagine a procedure more subversive of ownership. The
practices of the Fund flatly contradict the obvious good sense of the
World Bank report (1992a, p. 15) that "one good indicator of ownership is
the borrower's willingness and capacity to prepare the letter [of intent]."

Such modalities are apt to result in programs that governments do
not regard as their own and of which, therefore, they will implement
only the inescapable minimum. Consequently, some governments have
become adept at finding ways that do not formally contravene agreed

policies but that effectively restore the status quo ante. One of the difficulties is that, by insisting on major policy changes, the Bretton Woods institutions ipso facto become important players on the domestic political stage but do not have the ability to assemble a coalition of interests sufficient to sustain the reforms, particularly if the economic crisis abates and the pressures diminish.

Here is a classical principal-agent problem, with differences in goals and interests between the principals (the Bretton Woods institutions) and the agents (implementing governments); inadequate incentives for the agents to promote principals' objectives; asymmetrical information; and high enforcement costs.

There are hence large advantages to "homegrown" programs, which avoid such dilemmas. This helps explain the examples cited earlier of favorable Asian and Latin American experiences that apparently owed little to direct participation by the Bretton Woods institutions (as distinct from the positive indirect influence of their advice and technical assistance). The most successful adjusting group of countries are the East Asian "miracle" countries (note, for example, the Republic of Korea's successful response to its large debt problems of the mid-1980s), *but their efforts owe little or nothing to Bretton Woods institution adjustment programs.* Indeed, in important and well-known ways, most of them departed from the orthodoxies of the Bretton Woods institutions. The same local ownership appears to characterize the reform process in China and India. More tentatively, it is not clear that much of the restoration of creditworthiness in heavily indebted Latin American countries owes much to conditionality in structural adjustment programs. Conversely, sub-Saharan Africa has undoubtedly been subjected to more conditionality per capita than any other region—and has achieved the least adjustment. Politically motivated changes in domestic government attitudes to macroeconomic management appear to be the decisive factor.

Being a product of domestic political and policy formation processes, homegrown programs more faithfully reflect domestic goals and priorities and are less likely to be sabotaged during implementation. In the ideal case, the program will be consensual, based on wide consultation and public information. Even without that, the government must take into account how the resulting social costs and political opposition are to be managed—something the Bretton Woods institutions are not well placed to do. By definition, such programs are tailor-made to suit local circumstances, and they tap superior local knowledge of the economy. The probability of sustained government commitment to the chosen path of reform is enhanced.

Evidence is accumulating that the nature of a country's polity—and the interventions that emanate from it—exerts a decisive influence on national economic flexibility, for good or ill. Political systems have hampered adaptation in sub-Saharan Africa, which has been marked by long-term government persistence with dysfunctional policies. Conversely, it is widely agreed that governments in East Asia have been highly successful in promoting adaptation and experimenting with different policies, being quick to drop those that have not worked and to try alternative measures. The relative autonomy of the state in these countries, that is, its relative freedom from the influence of pressure from special interest groups, has been the central influence on the state's responsiveness and (tacitly) the resulting flexibility of the economy. Thus, Wade (1990) identifies the following factors to explain the success of Japan, the Republic of Korea, and Taiwan Province of China: centralization of a decision-making structure employing the best managers; insulation of decision makers from all but the strongest pressure groups; a powerful executive not beholden to the legislature; the absence of a powerful labor movement; the absence of conflicts between the owners of natural resources and manufacturers; and decision makers' perception that their legitimacy is grounded in economic success.

Thus, even though the thrust of the policy reforms promoted by the Bretton Woods institutions is desirable, their programs can get in the way by undermining the building of local capacities and responsive political systems that alone will permit adjustment to be sustained over time. They can get in the way for a more prosaic reason, too: the proliferation of conditionality aggravates the already formidable pressures on the cadre of key administrators in often weak and poorly manned public administrations, increasing the probability of slippage in program execution. Overall, the explosion of conditionality seriously affects the cost-effectiveness of structural adjustment programs. It increases the associated information and opportunity costs. The ever-growing influence of external agencies in socioeconomic policies, to say nothing of political processes, also increases investor uncertainties about the future policy environment and the sustainability of reform.

I do not want to argue that conditionality is *never* effective, however. It—and the money that comes with it—probably works best when it tips the balance between evenly poised domestic forces promoting and opposing policy reform, enabling vested interests to be bought off, or confronted. But in general, I suggest that, to be effective, measures to promote adaptation must emanate from an understanding by responsible ministers of the actions necessary, with policies emerging organically, as it were, through local decision and implementation processes, and tailor-made to domestic conditions in a way that is only feasible when designed locally. The success of homegrown programs is far from guaranteed, of course, because the possibility of misdesign is still present and shocks can supervene. However, they stand a better chance of success than the opposite case of Washington-designed programs that are to a substantial degree wished on more or less reluctant governments desperate for money.

Other Constraints on the Effectiveness of Conditionality

Besides the ownership problem, various other factors limit what it is realistic to expect to be achieved through conditionality.

First, the Bretton Woods institutions suffer from *resource problems*. Arguably the most serious of these is *inadequate knowledge*. The circumstances of each country differ. Each economy has its special structural characteristics and problems. Policies and other economic variables interact with each other in complex ways. To be effective, adjustment programs must be tailored to these local particularities. A great deal of in-depth country knowledge is therefore necessary for well-founded programs—more knowledge than it is often reasonable to expect of hardpressed staffs in Washington.

In the face of inadequate knowledge, the danger is that the institutions will fall back on institutional orthodoxies and more or less standard prescriptions. Moreover, the large number and ambitious scope of country programs described earlier add to pressures for the adoption of standard recipes. Pressure of work and the inherent limitations on the freedom of action of the Bretton Woods institutions increase the difficulties of coping with the complexities and uncertainties of devising tailor-made adjustment packages. Martin (1991, p. 35) has observed the consequences of these tendencies in Africa:

> IMF staff were overworked, especially because they had to reconcile positions with the World Bank and take account of creditor-government pressure. A larger number of African countries were applying for loans more often . . . ; and conditions were proliferating, demanding new expertise . . . . Time pressure, notably in functional departments, often meant that staff did not understand the country's economy or politics, or had not enough experience of African adjustment to be flexible. They tended to absorb the Fund's view of the country in the briefing paper.

The managements of both Bretton Woods institutions deny any mechanistic application of standard formulas and insist that their staffs tailor programs to country circumstances. But there is a frequently-complained-of gap between management aspirations and what happens in practice, to which there is no easy solution. It is an intrinsic difficulty with conditionality as a mode for achieving change. The danger, of course, is that some programs turn out to be ill fitting or unrealistic, and that they result in avoidable adjustment costs—another recurring developing country complaint.

The knowledge constraint is compounded by problems with *staffing*—problems of numbers and of turnover, not of competence. The numbers aspect has particularly affected the IMF, which in recent years has seen a large increase in the number and labor-intensity of its programs (particularly since the emergence of a major group of European economies in transition, the introduction of ESAF, the associated policy framework paper mechanisms, and the Fund's welcome increased use of review missions) while their boards have shortsightedly prevented them from recruiting parallel increases in professional staff.

The turnover aspect of the problem refers not so much to staff movements out of the Bretton Woods institutions (although their terms and conditions have become somewhat eroded, also because of board pressures), but to movements within each institution. Developing country officials complain often and strongly about the delays and other costs imposed by this turnover. Thus, an official of an African government in private correspondence has written of the problems caused by lack of continuity:

> To give an example, a new Exchange and Trade Relations (ETR) man was sent with the IMF mission earlier this year.[6] It took at least two missions for him to get to grips with [this country's] case, and only on his last mission did he look comfortable. However, he has been transferred so the next mission will bring a new ETR man. This will significantly increase my workload as I will have to "educate" him on [my country], answer endless questions and supply lots of information that has already been given in the past. This has also been the case in other areas of the "away team."

In addition to these extra costs, high turnover and the erosion of mission self-confidence that results aggravate the knowledge problem and can lead to an appearance of institutional inflexibility and arrogance in negotiations.

Finance is a third resource constraint. This, however, is too large a subject to go into here. Suffice it to say that there are still too many underfunded programs and that it is easy to exaggerate the extent to which structural adjustment programs have a catalytic effect on net inflows of capital from other sources.

A further constraint can be called the *rigor problem*, referring to pressures from major shareholders or managements for program measures to appear tough and far-reaching. This constraint is associated with the trend toward the proliferation of conditionality and has various adverse consequences. It discourages governments from seeking assistance (a large problem for the take-up rate under the ESAF) or leads them to delay until all other options have been exhausted, so that programs too often have to address crisis situations. They strain the lim-

---

[6]IMF negotiating missions are conducted by the relevant area department, with the participation of a representative of ETR (now called the Policy Development and Review Department).

ited policy implementation capabilities of borrowing governments, causing "noncompliance" and suspicions of bad faith.

Alternatively, when combined with continuing pressures on staff to maintain the level of adjustment lending, these pressures give rise to "paper programs"—the penning of ambitious-seeming commitments to reforms that both parties tacitly understand but which cannot or will not be implemented. Thus, Berg (1991, pp. 219–20) argues that conditionality

> tends to encourage a game in which differences are reconciled more on paper than in reality and agreements are framed so as to meet conflicting needs—the country's need for understated, flexible conditions that will not involve rigid, risky, or excessively difficult commitments, and the World Bank's desire for conditionality that is as firm and explicit as possible.

There is a good deal of pretense in conditionality: paper agreements that the staffs of the Bretton Woods institutions know cannot stick but that are intended to impress managements and boards and to "keep the money moving," or just to give the appearance that borrowing governments are being treated equally.

In either situation, a consequence is to reduce the credibility of reforms, reducing program capacity to influence expectations and investment decision making, and undermining the prospects for good responses to future reforms. This helps explain the sluggishness of private investment response reported earlier.

Finally, there is what can be called the *unequal treatment* constraint, which takes two forms. One occurs among borrowing governments, in breach of the Bretton Woods institutions' principle of uniformity of treatment, defined by the Fund to mean that "for any given degree of need the effort of economic adjustment sought in programs be broadly equivalent among members." Unequal treatment arises chiefly as a result of lobbying on behalf of favored countries (ex-colonies, strategic allies) by governments of major shareholders. It has been particularly a problem for the IMF, for which there are several well-documented cases, but it has also seriously affected the World Bank as it has moved into policy-related lending. It is perhaps now of diminishing concern, following the end of the Cold War.

The second form of unequal treatment is one of asymmetry between developing and developed countries, with the former required to endure a degree of institutional involvement in policy formation that would not be tolerated for a moment by governments of industrial countries, which routinely discount the "surveillance" advice of the IMF. Note that this is not strictly an asymmetry between deficit and surplus countries, as the position of the United States demonstrates.

Both these inequalities of treatment undermine the legitimacy of the Bretton Woods institutions' conditionality, weakening the motivation of governments confronted with demands to implement their commitments and further reducing the credibility of program measures.

Reconsidering the Link Between Adjustment Policies and Supporting Finance

Now to the hard part: to suggest alternatives to the approaches criticized above. If the Bretton Woods institutions are to diminish their reliance on conditionality as a mode for trying to achieve policy and institutional reform while still offering financial support for adjustment efforts, how should they proceed?

First, they should recognize what I believe is true, that their main contribution to successful adjustment in developing countries has been through their influence on the contemporary intellectual climate in which policy issues are debated and their persuasion of governments and their advisors through the regular contacts that occur. If there has been a tendency to overstate what has been accomplished through structural adjustment programs, there has also (because it is hard to demonstrate) been underacknowledgment of this intellectual influence on the "silent revolution" that has occurred in many governments' attitudes toward economic policies. On this view, the turnaround in Latin America can still be viewed as a success story for the Bretton Woods institutions, although not one achieved principally through the specific conditionality of structural adjustment programs.

An implication, then, is that the Bretton Woods institutions should seek ways of maximizing this influence. One possibility that suggests itself—desirable for other reasons, too—is that both the institutions should decentralize their activities and bestow more genuine authority on their in-country offices. Perhaps the World Bank should institute a tradition of regular consultations analogous to the Fund's Article IV consultations. The research activities of the two institutions have a crucial role to play in this, subject to two cautions: (1) they should avoid any tendency to confuse the reportage of research with propaganda, as seriously erosive of intellectual credibility; and (2) they should ensure that their researchers do not become estranged from field operations, so that the latter do not reflect best professional practice. Of course, none of these actions could guarantee that all governments would be sweetly reasonable. However, an incentive mechanism is at work here: governments that make a mess of their countries' economies are apt to become unpopular and fall from office.

It also follows from the earlier comparisons of the policy implications of the adjustment-as-catharsis and adjustment-as-continuous-adaptation views of the relationship between adjustment and development that a broader view and a longer time horizon are needed to comprehend the strategic importance for economic adaptation of such factors as the development of skills and institutions and industrialization, and to rely less on getting prices right (important though that is). Such a perspective might also encourage the Bretton Woods institutions to better focus on the main thrust of what programs are seeking to achieve over time, steering them away from the temptation of (an actually unattainable) "fine-tuning" of policies and economies and its associated proliferation of policy stipulations.

Above all, the Bretton Woods institutions should be willing to say "no" more often to governments with a weak commitment to reform and should insist that all programs be prepared by the borrowing governments. The willingness of governments to draft their own letters of intent or of development policy should be a *minimum* obligation; they should *never* be prepared by the institutions' staffs in Washington. The Bretton Woods institutions should refuse to play the paper conditionality game; their staffs should be assessed on the quality of the adjustment lending they undertake, not the volume—a recommendation at the macro level similar to that in the Wapenhans report on improving the quality of World Bank project lending (see also Wapenhans, 1994), but applicable also to the IMF.

Implementation of these recommendations should result in a reallocation of financial resources away from reluctant adjusters and client states, releasing more for the committed adjusters. If it is correct that domestically designed adjustment programs are more effective, they should further induce larger additional inflows of foreign capital, private and public (as again apparently exemplified by Asian and Latin American cases).

It would, however, be important not to confuse unwillingness to adjust with the limited technical capabilities of some developing country governments. Technical assistance to enhance such capabilities should be even more freely available, but it should be independent of the Bretton Woods institutions, so as to minimize conflict of interest problems, and this assistance should *never* be imposed. Imposed advisors are no more effective than imposed policy reforms, as forcefully conveyed by the World Bank Vice President responsible for Africa (Jaycox, 1993):

> Donors also relied too heavily on foreign experts, even when qualified Africans were available. This did little to foster a receptive environment for the transfer of skills. In fact, it was often bitterly resented. Overreliance on technical assistance also brought many difficulties. Expatriates were frequently chosen for their technical skills rather than their ability to pass on those skills. This, coupled with operational difficulties, pulled foreign consultants into operational support at the expense of capacity building.

A further implication of my recommendations is that the required broadening of programs and insistence that they be home designed would require the Bretton Woods institutions to be more pragmatic and pluralistic in their assessments of programs. Willingness by the World Bank to countenance measures of the type associated with Japan, Korea, and Taiwan Province of China are an example. Moreover, the recommendation of greater country selectivity would necessitate greater restraint by governments of major shareholders from lobbying on behalf of favored applicant governments. The end of the Cold War will, it is hoped, facilitate such restraint.

References

Berg, Elliot, "Comment" in *Restructuring Economies in Distress*, ed. by Vinod Thomas and others (Oxford: Oxford University Press for the World Bank, 1991).

Corbo, Vittorio, and Patricio Rojas, "World Bank-Supported Adjustment Programs: Country Performance and Effectiveness," World Bank Working Paper WPS 623 (Washington: World Bank, March 1991).

Elbadawi, Ibrahim A., Dhaneshwar Ghura, and Gilbert Uwujaren, "Why Structural Adjustment Has Not Succeeded in Sub-Saharan Africa," World Bank Working Paper WPS 1000 (Washington: World Bank, October 1992).

Hewitt, Adrian, and Tony Killick, "Bilateral Aid Conditionality: A First View" in *Foreign Aid in the 1990s: Experiences and Challenges*, ed. by Olaf Stokke (London: Frank Cass and Co., forthcoming, 1995).

Jaycox, Edward V.K., *Capacity Building: The Missing Link in African Development* (Reston, Virginia: African American Institute, 1993).

Khan, Mohsin S., "The Macroeconomic Effects of Fund-Supported Adjustment Programs," *Staff Papers*, International Monetary Fund, Vol. 37 (June 1990), pp. 195–231.

Killick, Tony, *The Adaptive Economy: Adjustment Policies in Low-Income Economies* (Washington; London: World Bank and Overseas Development Institute, 1993).

_____, "Can the IMF Help Low-Income Countries? Experiences with its Structural Adjustment Facilities," a review article of Schadler and others (1993), in *World Economy* (forthcoming, 1995).

_____, ed. *The Flexible Economy* (London: Routledge and Overseas Development Institute, 1995).

Martin, Matthew, *The Crumbling Facade of African Debt Negotiations* (London; New York: Macmillan and St. Martins Press, 1991).

Mosley, Paul, Jane Harrigan, and John Toye, *Aid and Power: The World Bank and Policy-Based Lending*, 2 vols. (London: Routledge, 1991).

North, Douglass C., *Institutions, Institutional Change, and Economic Performance* (Cambridge: Cambridge University Press, 1990).

Olson, Mancur, *The Rise and Decline of Nations: Economic Growth, Stagflation, and Social Rigidities* (New Haven, Connecticut: Yale University Press, 1982).

Polak, Jacques J., "The Changing Nature of IMF Conditionality," *Essays in International Finance* No. 184 (Princeton, New Jersey: Princeton University, September 1991).

Schadler, Susan, and others, *Economic Adjustment in Low-Income Countries: Experiences Under the Enhanced Structural Adjustment Facility,* Occasional Paper 106 (Washington: International Monetary Fund, September 1993).

Tanzi, Vito, "Fiscal Policy, Growth and the Design of Stabilization Programs" in *Fiscal Policy, Stabilization, and Growth in Developing Countries,* ed. by Mario I. Blejer and Ke-young Chu (Washington: International Monetary Fund, 1989).

Wade, Robert, *Governing the Market: Economic Theory and the Role of Government in East Asian Industrialization* (Princeton, New Jersey: Princeton University Press, 1990).

Wapenhans, Willi A., "Efficiency and Effectiveness: Is the World Bank Group Well Prepared for the Task Ahead?" in *Bretton Woods: Looking to the Future,* Vol. 1, Commission Report, Staff Review, and Background Papers (Washington: Bretton Woods Committee, July 1994).

World Bank (1992a), "World Bank Structural and Sectoral Adjustment Operations: The Second OED Overview," Operations Evaluation Department Report 10870 (Washington: World Bank, June 1992).

_____(1992b), *The Third Report on Adjustment Lending: Private and Public Resources for Growth* (Washington: World Bank, 1992).

_____, *Adjustment in Africa: Reforms, Results and the Road Ahead* (New York: Oxford University Press for the World Bank, 1994).

Alassane Ouattara

I have prepared a formal paper for this session on the experience of the low-income countries with adjustment and growth (see annex). Taking a look at the audience for today's session, I see many familiar faces and many former colleagues in both the Fund and the World Bank but also in government—colleagues with whom I have worked on the implementation of reform policies and with whom I have shared the difficulties of trying to create growth in very low-income countries. I think that many of them would be disappointed if I were merely to read a paper. I propose instead to review a few of the major items on our agenda and to share my thoughts and experiences with you. In turn, I will to try to draw on this experience in order to convey some of the lessons for adjustment and growth. In the process, I hope to touch on a wide range of issues: what developing countries are currently doing, what they could do better, what they should do better, how they could be helped, how they are not helped sometimes, and the social and economic environment for many of these countries, which continues to be difficult.

As the only former Prime Minister in the Fund's management team, I have a responsibility for ensuring that the political perspective of the adjustment process is shared with the Executive Board of the Fund.

Although at the technical level neither the Fund nor the World Bank has any wish to interfere in this area, it is important that we begin to look more closely at the political process in each case, which, in the final analysis, is what shapes decisions. One can design the best adjustment program and have the best people in office, but if the political commitment is not present, even the best program will remain, as Professor Killick said, merely a program on paper. Adjustment programs are also influenced by factors of chance: the terms of trade, international interest rates, the generosity of the industrial countries, and so forth, all of which can help to improve the outcome of the adjustment process in developing countries even in the absence of longer-term structural measures.

I will not bore you with a detailed account of the experience of these countries in the 1980s and the early 1990s, with which we are all familiar. The results have been disappointing for many countries, both in Africa and in some other areas of the world. As noted in my background paper, the results have been mixed in part because individual country performance has been mixed, in terms of both policies and the time path that was envisaged. To be sure, the external environment over the past 15 years has also been a mixed blessing for low-income developing countries: changes in the prices of commodities benefited some countries and burdened others, while the high level of interest rates and other exogenous factors have essentially determined the evolution of some economies from time to time. The accumulation of large amounts of external debt is another important element in the analysis of the adjustment and growth of low-income countries since 1980.

What, then, are the lessons for adjustment and growth? As I said, the economic performance of the low-income countries has been weak, and their efforts to raise saving to support investment, growth, and development have been very disappointing. In drawing lessons from this experience, policymakers in the countries concerned and outside advisors need to understand how the policies and prospects of low-income countries can be strengthened, especially in terms of sustained higher growth and improved living standards for the people of these countries.

These observations lead me to the central question: has our approach to adjustment been a failure, as Professor Killick indicated, or has there instead been a failure to adjust? To address the first aspect of this question, whether adjustment programs are supportive of growth, we must first ask another question: what conditions are most conducive to generating higher growth? We know that there is no simple set of policy prescriptions. Nevertheless, in all regions of the world and across the political spectrum, there is now basic agreement on the main thrust of economic policy. It is now widely understood that a country cannot run a large fiscal deficit over a long period without consequences for inflation and the external accounts. It is also evident that a restrictive monetary policy is not possible in all low-income countries, given the structural elements of their economies. Moreover, as a former governor of a central bank, I would also say that it is now clear that monetary policy cannot by itself work to reduce inflation, ensure an adequate level of financing in the economy, and instill the necessary confidence in the economy. Fiscal policy, therefore, is at the core of the adjustment process, especially for low-income countries.

Different economic and social settings clearly influence the level of saving, the trend of saving, and the capacity to save. Looking at specific policy actions, a great deal of reliance has obviously been placed on measures to raise fiscal revenue, however defined. In many low-income countries, for various reasons, the level of taxation is very high; it is very difficult to bring this level down, of course, owing to the need to finance current outlays and, in particular, to provide for investment. How, then, does one deal with a system in which very high tax rates, especially customs duties, coexist with very low wages for the officials charged with implementing these policies? Such a system would seem to meet, albeit unconsciously, all the requirements for corruption. Take, for example, the circumstances of a typical civil servant in an African country: this individual might very well be responsible for the well-being of 10–20 family members, or even a whole village; clearly, a very high level of expenditure has been imposed on him by social factors, and he finds himself in a job in which clearly not all the mechanics are working properly. These are the kinds of issues that I think we need to look into in more detail when we give advice to the officials of low-income countries. As I have already noted, there is now a broad consensus on which policies are right, but also on which policies are wrong.

I would now like to turn to certain elements of structural reform and, in particular, the need to improve efficiency in the allocation of resources in low-income countries. Typically, low-income countries have a large number of public enterprises, mainly because of historical factors, such as the lack of private saving and the relatively favorable terms of trade for many of these countries in Africa in the first years of independence, and because the public sector is widely viewed as the main provider of employment and investment. Public enterprises are intended, at least in the minds of many politicians, to help to improve the social conditions of the country, but they have increasingly become merely institutions that provide employment. To sustain a high level of public sector employment and meet the increasing costs of operating public enterprises, tariffs had to be raised. This, in turn, has led to a situation in which public enterprises are overindebted and their capital stock is ill suited to the needs of a developing economy. In the transportation sector, for example, trains and buses are typically old and have not been well maintained.

How does one go about ensuring a healthier public sector? Should public enterprises be restructured, as is often suggested, or privatized?

Should subsidies be eliminated over an agreed period? As everyone recognizes, politicians clearly prefer the smoothest approach. In a low-income country dependent on external financing and the external environment, over which it has no influence, the best approach is to take a bold decision and to implement forceful measures. In my view, trying to restructure a public enterprise whose financial operations are wildly out of line with good management practice is more difficult than opting for privatization; and it is certainly easier to go in the direction of changes that will create higher and more sustained employment.

In addressing these issues, it is helpful to keep in mind the underlying aim of economic policy, namely, to improve living standards for the majority of the population. Better living standards mean, among other things, lower tariffs for the consumer and more plentiful buses and trains. Obviously, political circumstances differ in each case: for example, whereas some countries can see merit in keeping a number of enterprises in the public domain—the so-called strategic sectors—others consider it necessary for domestic political reasons to keep certain enterprises in the public sector but to operate them in accordance with the principles governing private sector entities.

On the problem of external debt, I would note at the outset that the responsibility for the rapid accumulation of external debt by low-income developing countries does not reside with these countries alone. The debt situation has evolved over the years, and the international community has done much to try to alleviate some of these difficulties. Even after a low-income country has rescheduled part of its external debt on the generous terms set forth in Toronto, Trinidad, and Dakar, however, policymakers are often faced with a situation in which they must choose between servicing external debt and mobilizing sufficient resources to pay wages and salaries for civil servants. It is clear which option most officials would choose in such a situation. In looking at ways to assist low-income countries, therefore, it is important to avoid the mistakes of the past: we would do well to remember that debt has both external and domestic aspects. In this context, I would underscore the need to ensure that beyond closely monitoring the financial position of the central government itself, peripheral agencies of the public sector should not be allowed to act as debt-creating vehicles. Global management of the public debt is indispensable; debt should be managed both externally and domestically.

Allow me to make a few comments on the broad issues of governance and transparency, upon which Professor Killick has already touched. These are important issues for every country. It is clear that government operations cannot be made transparent in the absence of a democratic environment. For any country, of course, the particular political system that is chosen is a matter for the people of that country to decide. When a country is dependent on the international community for part of its survival through financial and other forms of support, however, those countries making their support available cannot remain indifferent to the extent to which government operations are conducted in a transparent manner and as part of a democratic process. Low-income countries have to implement very difficult reforms because problems have been allowed to accumulate over the years. Resolving these problems can best be done in an environment in which there is a broad consensus on what needs to be done and how to do it. Thus, it is important to make sure that the general public understands fully the problems facing the country so that it can more readily accept the adjustment measures proposed by the government. It is not sufficient, as Professor Killick suggested, for a country to develop a program of its own and to obtain the approval of the international community; government officials have to make sure that the population understands the problems, and political leaders need to explain why certain measures are necessary, what type of time frame is necessary to implement them, how the burden will be shared, and, especially, that those who have most will contribute most to the solution. The political situation of adjusting countries is clearly not in the domain of the Bretton Woods institutions, but looking carefully at the nature and strength of the political process as it relates to policy implementation is, in my view, indispensable.

Finally, a piece of advice for those of us who offer advice to countries, especially to low-income countries: one should not be ashamed of accepting second-best solutions, because the political authorities must be able to explain the solution to the country as a whole to ensure that decisions are well understood, are accepted, and can be implemented on a sustained basis over a long period. Thus, when an opportunity to make progress presents itself, it should be seized. Demonstrating a better understanding of the difficulties facing the authorities in the process of implementing reforms is, in my experience, as indispensable to the success of an adjustment program as any assistance that may be offered along the path of reform.

General Discussion

Ariel Buira remarked that Killick had made a number of very important points with which he was in very substantial agreement. Part of the problem with adjustment programs was that the Fund traditionally had felt that it did not have a responsibility for development, and that its responsibility was very short term in nature. That perspective was evident in the view that the Fund was a monetary institution, and that it had to preserve its monetary character and the revolving nature of its resources. In the light of its perceived role as a short-term monetary institution, the Fund had tended to rely very heavily on demand-management policies, leaving aside other aspects of adjustment and development. Killick was absolutely correct in saying that successful adjustment required a much longer and broader view; the process went far beyond demand management and required a number of structural changes, including in areas such as education and technological development.

Taking a longer and a broader view required substantially more financing, but the Bretton Woods institutions were subject to limited resources. The major contributing countries had difficulty in increasing those resources; in fact, over the years, the relative size of the Fund had declined to the point where its resources were minuscule in proportion to world trade. Furthermore, the Fund did not make use of all available resources: the Fund had an enormous amount of liquidity, even leaving aside its gold holdings. Currently, annual access to the Fund's general resources was set at a limit of 68 percent of a member's quota, but in practice average access was closer to 40 percent of quota.[7]

The underlying reason for not making better use of the Fund's resources lay in the tension between countries that were creditors to the institution and those that were its debtors. Creditor countries wished, not unreasonably, to take the view of lenders, lending as little as possible with as many conditions as possible. Killick rightly pointed out that such a policy became somewhat self-defeating, in that the success of programs had been limited, they were overburdened with conditions, and governments did not identify to any great extent with them. He was also correct in saying that success depended on governments' identifying with the policies of the program, which meant that successful programs were those designed by the governments themselves. Implementation of such a policy required placing a certain amount of trust in the governments to which the Fund was lending, giving them considerably greater leeway than at present to design their own programs. Clearly, that was the right approach.

Ishrat Hussain commented that the useful distinction that Killick had drawn between adjustment as a transition and adjustment as a continuous adaptation could be reconciled by reference to the different initial conditions that countries faced. In countries that had allowed their economies to accumulate significant distortions over time, characterized by the accumulation of large black market premiums, large fiscal deficits, and large losses in the financial sector and public enterprises, there was a need for large, discrete changes in the economy—what might be called a purging process. Once those roadblocks had been removed, it would be possible to move to a process of continuous adapta-

---

[7]Two days after this conference, the Interim Committee recommended increasing the Fund's access limits. Three weeks later, the Executive Board approved raising the annual limit from 68 percent to 100 percent. The cumulative limit of 300 percent was retained.

tion, in which marginal changes could be made in response to either external or internal shocks. A useful analogy in that respect was of a road littered with boulders and big stones, which took a long time to remove; once they were removed, however, one could accelerate, slowing down from time to time only to remove small pebbles. Such an analogy was certainly relevant to the East Asian example, where countries had continued to adapt and respond to changes. They had not allowed distortions to multiply and accumulate over time and, therefore, had not needed to make the types of nonmarginal changes that had been necessary in Africa.

Layeshi Yaker noted that it was generally agreed that in the rapidly changing global economic environment, all economies—whether small or large—had to adjust and adapt to the changing environment. The center of the debate, however, was whether existing structural adjustment programs, especially in Africa, were an adequate framework for promoting sustainable development. Many had expressed doubt on the point, and the overall performance of African economies during the past decade and a half appeared to support the view that the current strategy was flawed. Indeed, the Managing Director of the Fund had recently noted that, while a number of developing countries had in recent decades achieved impressive rates of growth, "the main problem is, of course, that economic progress has been so uneven, bypassing hundreds of millions of the world's poorest. About one in six of the population of the developing world live in countries where real per capita incomes have actually declined in the past decade, creating a fourth world that is concentrated in Africa."[8] During the 1993 Annual Meetings of the World Bank and the Fund, the Managing Director had vividly characterized the plight of Africa as "a sinking continent." Yaker wondered whether those statements implied there was a need for an alternative framework, taking into account the failure of the current development strategies to engender sustainable growth and significant poverty reduction.

In Yaker's view, it should be acknowledged that the continent of Africa, in crisis but with considerable potential, would benefit from a different development strategy; global security and sustainable and equitable world development could not otherwise be achieved. Against the rapid development of regionalism, especially within the OECD, the whole continent of Africa was in need of structural adjustment. Within that framework, an Africa in transition—including democratic South Africa—and Africa's partners in the development process had the means to reverse those disturbing trends. A real solution to the debt problem would require adequate trade policies in favor of Africa—the

---

[8]Michel Camdessus, "The World Economy—Prospects and Challenges," address at the Palace of Regional Government, Barcelona, Spain, July 4, 1994.

only loser in the Uruguay Round—and a massive international plan for human and technology development, including infrastructure. In that context, it was worth mentioning that the treaty establishing a Pan-African Economic Community, which had been ratified by 53 African states, including South Africa, would shortly come into effect. More meaningful cooperation with the continental and regional institutions of Africa—including the Economic Commission for Africa, the African Development Bank, the Southern African Development Conference, the Economic Community of West African States, the Preferential Trade Area for Eastern and Southern African States, and the Maghreb Union—would bring about far-reaching positive results, providing development in Africa, employment in OECD countries, and improved global security, democracy, and human rights; in other words, a more equitable and harmonious world order.

Jo Marie Griesgraber said that she shared Yaker's views. On the debt issue, many people had been working with the commercial banks, the Paris Club, and the U.S. Treasury to encourage the Treasury and the U.S. Congress to provide money for African debt relief. She asked Ouattara to explain, in his capacity as a senior Fund official, the responsibility of the Fund to assist countries, particularly in Africa, in reducing their debt to the Fund. The community of nongovernmental organizations was very supportive of the stated position of the U.K. Chancellor of the Exchequer on the possible sale of part of the Fund's gold holdings for that purpose.

On the matter of transparency, and on the importance of politics noted by Ouattara, she wondered what was the institutional position of the Fund in terms of opening up its own procedures and its papers, particularly the Article IV consultation documents—a move that the Governments of the United States and Switzerland, among others, appeared to endorse. As an intergovernmental institution, of course, the Fund was guided by the wishes of its member governments, but those same governments often argued that they had no direct influence over the decisions of the World Bank and the Fund. Therefore, it would be interesting to know what kind of example the Fund would make in terms of the transparency of its own documents and policies.

Manuel Guitián said that his comments were prompted by the very persuasive presentation by Killick, with whom he had had an exchange of views over an extended period. His impression was that the debate was often burdened by its terminology. He did not see adjustment as being equivalent to conditionality. In the Fund, adjustment was a continuous process, along the lines of the second of Killick's characterizations. It was a process in which members regularly discussed their policies with the institution; the Fund did not deal with adjustment only when the use of its resources was requested. In that sense, the Fund had gone much further along the lines on which Killick had concluded his presentation: the influence of ideas on the process was very important; and influence was a two-way road, coming both from members to the institution and from the institution to members.

Perhaps the most important consensus that had emerged in the past 50 years was the importance of macroeconomic stability, policy measures to support the market, and international openness. All members had opened their economies to an extent that had not been foreseen at Bretton Woods—in respect of trade, as well as other current and capital account transactions. Guitián noted that Killick viewed that consensus as a paradox, however, because he saw very little relation between the policies and the achievement of the objectives. Perhaps the only way to reconcile the apparent paradox was to review the evidence that had led to his conclusion that the policies had not been effective.

Leszek Balcerowicz remarked that it would be a grave error not to distinguish between the principle of conditionality and the concrete manifestation of conditionality. The rejection of that principle would imply a return to project lending or nonconditional lending. One could certainly criticize details, such as inappropriate or excessive conditions, but the core principle of conditionality should be retained.

Killick responded that he could agree with many of the points raised by other speakers. He shared Buira's view that pushing the Fund, and indeed the World Bank, in the direction of longer-term programs implied a need for more resources. It was important to bear in mind, however, as he had stated in his presentation, that the institutions should at the same time be more selective about the governments to which they provided support. Greater selectivity was a form of rationing and should, therefore, release additional resources in support of those programs endorsed by the institutions. Furthermore, he was less pessimistic than some about the prospect of obtaining more resources for the Fund and the Bank. The Fund's ESAF, for example, was a relatively new source of additional financing; moreover, the U.K. Chancellor of the Exchequer had recently proposed what might be called a "super ESAF," which would provide even longer-term support.

On Guitián's point about the evidence, or the lack thereof, of the success of the consensus, he would refer to the evidence that he had cited earlier. In addition, he would note that a senior member of the Fund's research staff, Mohsin Khan, had concluded a survey article on the evidence of the impact of Fund-supported programs with the observation that it would be hard to draw any strong conclusions from the evidence.[9]

---

[9]Mohsin S. Khan, "The Macroeconomic Effects of Fund-Supported Adjustment Programs," *Staff Papers*, International Monetary Fund, Vol. 37 (June 1990), pp. 195–231. After observing (p. 222) that the evidence "from existing studies . . . is fairly inconclusive," Khan continues: "More definitive evidence emerges from the tests performed in this paper."

Ouattara observed that the financing of an adjustment program was clearly related to its strength. In his remarks, therefore, he had advised low-income countries that, taking into account the external environment, it would be better to undertake stronger programs. Such an approach, in turn, implied a need for better communication within adjusting countries to garner the necessary support for the program and for the difficult measures that would be taken. Similarly, the prospects for resolution of the debt problem for low-income countries clearly depended on the sustainability of programs and the proper management of debt under various arrangements, such as the Paris Club.

With respect to transparency, further steps had been taken recently in the area of publishing Fund documents. As he had indicated in his remarks, however, adjustment programs should not be viewed as "Fund programs." They should be viewed as programs of the Fund's member governments; indeed, many countries had demonstrated the capacity to develop their own adjustment programs. The process of designing and implementing programs was continuous, of course, and by explaining the objectives and details of those programs within their own countries, governments could go a long way toward informing the international community at large about the work of the Fund. In any event, the Executive Board of the Fund was continuing to examine the issue with a view to making further progress.

In concluding the session, the Chairman, *Luis Angel Rojo,* commented that Ouattara appeared to side with those who were relatively optimistic about structural adjustment programs and who considered that, on balance, these programs had achieved a considerable measure of success in strengthening economic performance, even while admitting that growth performance in many cases had been disappointing. Killick seemed to fall on the more skeptical side, considering that the record of those programs was, as he had said, "patchy, at best," and that they did not have much impact on inflation or economic growth, taking into account the available empirical evidence.

In fact, both speakers were in general agreement in underlining the need to pay much more attention to long-term considerations, to factors that affected the flexibility of the economy to face the continuous challenges of a changing environment. They had also both stressed the importance of institutional reforms and of structural adjustments, such as improving human capital and economic administration.

Killick had raised a somewhat polemic point related to conditionality, asking whether there had been an "explosion" of conditionality in recent years. He had gone on to question whether conditionality in fact negatively affected the results of adjustment programs and at the same time gave "recipient" governments the impression that the programs were not homegrown but imposed by an external institution. The issue was clearly controversial and, as in so many matters, reasonable people could be expected to disagree.

Annex: Alassane Ouattara

Experience of the 1980s and Early 1990s

Following broadly satisfactory growth, inflation, and external performance during the 1960s and 1970s, many low-income developing countries encountered serious economic difficulties in the early 1980s. These difficulties were the product of several factors: weak productive bases; periodic disruptions from poor weather and civil strife; and a clash between stark reversals of the terms of trade and rising borrowing costs on the one hand and expansionary financial policies on the other. Longstanding structural weaknesses were exposed and placed countries in a poor position to adjust to their setbacks while sustaining growth: elaborate networks of state intervention, ostensibly to make up for the fragile productive base, rendered the supply side of the economy inefficient and unresponsive to market signals. Often, the first response to the adverse developments was to borrow more to maintain domestic absorption in the face of a sharp drop in income. By the mid-1980s, in the absence of effective adjustment and recovery in the terms of trade, many of the poorest countries faced not only massive stabilization problems but also unmanageable external debt problems.

In the face of these harsh circumstances, there has been a growing realization by governments of the virtues of macroeconomic stability and financial policy discipline. Since the mid-1980s, with the support of the IMF and World Bank, many low-income countries have implemented major structural adjustment programs. How have the achievements under these programs measured up to the goal of higher sustainable growth and a broad-based improvement in living standards? When viewed against a backdrop of very weak starting positions and, for many countries, serious and persistent declines in the terms of trade, a considerable measure of success was achieved in strengthening economic performance. On average, output growth, trade volumes, inflation performance, and external debt ratios strengthened. There was, of course, considerable variation between individual countries.

But there have also been disappointments, particularly in countries in which the response thus far of investment to adjustment policies has been relatively small, and low domestic saving has persisted. This experience stands in contrast to that of other more successful developing countries, especially in East Asia, in which investment and savings performance has been strong. Also, notwithstanding the reform efforts undertaken and the progress achieved, conditions in many low-income countries remain harsh and their economies weak: during the 1980s and early 1990s, low growth rates have failed to keep pace with population growth in sub-Saharan Africa and have prevented a fundamental attack on poverty in Bangladesh, Pakistan, and India; the level of social indicators, such as health, nutrition, and access to primary education in Africa is poor and in a number of countries has worsened; and most of these countries, particularly in Africa, have seen little diversification of their economies and continue to rely on a limited number of commodity exports.

Lessons for Adjustment and Growth

The mixed economic performance following the renewed adjustment effort in low-income developing countries, especially the weak response of savings and investment, which are essential underpinnings to sustainable higher growth, raises several important questions. Looking to the past, has there been a failure in our approach to adjustment, or instead has there been a failure to adjust? Drawing upon the lessons of the past, how can we—policymakers and advisors—better fashion adjustment policies to strengthen prospects for sustainable higher growth and improved living standards?

To address the first question—whether adjustment programs are supportive of growth—we must ask another: what are the conditions most conducive to generating higher growth? Experience has shown us that there is no simple set of policy prescriptions that will yield higher and sustained growth: the links between policies and growth are both complex and indirect, and much remains to be learned about the underlying causal relationships. Different economic, social, and political settings influence the effectiveness of policies in promoting growth. Also, fostering sustainable growth is often a protracted process, yielding clear gains only beyond the short term and requiring steady policy efforts over a long period.

Nevertheless, there is now a broad consensus among researchers and policymakers on some of the more important policy conditions necessary for sustained growth. A key element of this consensus is that macroeconomic stability is an essential foundation for sustained growth. For countries with severe financial imbalances, adjustment therefore sets the stage for stronger growth in the long term. At the same time, to reap the reward of higher growth, adjustment must not rest upon unsustainable restraint of domestic demand but should rather stem from policies that will help countries realize their long-term growth potential.

The main elements of adjustment programs are based on this consensus: first, a monetary policy consistent with low inflation; second, a public sector deficit that does not crowd out private investment and does not require inflationary bank financing or unsustainable borrowing from abroad; third, an exchange rate that is consistent with fundamentals and does not need to be supported artificially by unsustainable borrowing or exchange restrictions; fourth, outward-looking policies for trade and investment that encourage competition, the inflow of technology, and efficient resource allocation; and fifth, structural reforms aimed at improving the efficiency of resource use and promoting a supply response. Structural measures are crucial for improving growth prospects, without which domestic demand restraint will bear heavily on living standards and consumption and may undermine the political sustainability of the adjustment process. Structural reforms are also essential for financial stability: in many countries, distortions and rigidities stemming from official controls, poorly designed tax and expenditure policies, and weak public enterprises perpetuate economic weakness and are a stifling drain on the economy's resources.

How does this consensus on adjustment for growth stand up against the experience of low-income developing countries? The evidence indicates that the largest improvements in macroeconomic performance occurred in countries that undertook stronger financial adjustment measures and, most strikingly, the most forceful structural reforms. By the same token, weak performance was the product of a failure to adjust sufficiently. Of course, policy adjustments were not the only factor at play during this period; others include the terms of trade, civil strife, and the degree of political commitment to reform.

Notwithstanding the progress achieved under many adjustment programs, there have been weaknesses: insufficient attention to rectifying social inequity, reducing poverty, improving the quality of public expenditure, building institutions, strengthening administrative capacity, and improving governance. An inadequate focus on these areas has, in turn, weakened the adjustment process and prospects for growth, as well as the domestic consensus for reform.

How Can We Strengthen the Growth Response of Adjustment Programs?

Reflecting upon past experience, there is clearly scope for efforts to improve our choices of policies so as to improve the size and speed of the response of savings, investment, and growth. Even if our understanding of all the issues is imperfect, this only makes them more deserving of attention; incomplete knowledge does not absolve the policymaker of the responsibility to make policy decisions.

At the same time, we must be realistic: even though policies can be improved, the fruits of adjustment in terms of higher growth may become tangible only over time. In the short run, adjustment will involve inevitable costs for countries experiencing severe financial imbalances and facing external financing crises. In these circumstances, there is a pressing imperative to restrain domestic absorption and inflationary pressures, which may have a negative impact on growth in the short term. Also, while front-loaded structural reform is crucial to encouraging an early supply response, output may in the initial phase be adversely affected as capital and labor move to more productive uses in response to new market-based incentives and the dismantling of regulations. In this context, the availability of external financing—on appropriately concessional terms that do not compound the initial debt problems of these countries—can help ease the path of adjustment and reduce the adverse short-term impact on growth.

How can we improve the influence of policies on growth? As a first step, a number of policy areas deserve more attention by policymakers, advisors, and researchers.

First, the quality of fiscal adjustment must be emphasized. In deciding upon the mix and nature of revenue and expenditure adjustments, policymakers must be sensitive to their likely effects on growth. The quality of expenditure needs to be improved, and expenditures that are especially important for growth in the long term must be safeguarded during the stabilization effort. Attention should be paid to sound public investment projects, such as infrastructure that complements private investment and thereby maximizes their developmental impact. Unproductive expenditures, including excessive military spending, must be reduced, while nonwage outlays on education and health must be adequately funded. Investment in human capital is essential for stronger growth, as evidenced by the experience of the fast-growing economies of East Asia; it is the key to unlocking the full rewards of structural reforms and liberalized markets.

Improvements in the structure of fiscal revenues must also be sought. Tax reforms, including the reduction of high marginal tax rates, the broadening of the tax base, and strengthened administration, will enhance incentives for savings and investment, as well as improve fiscal management. Finally, a critical element in the fiscal adjustment process is the formulation of a clear medium-term fiscal strategy: expenditure and revenue adjustments in the short term in response to unforeseen developments should take account of their longer-term implications for savings, investment, and growth.

Second, policymakers must pay attention to the design of policies to speed the response of private investment in many adjusting countries. A number of factors come into play in this area. Where existing structural distortions are large, timely and strong reforms are essential. In particular, evidence suggests that for structural reforms to have a significant impact on growth, a critical mass is important. Also, to overcome the wait-and-see attitudes of private investors, it is important that policy commitments are seen to be both credible and sustainable. In this context, firm, preannounced plans for structural reforms, which in many instances take time to implement, can help encourage an early investment response. Although price, exchange, and trade liberalization has been implemented relatively quickly and can have rapid effects on growth, other crucial reforms—such as the modernization of the financial sector and restructuring of public enterprises—often take longer and need to be resolutely pursued for the desired efficiency gains to be realized. All of these measures call for a strong, credible, and sustained reform effort, which, in turn, takes political leadership and consultation: the public must be supportive of the thrust of reform.

Third, policymakers must work to strengthen policy institutions and overcome administrative constraints, so as to improve the ability to design and implement policies. In this regard, efforts must continue to focus on making effective use of the technical assistance provided by international financial institutions and other organizations. Progress in this area will also help improve the domestic ownership of policies. The transparency of operations of key institutions is also essential, so as to provide a clear set of rules by which the private sector can guide its decisions.

Fourth, more attention must be given to promoting efficient trade and diversification through maintaining an adequate level of competitiveness and strengthening the human capital and physical infrastructure. Such measures would place countries in a stronger position to respond to the challenges and opportunities presented by the completion of the Uruguay Round and reduce their vulnerability to the terms of trade. The process of economic diversification, however, takes time, and in the short term a level of reserves and external support sufficient to smooth the income losses stemming from temporary adverse movements in the terms of trade is important.

Fifth, external debt is an important factor in the equation for growth. By the mid-1980s, many low-income countries had high and often rising debt and debt-service ratios. If policies aimed at stronger growth are to yield durable gains, output growth must be based on sustainable financing inflows. Yet for many countries, the need to reduce large external borrowing requirements, as well as to meet obligations on a large debt stock, implies a significant reduction in the share of income that could be channeled into domestic absorption. They have been long in coming, but we are now on the verge of having in place mechanisms that, if implemented with sufficient flexibility, should bring the burden associated with the stock of debt to manageable levels. As these mechanisms are implemented, attention must shift from the debt "crisis" to the need for governments to adopt sound debt-management policies so as to maximize the development value of external borrowing. Such policies, together with firm and sustained domestic adjustment and re-forms, are important for preventing the re-emergence of debt-servicing problems. Policies that can attract non-debt-creating flows are also im-portant complements to prudent debt management. In addition, offi-cial financial support—on as concessional terms as possible—needs to be maintained to finance the enormous development requirements of these countries.

The implementation of adjustment and structural reform programs has, in certain cases, had a favorable impact on savings, investment, and economic growth. In other cases, however, the results have fallen short of program expectations. In reviewing these cases, it is necessary to note that international institutions cannot or indeed should not sub-stitute for governments' responsibilities to their people. For sustained economic growth in developing countries to materialize, governments must pursue this objective relentlessly and demonstrate their commit-ment to it continuously. Certain habits in the area of economic manage-ment and, more broadly, management of the public good must be put in place.

The progressive transformation of attitudes, the modernization of so-cial structures, the emergence of consensus in countries adopting demo-cratic structures, and the reinforcement of institutions are important ele-ments for economic growth—elements that are not addressed today in adjustment and reform programs. Accordingly, while these programs contribute to placing economies on the path of sustained growth, gov-ernments should pursue sufficiently decisive actions to accelerate the process of development essential for a determined reduction in poverty and for an appropriately broad distribution of the benefits of adjustment and reform. The responsibility of governments and the efficient man-agement of public affairs need to be closely associated with the more tra-ditional aspects of programs if these programs are to meet their poten-tial in contributing to growth and the well-being of the population.

As a concluding point, it is important to remember that the opportu-nity to implement sound policies and reforms should be seized when it appears, even when it may involve compromises. Although the luxury of first-best policies—and we have seen that the list is long—is one for which we should aim, it is often, in practice, one for which we can ill af-ford to wait.

9

Sustainable Poverty Reduction

The session on sustainable poverty reduction aimed at examining two aspects of the problem: developing strategies for reducing poverty through economic growth and human resource development; and making poverty reduction sustainable by taking account of environmental, financial, and political constraints. The three featured speakers brought quite different perspectives to bear on these issues. The first speaker was Professor Widjojo Nitisastro, Economic Advisor to the Government of Indonesia, who spoke on the reduction of poverty in that country. In addition to his distinguished service in major ministerial positions, he was formerly Dean of the School of Economics at the University of Indonesia, and he has published a number of papers on development issues. He was followed by Professor Albert Fishlow of the University of California at Berkeley, who has worked extensively in Latin America and is a Co-editor of the Journal of Development Economics. *His presentation dealt with the relationships between equity in income distribution, the alleviation of poverty, and economic growth. The third speaker was Fazle Hasan Abed, the founder and Executive Director of the Bangladesh Rural Advancement Committee and the author of many publications on development issues. The session was chaired by Musalia Mudavadi, the Minister of Finance of Kenya. Owing to the shortage of time, the general discussion that had been planned for this session was folded into that of a later session (Chapter 12).*

Musalia Mudavadi

The Bretton Woods conference of 1944 focused on the problems to be encountered in postwar reconstruction, including projects for development and rehabilitation, as well as short-term solutions to temporary balance of payments disequilibria. New problems have now been identified, many of which relate to development in its market-oriented context and the requirements brought about by change in emerging economies, rather than the need to re-establish order in mature ones. The concept of poverty has changed from being a problem of an enclave to being the problem of the nation as a whole. Solutions are no longer, therefore, to be found in simple, targeted interventions. They depend more on augmenting a nation's resource base than on its redistribution.

Not so long ago, discussions of development occupied the minds of those managing the World Bank and the Fund; then the pendulum swung, and the conscience of those institutions was disturbed by the plea that development must have a human face. Moreover, faith in trickle-down effects and balanced growth declined, and governments were called on to identify those who were bypassed by prosperous change. Women, the rural landless, the urban poor, and a whole multitude of vulnerable groups became the focus of special programs.

To reduce the incidence of poverty on a sustainable basis requires the vertical mobility of many of these groups, not just an alleviation of suffering, which may merely be a temporary palliative. Unfortunately, some changes, such as those relating to the status of women, do not immediately relieve poverty and, by diverting resources, may temporarily worsen it.

Change is always painful to some. Not all have the ability to voice their distress to sympathetic ears; some may easily gain attention, and others may be able to express their pleas for lost privileges. It is always difficult, therefore, to set about long-term poverty reduction where the method of intervention is either an appeal to efficiency, equity, or charity. It is my hope that today's discussion will not just bring to light the causes of poverty but will also explore what strategies are feasible for eradicating it in the economies of the third world. We must not launch into programs that are unsustainable, because the frustration of failure and of falling back into poverty creates far greater distress.

Widjojo Nitisastro

Let me first say how honored I feel to be invited to speak on the topic of sustainable poverty reduction at this conference on the occasion of the fiftieth anniversary of the World Bank and the International Monetary Fund. I would like to express my good wishes to the IMF and the World Bank Group on this most important event. The choice of sustainable poverty reduction as a topic for discussion reflects the commitment of the two institutions to support developing countries in their endeavors to reduce poverty and improve living standards.

As to poverty reduction, I am familiar only with the experience of Indonesia. Therefore, my contribution to this conference will be limited to poverty reduction in Indonesia. Let me start with a few statistics.

The 1994 *Annual Report* of the World Bank indicated that

> Among regions, East Asia and Pacific stands out as the one that has made the most impressive gains in poverty reduction, as well as being the fastest growing .... The most impressive gains have been made in Indonesia, where the percentage share of absolute poverty has fallen

from 60 to 15 percent of the total population over the period [1970–1990], and China, where it fell from 33 to 10 percent.

The analysis of poverty over time is difficult and controversial. Nonetheless, estimates on poverty in Indonesia have reached a fair degree of consensus: poverty has fallen rapidly over the past 25 years. The proportion of the population below the poverty line fell from about 60 percent in 1970 to about 29 percent in 1980 and to about 14 percent in 1993. The absolute numbers of those in poverty fell from about 70 million in 1970 to about 26 million in 1993. Total population in 1993 was almost 190 million. More than 110 million live on the island of Java, which has an average density of more than 800 people per square kilometer. Of the 26 million below the poverty line, 15 million, or 58 percent, are in Java.

What explains the sharp drop in poverty in Indonesia? The most important factor seems to be sustained rapid economic growth, which was broadly based and labor intensive. The effects of this growth were reinforced by an array of policies that improved the health and education of the poor, reduced population growth to manageable levels, and provided infrastructure. In economic terms, the rate and pattern of growth generated a strong demand for labor, while the policies in education, health, and infrastructure enabled the poor to take advantage of this demand to improve their incomes.

Let us first discuss the growth process. Between 1970 and 1993, real GDP increased by about 6.5 percent annually. With population growing by about 2.2 percent on average, per capita GDP grew by over 4 percent a year. Of key importance to poverty reduction in the 1970s and early 1980s was the high rate of growth in the agricultural sector, on which most of the population and the poor depended. Production of rice, the most important crop, grew by nearly 5.3 percent a year between 1971 and 1983.

The sources of rapid growth in rice production have been a combination of the rapid spread of irrigation, the provision of key inputs, and the spread of high-yielding varieties. At the same time, investment in rural infrastructure, as well as price policy, public procurement, and price stabilization, increased the level and stability of the prices received by the farmer. This early emphasis on agriculture played a decisive role in breaking the downward cycle of poverty, population growth, and environmental degradation.

In the second half of the 1980s and the 1990s, a different process became important in generating high growth and reducing poverty—the rapid growth of exports of labor-intensive manufactures, which generated employment growth in manufacturing of about 7 percent a year after 1985. In addition, the growth in manufacturing employment was accompanied by rapid growth of construction and employment in the construction sector. During the three-year period from 1984 to 1987,

Indonesia's total outstanding debt increased from $31.2 billion to $50.2 billion, an increase of 60 percent. Its annual debt-service payment increased from $4.2 billion in 1984 to $6.9 billion in 1987, an increase of 64 percent.

The very sharp increase in both total debt outstanding and annual debt servicing was mainly due to the realignment of world currencies, in particular the rapid depreciation of the U.S. dollar against the Japanese yen and other major currencies. However, a substantial proportion of Indonesia's debts was denominated in yen and currencies other than the U.S. dollar. It has been estimated by the IMF that more than 80 percent of the increase in the stock of outstanding debt and about two thirds of the increase in debt-service payments were attributable to the valuation effects of the depreciation of the U.S. dollar.

The impact of the sharp depreciation of the U.S. dollar on Indonesia's development was even worse because of its timing. It coincided with the sharp decline in the international price of oil in 1986. Indonesia's development was thus receiving a double blow: the sharp fall in oil prices and, at the same time, the sharp depreciation of the U.S. dollar. As a response to the new challenges, Indonesia embarked on a comprehensive set of economic reforms, policy adjustments, and restructuring. These measures included the postponement of major capital-intensive projects, devaluations, flexible exchange rate management, prudent fiscal and monetary policies, tax reforms, financial sector reforms, waves of deregulation of foreign trade and industry, the rollback of nontariff barriers, tariff reform, improvement of the climate for investment, development of the stock exchange, and an all-out effort to capture foreign markets for non-oil exports.

All these measures, which were implemented in a consistent manner, resulted in a substantial growth of exports, employment, and investments. Instead of capital flight, the country had a vigorous capital inflow.

An issue that attracted wide-ranging interest was whether all those economic reforms, policy adjustment, and restructuring did not result in an ever-increasing burden for the poor. A number of studies carried out to measure the incidence of poverty and its trend concluded that the incidence of poverty declined from 22 percent in 1984 to about 18 percent in 1987, implying an absolute decline in the number of poor Indonesians from about 35 million in 1984 to about 30 million in 1987. The success in reducing poverty during the difficult adjustment period in the 1980s was due to three factors:

- First, the development efforts before the adjustment period were directed at establishing a strong rural economy and establishing an extensive network of social and physical infrastructure, such as primary schools leading to universal primary education; integrated

centers for health, nutrition, and family planning; and rural networks of roads, irrigation facilities, and support for flood control.
- Second, the economic reform and policy adjustments introduced contained elements geared toward sustaining progress on poverty reduction. Budgetary expenditures in poverty-related sectors—such as agriculture, human resource development, and transfers to regional governments—were protected relative to other sectors.
- Third, the combination of trade and industrial deregulation and real exchange rate adjustments led to a rapid recovery in investment and employment in manufacturing and agriculture.

These policy changes were supported by the World Bank, the IMF, and bilateral donors. The inflow of funds from these sources cushioned the fall in oil prices, allowing government spending and aggregate demand to be maintained while avoiding high levels of inflation.

In summary, rapid, sustained, and labor-intensive growth was a major factor in reducing poverty in Indonesia. This close linkage between growth and poverty reduction is reflected in Indonesia's particular growth process: initial rapid growth in agriculture followed by rapid growth in labor-intensive manufactures—and in the policy packages that generated it.

Let me now turn to another important factor accounting for poverty reduction in Indonesia: the slowdown in population growth. Annual population growth rates in Indonesia fell from 2.5 percent in 1970 to about 1.7 percent at present. This drop was the result of a pronounced reduction in fertility rates at the same time as mortality rates fell rapidly. A successful family planning program, as well as rapid educational and employment gains among women, played a crucial role in reducing population growth. Indonesia's total fertility rate was nearly halved in two decades—from 5.5 in 1970 to 3.0 in 1990. Child survival rates improved, owing to the provision of health care, especially through programs such as universal child immunization, improved nutrition, and rapid gains in female education. The gross enrollment rate for females in primary education increased from about 73 percent in 1970 to 114 percent in 1990,[1] and in secondary education from 16 percent in 1970 to 45 percent in 1990. The effect of these factors on reducing population growth is now well recognized.

In sum, as I have tried to illustrate, Indonesia was able to reduce poverty rapidly, first, through sustained, broad-based and labor-intensive growth based on rapid growth of agriculture, and then through rapid growth of labor-intensive manufacturing exports. Second, the poor

---

[1] "For some countries with universal primary education, gross enrollment rates may exceed 100 percent because some pupils are younger or older than the country's standard primary school age" (World Bank, *World Development Report 1994*, p. 243).

were able to participate in that growth because of substantial improvements in education and health and investments in infrastructure. Third, population growth fell sharply.

What lessons can be drawn from Indonesia's experience in achieving a rapid reduction of poverty? First and foremost is the need for a true commitment to achieving it. It has to be a true commitment as opposed to adhering passively to possible fashions in the development debate. Such a commitment has to be translated into operational policies and programs to be implemented in a consistent manner. These policies and programs have to be internally designed and self-imposed rather than being parts of conditions attached to loans or grants. The test of a true commitment arrives when the availability of resources is rapidly declining: whether to forgo other claims or to yield to pressures and sacrifice the poverty-reduction programs.

Another critical requirement is the development of capabilities, both individual and institutional, to identify problems and opportunities and to design and implement poverty-reduction policies and programs. However, poverty reduction should not be postponed until such capabilities are completely developed.

The Indonesian experience with poverty reduction also shows clearly the important role of broadly based labor-intensive economic growth, together with the rapid growth of primary education and the effective delivery of health care and family planning services. It follows that the pattern of growth pursued in a country is of great importance for achieving the objective of poverty reduction. Broad-based labor-intensive growth in Indonesia was primary in agriculture during the 1970s and shifted toward labor-intensive manufactured exports in the 1980s and 1990s.

Education and health are ends in themselves, but they also have a great effect on the pace of labor-intensive growth of the economy. In particular, the education of women is of great social and economic benefit.

Finally, what can or should the international community do to assist developing countries in achieving poverty reduction? Needless to say, poverty reduction is the responsibility and, therefore, the homework of the individual country concerned. However, to be successful in carrying out a poverty-reduction program, there is a serious need for an enabling external environment—a world economic environment that is supportive. The following are some examples.

Volatile exchange rates between the major currencies can have a devastating impact on a developing country's economy. Thus, the rapid depreciation of the U.S. dollar against the yen could have wiped out Indonesia's endeavors in poverty reduction. The two economic superpowers in the Pacific certainly did not intend to harm another country in the Pacific, but in trying to find solutions to their problems, they did not take into account the impact of their actions on the developing countries.

The establishment of a stable and predictable exchange rate system can be achieved only by the major developed countries.

Another important enabling external environment is related to market access. Manufactured exports of developing countries, such as textiles and garments, are facing nontariff barriers in accordance with the Multifiber Arrangement (MFA). Everybody is happy that the Uruguay Round was agreed upon by all countries, but the MFA will remain in force for another ten years. We have to wait ten years before there will be real market access for our textiles.

The burden of debt repayment can be very severe for developing countries. Let me describe Indonesia's experience with debt. When there was a change in government in 1966, Indonesia had a huge debt in relation to exports, reserves, and GNP. At that time, Indonesia had arrears, and what it did, of course, just as any other developing country, was to go to the Paris Club and negotiate a rescheduling. We came out with an agreement, namely, rescheduling for eight years with three years' grace period. Following that agreement, we had to go to the Paris Club for another rescheduling, and then again. In addition, we had to negotiate at that time with 22 creditor countries. There was complete uncertainty about what would happen the following year. That was very much in our mind. If you ask people working in a country to take care of poverty problems while worrying about the payment of debt the next year, I think that is too much to ask.

What happened next was that the Paris Club agreed to ask a third party to study the problem of Indonesia's debt and come up with a proposal for a solution. After some time, we agreed to ask the late Dr. Hermann Abs of the Deutsche Bank—which at that time was not one of Indonesia's creditors—to make a study of Indonesia's debt problem for the Paris Club and for Indonesia. In his work, Dr. Abs was assisted by many able officials from the World Bank and the Fund.

Dr. Abs came up with three proposals. The first was that the settlement of the debt should be a once-and-for-all settlement that did not have to be repeated every year. Once done, that was it; no more negotiations. The second principle was that Indonesia must be able to pay; the settlement was to make Indonesia creditworthy so that it could have normal financial relations. Creditworthiness was the objective. And third, there should be a nondiscriminatory treatment of all debt.

Indonesia was lucky because the Paris Club countries agreed at that time to these three proposals. Unfortunately, the Paris Club said that this was a unique case that could not be used as a precedent for other developing countries.

This history is just to give you an example of the big difference it made to Indonesia to have its debt settled—and settled in a way that can be called a final settlement. Because of that, we were able to concentrate all of our efforts on the development of the country and on poverty

on. The settlement of Indonesia's debt on the basis of the princi-
.t forward by Dr. Hermann Abs (once-and-for-all settlement,
cɪ⌵ ⌵orthiness as an objective, and the principle of nondiscrimina-
tion) could be considered more generally for the settlement of debts of
other developing countries.

Albert Fishlow

Income distribution entered the postwar discussion of economic development relatively late. Up to the 1960s, much of the focus was on industrialization and the need for capital accumulation as a motor for
more rapid expansion. It was an era, moreover, of large flows of external
assistance, much of it to the European economy, in the midst of global
division between East and West. Indeed, not until the mid-1950s did the
World Bank turn its focus to the developing countries, and then only
gradually. And already by that time, the flows of assistance from industrial countries, primarily the United States, were beginning to diminish
proportionally.

Moreover, that early period saw the end of colonization and the beginning of new national units throughout Asia and Africa. For them, the
focus became economic expansion as a means of achieving political
identity. Rapid population growth, associated with great declines in
mortality, focused attention on the acceleration of production required
to keep pace. Overall, the period saw much higher rates of aggregate expansion than had been experienced previously. And there was even acceleration: per capita growth increased from 2.4 percent a year in the
1950s to 3.5 percent in 1965–70. Indeed, in this latter period, growth
rates were not only positive in every region, but the lowest, for sub-Saharan Africa, amounted to an annual increase of 2.3 percent per capita.

In the late 1960s and early 1970s, in the context of positive achievement, there emerged a new interest in income distribution. On the academic side, a new series of studies called attention to continuing significant inequality and the failure of widespread economic growth to
remedy the problem (see Adelman and Robinson, 1989). On the practical side, Robert McNamara's interest in the subject stimulated the
World Bank study by Chenery and others (1974), an important effort to
define new policies and strategies that could be effective in combining
increased equity with improved aggregate performance.

In the event, distributional issues, soon extending into new attention
to basic needs—a policy approach emanating from the World Bank—
had only a brief moment on center stage. Most important, the rise in oil
prices in 1973 set in motion a sequence of excessive dependence by developing countries on foreign debt, initially quite cheap but soon impossible to sustain, which dominated attention in the 1980s and beyond.

Adjustment dominated. Suddenly, the IMF became a central element in providing assistance to developing countries, something it had not done in great measure before. The balance of payments became the determining factor in policy. Countries were necessarily focused not only on getting their macroeconomic policies right but also on a whole range of related issues. These involved questions like internal wage and interest rate policy, government subsidies, and, inevitably, the role of the state in guiding the development process.

Growth, or lack thereof, increasingly became the burning issue among developing countries. Since the 1980s, we have seen wider differences in regional performance than at any other time in the postwar period. Africa and Latin America have experienced stagnation while Asia has moved rapidly ahead. Yet in the midst of more widespread democratization than has occurred at any previous time, increasing concerns about the fate of the poor and their future become virtually inevitable. With renewed global expansion, as finally now seems the case, the question of income equality and what can be done will surely again command attention.

In this paper, I briefly take up three central questions: the state of income inequality currently; policy measures that can be adopted to help the evolution of the poor more generally; and the state of recent research on the relevance of inequality to the growth process. I conclude with some final observations.

The Record

The *World Development Report 1994* of the World Bank reports in its statistical annex, as it has for many years, recent data accumulated on the measurement of income inequality (Table 1).[2] These data reveal that shares of income received by the top 10 percent of the population in developing countries vary from more than 50 percent in Brazil to about 25 percent, shared by a number of countries; the inclusion of Eastern Europe, showing the effects of socialist equalization, brings that minimum closer to 20 percent. The range among developed countries is much narrower, and concentrates at less than 25 percent; income inequality is obviously smaller.

What is apparent from these numbers, now available more accurately and widely than before, is that the simple U-hypothesis advanced by Simon Kuznets does not seem to hold as universally as was first thought (see Kuznets, 1955; and Robinson, 1976). That conception, in which low-income and high-income countries would share lower levels of inequality owing to greater homogeneity of their labor forces first in agriculture

---

[2]Measurement of income inequality, despite significant advances over the years, is still inadequate. For useful discussion of many of the problems, see Fields (1994, pp. 87–102).

Table 1. Income Distribution
(Percent share of income or consumption)

	Year	Lowest 20 percent	Second quintile	Third quintile	Fourth quintile	Highest 20 percent	Highest 10 percent
Low-income economies							
Ethiopia	1981–82	8.6	12.7	16.4	21.1	41.3	27.5
Tanzania	1991	2.4	5.7	10.4	18.7	62.7	46.5
Nepal	1984–85	9.1	12.9	16.7	21.8	39.5	25.0
Uganda	1989–90	8.5	12.1	16.0	21.5	41.9	27.2
Bangladesh	1988–89	9.5	13.4	17.0	21.6	38.6	24.6
Guinea-Bissau	1991	2.1	6.5	12.0	20.6	58.9	42.4
Rwanda	1983–85	9.7	13.1	16.7	21.6	38.9	24.6
India	1989–90	8.8	12.5	16.2	21.3	41.3	27.1
Kenya	1992	3.4	6.7	10.7	17.3	61.8	47.9
Pakistan	1991	8.4	12.9	16.9	22.2	39.7	25.2
Ghana	1988–89	7.0	11.3	15.8	21.8	44.1	29.0
China	1990	6.4	11.0	16.4	24.4	41.8	24.6
Mauritania	1987–88	3.5	10.7	16.2	23.3	46.3	30.2
Sri Lanka	1990	8.9	13.1	16.9	21.7	39.3	25.2
Zimbabwe	1990–91	4.0	6.3	10.0	17.4	62.3	46.9
Honduras	1989	2.7	6.0	10.2	17.6	63.5	47.9
Lesotho	1986–87	2.9	6.4	11.3	19.5	60.0	43.6
Indonesia	1990	8.7	12.1	15.9	21.1	42.3	27.9
Zambia	1991	5.6	9.6	14.2	21.0	49.7	34.2

Middle-income economies¹

Côte d'Ivoire	1988	7.3	11.9	16.3	22.3	42.2	26.9
Bolivia	1990–91	5.6	9.7	14.5	22.0	48.2	31.7
Philippines	1988	6.5	10.1	14.4	21.2	47.8	32.1
Senegal	1991–92	3.5	7.0	11.6	19.3	58.6	42.8
Peru	1985–86	4.9	9.2	13.7	21.0	51.4	35.4
Guatemala	1989	2.1	5.8	10.5	18.6	63.0	46.6
Morocco	1990–91	6.6	10.5	15.0	21.7	46.3	30.5
Dominican Republic	1989	4.2	7.9	12.5	19.7	55.6	39.6
Jordan	1991	6.5	10.3	14.6	20.9	47.7	32.6
Bulgaria	1992	10.4	13.9	17.3	22.2	36.2	21.9
Colombia	1991	3.6	7.6	12.6	20.4	55.8	39.5
Jamaica	1990	6.0	9.9	14.5	21.3	48.4	32.6
Tunisia	1990	5.9	10.4	15.3	22.1	46.3	30.7
Algeria	1988	6.9	11.0	14.9	20.7	46.5	31.7
Thailand	1988	6.1	9.4	13.5	20.3	50.7	35.3
Poland	1989	9.2	13.8	17.9	23.0	36.1	21.6
Costa Rica	1989	4.0	9.1	14.3	21.9	50.8	34.1
Panama	1989	2.0	6.3	11.6	20.3	59.8	42.1
Chile	1989	3.7	6.8	10.3	16.2	62.9	48.9
Brazil	1989	2.1	4.9	8.9	16.8	67.5	51.3
Botswana	1985–86	3.6	6.9	11.4	19.2	58.9	42.9
Malaysia	1989	4.6	8.3	13.0	20.4	53.7	37.9
Venezuela	1989	4.8	9.5	14.4	21.9	49.5	33.2
Hungary	1989	10.9	14.8	18.0	22.0	34.4	20.8

Table 1 (concluded)

	Year	Lowest 20 percent	Second quintile	Third quintile	Fourth quintile	Highest 20 percent	Highest 10 percent
Mexico	1984	4.1	7.8	12.3	19.9	55.9	39.5
Korea, Rep. of	1988	7.4	12.3	16.3	21.8	42.2	27.6
High-income economies							
New Zealand	1981–82	5.1	10.8	16.2	23.2	44.7	28.7
Israel	1979	6.0	12.1	17.8	24.5	39.6	23.5
Spain	1988	8.3	13.7	18.1	23.4	36.6	21.8
Hong Kong	1980	5.4	10.8	15.2	21.6	47.0	31.3
Singapore	1982–83	5.1	9.9	14.6	21.4	48.9	33.5
Australia	1985	4.4	11.1	17.5	24.8	42.2	25.8
United Kingdom	1988	4.6	10.0	16.8	24.3	44.3	27.8
Italy	1986	6.8	12.0	16.7	23.5	41.0	25.3
Netherlands	1988	8.2	13.1	18.1	23.7	36.9	21.9
Canada	1987	5.7	11.8	17.7	24.6	40.2	24.1
Belgium	1978–79	7.9	13.7	18.6	23.8	36.0	21.5
Finland	1981	6.3	12.1	18.4	25.5	37.6	21.7
France	1989	5.6	11.8	17.2	23.5	41.9	26.1
Germany	1988	7.0	11.8	17.1	23.9	40.3	24.4
United States	1985	4.7	11.0	17.4	25.0	41.9	25.0

Norway	1979	6.2	12.8	18.9	25.3	36.7	21.2
Denmark	1981	5.4	12.0	18.4	25.6	38.6	22.3
Sweden	1981	8.0	13.2	17.4	24.5	36.9	20.8
Japan	1979	8.7	13.2	17.5	23.1	37.5	22.4
Switzerland	1982	5.2	11.7	16.4	22.1	44.6	29.8

Source: World Bank (1994), Table 30.

[1]Brazil, Botswana, Malaysia, Venezuela, Hungary, Mexico, and Korea are considered "upper-middle-income" economies; remaining countries in this group are considered to be "lower-middle-income" economies.

and then in nonagricultural activities, has been carefully re-examined in recent years.[3]

Over the range of developing countries, there seems to be little regular variation with income level. Thus, a simple relationship trying to fit a parabola to the income share of the bottom 40 percent to level of income, whether as estimated by Summers and Heston (see, for example, Summers and Heston, 1991) or using more conventional values, does not work for recent periods. This is true both for a sample of countries similar to that used by Ahluwalia (1976) and a broader one that incorporates more recent entries. Anand and Kanbur (1993) utilize a series of different measures of inequality and find, first, that these different indices yield widely disparate turning points; second, that the statistical results indicated by a strict theoretical derivation are generally poor, especially when developing countries alone are considered, and that implied restrictions on the arithmetic value of coefficients are not satisfied; and third, that the change in relationship between means of agricultural and urban labor forces imposes new and still more rigorous limitations on the data.

The problem exposed, however, seems less with the inherent consistency of the initial Kuznets hypothesis than with the reality of substantial intervention in the economic system. Although not contemplated in the original formulation, policy in individual countries does differ widely with respect to the incidence of land redistribution, as well as with utilization of the rural labor force. It also varies in the urban areas, where the levels of employment and wage rates, and of capital intensity and profitability, are much affected by the industrial strategies pursued. Moreover, for most of the developing countries chronicled, the share of the population engaged in agriculture already has fallen significantly in recent years, suggesting that many should be on an equalizing course already.

If one goes on to more complex statistical relationships that introduce a number of other relevant variables to the analysis, inequality seems again to vary parabolically with income. I provide some indication of these findings in Table 2. What these relationships also show is clear indication of the much higher inequality in Latin America, once that regional distinction is introduced; the importance of secondary school attendance, past population growth, and share of income generated by agriculture as determining variables; and, both for developing countries alone and for a broader sample, including the developed countries, some tendency for income distribution to improve at higher levels of per capita income.[4] The important point is that inequality is not merely a random variable.

---

[3]Initial article by Ahluwalia (1976), and a recent reference by Anand and Kanbur (1993).

[4]For the equations in Table 2, turning points for the parabolas are as high as $5000 in 1980 Summers-Heston dollars. This compares with much lower real values found by Paukert (1973).

Table 2. Regression Estimates of Inequality[1]

	All Countries[2]		Developing Countries[3]	
	Income Share of Bottom 40 percent	Theil Index of Inequality	Income Share of Bottom 40 percent	Theil Index of Inequality
Constant	−121.5	696.7	−111.5	479.8
	(3.8)	(8.1)	(2.1)	(5.7)
Income[4]	32.5	−82.5	29.3	−39.5
	(4.2)	(4.0)	(2.0)	(1.6)
Income squared[4]	−1.91	4.59	−1.67	2.68
	(4.2)	(3.7)	(1.7)	(1.4)
Education[5]	0.03	−0.09	0.04	−0.23
	(1.0)	(1.1)	(.8)	(1.8)
Agriculture[6]	0.22	−4.4	0.23	−0.53
	(3.8)	(1.4)	(3.5)	(2.6)
Population growth[7]	−1.32	2.26	−1.14	3.72
	(2.1)	(1.4)	(1.4)	(1.6)
Latin America[8]	−6.2	18.5	−6.4	15.3
	(5.3)	(5.8)	(4.3)	(3.6)
R squared	0.55	0.61	0.53	0.41

Sources: World Bank, *World Development Report 1994*; *Social Indicators of Development*, 1994; and *World Tables*, 1994.

[1] t-values are in parentheses.
[2] Includes 64 countries.
[3] Includes 45 countries.
[4] Logarithm of the level of Summers-Heston income.
[5] Average percent of age group enrolled in secondary education, 1965–90.
[6] Average percent of aggregate income generated by agriculture, 1977–92.
[7] Average annual population growth, 1977–92.
[8] Dummy variable to represent inclusion in Latin America.

Clearly, the transformation of economies from low levels of income can create inherent tendencies toward higher levels of inequality, but what the record obviously suggests is that policies can make a palpable difference in averting them. Equally, and much more disturbing, is the continuing unaltered concentration of income in several countries despite intervening rises in income; interestingly, that leads to higher parabolic turning points in recent estimates than was characteristic of the earlier statistical analyses. That is particularly true of inequality in Latin America.

New and more vigorous efforts are necessary in the laggards, and at an early juncture, lest the democratic trend of the past decade be reversed. Perhaps the most important two interventions, whose economic effects are clearly visible, are those relating to physical asset structure and to rapid accumulation of human capital.

Of the possibilities associated with redistribution of wealth, land stands out as clearly the most potent variable. Land reform, where used, has been a powerful factor in affecting income distribution. The Republic of Korea and Taiwan Province of China stand out as the two most obvious cases where an initial commitment to equalization played a major role; the implications of that experience are currently very much being re-examined in an attempt to find methods to generalize it (see World Bank, 1993; but also Fishlow and others, 1994, for a critical evaluation). But in addition to those two cases, the experiences of China and Viet Nam, now showing signs of quite rapid and vigorous expansion, should not be forgotten. In those countries, an imposed equality generated relatively little growth until combined with greater personal incentives and opportunities for productivity improvement. Strict communist doctrine did not work, but its initial redistributive measures served as a powerful equalizing device that those countries subsequently could draw upon to their advantage.

Where there is a large rural population, productivity and equality are both served by such efforts. There is little doubt that the high rates of inequality found in Latin America trace back to the initially much higher inequality of land distribution in the region dating from the nineteenth century and, in some cases, even before. That inequality preceded the later commitment to import-substituting industrialization. Also, there can be little question, despite the lesser enthusiasm now available, that fairer allocation of this basic asset can serve as an important stimulant to broadly based development. For many reasons, there is a seeming reluctance to act; land reform seems to await war or revolution for its imposition. Yet where land is poorly utilized and its productivity can be much enhanced, redistribution—even with the payment of current capital value—can be quite economical.

What must be stressed, however, are the essential additional public inputs required for any distributive policy to be effective. Reallocation alone will not work. Only if viewed as a means toward the end of greater efficiency and output can any effort be successful. Too frequently, reform initiatives have encountered significant opposition from landholders reluctant to give up their command over resources, even when poorly utilized.

Human capital is a second area in which public actions can make a large difference. And it is one to which developing countries have made significant commitments over the postwar period. One need only cite the record from 1960 to 1991. For low-income countries, enrollment in primary school has increased from 54 percent to 101 percent (see also footnote 2, above); for secondary school, from 14 percent to 41 percent; and for tertiary, from 2 percent to 5 percent. For middle-income countries, enrollment has risen from 81 percent to 104 percent; from 17 percent to 55 percent; and from 4 percent to 18 percent, respectively (World Bank, 1994). Many countries have substantially increased their expenditures in this area.

There is good reason for these actions, in two dimensions. First, there is a quite high social return from the investment. The World Bank finds rates in excess of 25 percent for primary education, 15–18 percent for secondary, and 13–16 percent for tertiary. There is even a positive relationship with years of schooling: East Asia, with an average of six years, yields a higher increase in GDP for additional investment than do other regions (Psacharopoulos, 1985). What this reinforces is the importance of achieving adequate *minimal* training: many students in rural areas, through grade repetition and lack of completion, wind up little better for it. Note as well that female education regularly has an indirect, negative feedback on fertility, as well as positive effects on family health and nutrition.

The second benefit from education is in the realm of income distribution. For a large variety of countries, where some type of decomposition of the sources of inequality has been undertaken, variation in education typically shows up as the principal explanatory variable. Its range of importance extends from 10 percent to more than 20 percent of observed inequality. Those who are better schooled regularly receive higher incomes, holding constant age, sector, etc. Typically, at the bottom of the income distribution, education is more important: one recent study cites those with no schooling as having a 56 percent probability of being in the lowest 20 percent, whereas those with university training had only a 4 percent chance (Behrman, 1993, p. 196). Undoubtedly, education is partially serving as a proxy for other associated factors, such as family characteristics, school quality, and labor market characteristics. However, its repeated relevance, even discounting some of the gross effect, gives it a crucial role as a policy contributing to greater distributional equality.

More active participation by government is necessary, particularly at local levels, where efforts must be undertaken to ensure attendance and maintenance of school quality. But beyond this, curricular reform in many instances is badly required. It does little good to provide a standard training that leads simply to grade repetition rather than the acquisition of skills. Whatever their many deficiencies, moreover, the record of the former communist countries stands out in the speed with which they achieved universal education. It remains as a task to show that market-oriented economies can do as well.

Beyond education itself, there is a whole range of ancillary activities whose effects are similar in improving the quality of labor: these include nutrition, health, and other social investments. Indeed, for very low-income countries, the returns from such outlays may be greater than those received from education, exactly because the latter is insufficient to have a direct impact. Countries that have made early and substantial commitments to universal access to this human capital have been rewarded by lower inequality as growth proceeds; in turn, the social returns from expanded investment in education have permitted simultaneous gains in real product.

There is also a generational phenomenon. Today's outlays will not have an immediate and observable impact on output, but one that is delayed. That makes it easier to postpone these outlays when fiscal stringency is necessary. One of the great tragedies of the 1980s in Africa and Latin America is not merely the poor economic performance that occurred but also the simultaneous reductions in government expenditures that were necessarily imposed. In many ways, it was much easier to cut back in areas that had initially failed to be universal in scope. This, in turn, meant shortfalls in reaching the very groups initially excluded from adequate coverage. In most cases, private outlays for education, health services, etc., continued, thus extending initial divisions between those who were better off and those with limited initial access. These kinds of delayed response are still to be felt in future decades, even as growth recovers. Not only has there been a "lost decade" of growth, but potentially a "lost generation" deprived of skills and any capacity to acquire them.

There is now greater realism in understanding that major efforts to achieve better distribution of income cannot rely on populist promises of higher wages and extensive direct economic controls and regulations. These efforts are temporary at best. The evidence of failure—in Chile in the 1970s and Peru and Nicaragua in the 1980s—is quite marked. Such paths of initially improved distribution come from arbitrary gains in income, gains that subsequently evaporate as inevitable adjustment occurs. Even without such extremes, policies adopted that rely heavily on subsidies, whether to agriculture or industry, frequently translate into efforts that distort incentives and benefit well-placed groups; the multiplicity of interventions ironically cancel out any real allocation effect that had been anticipated.

Indeed, the triumph of the market is now widely recognized, even where it had once been resisted. But conversely, the recognition that markets should play a wider role in the development process is still consistent with important areas of public responsibility. A danger is that the fear of excessive and inefficient government intervention excludes productive investment that can yield growth as well as improve income distribution. That would be a great tragedy in the midst of the present policy convergence. The commitment must be not merely to ensure current increases in product but also to guarantee them in the future through a strategy of continuing public investment and taxation.

Scope for progressive taxation is necessarily limited when (simultaneously advance private savings and investment. On assess positive gains from redistribution without paying attention to potential negative consequences. But equally, one cannot ignore possibilities for utilizing enhanced revenues productively. The real challenge for the future is creating an efficient public presence. Nowhere is it more important than in the realm of income distribution.

Poverty Alleviation

Much of the attention in the last 15 years has turned away from dealing with income inequality to the task of ameliorating poverty. These tasks are not the same. In this effort, the World Bank has led the way. Its *World Development Report* in 1980 was centrally directed to the poverty question, not to that of income inequality. First, such a shift meant more concern with those who were worst-off—the poorest of the poor. Second, the geographic focus was necessarily changed: the concern with the poor necessarily meant greater attention to the populations of Asia, where incomes were lower. Third, attention was necessarily concentrated on the rural sector, where the poverty burden was larger. Finally, this new focus reduced tension between the objectives of improving the distribution of income and accelerating growth. Increasing incomes at the bottom could occur with greater product although the distribution of income was to remain as unequal, or even more unequal, than it had been; trickle-down effects could produce significant gains.

I have argued above that income distribution does matter. How much is available to the top groups relative to the bottom can make a difference to perceived welfare. In the next section, I will return to that theme. But here, I wish to pay attention to the special problems of coping separately with those with inadequate incomes. Unlike the poverty population in wealthier countries, these are groups that regularly work but whose incomes are insufficient to provide them with adequate nutrition, housing, education, etc. In many ways, dealing effectively with the poor is simply a means of ensuring attention to their particular problems; done well, the implications for inequality can certainly be positive. But it does lead to a different, if not independent, policy approach.

A leading part in this initial effort to focus attention on poverty was played by the "basic needs" approach (see World Bank, 1980 and 1990; and Lipton and Ravallion, forthcoming). This approach emphasized the importance of separating generalized income increases from the more significant attainment of requirements essential to permanent poverty reduction. Among the latter were improvements in health, access to more nutritional food, more education, and better shelter.

Three arguments were advanced for adopting this view. First, many poor people are themselves not producers but are part of the dependent population; as a consequence, they have no direct earnings of the kind that are typically evaluated in distribution studies. Second, even increased income may be inadequate to lead to its expenditure on essential required services: neither better medical care nor safe drinking water nor better housing may be available. In such circumstances, individuals are nominally better off, but not in reality. Third, households vary in their ability to spend wisely and effectively; they may irrationally prefer "better" consumption goods whose contribution to welfare may be inferior.

In the end, basic needs vanished as a tracking device, perhaps as much because of difficulties of practically aggregating them as any other. But the attention it directed, first to the poor, and then to the policies required for improving their lot, has persisted over the years. The *Human Development Report 1993* by the United Nations Development Program is illustrative (p. 3) in distinguishing between income and its potential applications: "The purpose of development is to widen the range of people's choices. Income is one of those choices—but it is not the sum-total of human life." Or, to put it differently, the negative correlation between income and the extent of poverty does not negate the relevance of public policies specially directed to the poor.

One consequence of this attention to the poor is the much greater attention it gives to the importance of safety nets to ensure their welfare. As more traditional mechanisms, like patron-client or kinship-based systems, have diminished in the midst of development, there is a clear role and scope for public intervention. More countries have adopted such programs, some stimulated by the absolute declines experienced in the 1980s, but their extent is still partial and inadequate; in some instances, these attempts serve more to ensure survival of a bureaucracy than to direct resources where they are urgently needed.

But this requirement is not alone. The *World Development Report 1990* of the World Bank, once again addressed to poverty, adds two further essentials (see Chapter 9): attention to labor-intensive growth, especially in the agricultural sector, which may additionally contribute to exports; and an emphasis on primary education and health, whose relevance to the distribution of income we have already seen.

On the first of these, there is little doubt. Poor people, even in rural areas, are food purchasers, and their position depends upon an adequate local supply. Yet agriculture has frequently been discriminated against in the drive to build up industry, both through inadequate investment in the rural area and through trade protection that levies negative effective tariffs on the sector. When such discrimination has occurred, the ultimate losers are typically the very poor, who have less preparation and opportunity for other employment.

On the second essential, I have already commented at length. What may simply be added in this context is the importance of ensuring education within rural areas, where poverty is much more pronounced. Flexibility of sessions to allow for needed assistance of older children with harvests and other economic needs is one possibility; another, general need is improved teaching capability through better training and salaries. In too many countries, free university education is featured at high expense while primary school personnel costs are kept to a minimum, dictated by the need to control government outlays.

Still a further dimension, recently emphasized by Bardhan (1993) and explicit as well in the UNDP *Human Development Report 1993*, merits discussion. On the one side is the market-oriented approach, with its safety net provisions for those who fail to be absorbed in productive employment; on the other is the basic needs emphasis on the need for public intervention on a large scale to meet the requirements of the poor for a range of essential services. Bardhan (1994, p. 14) encourages a third alternative, relying "instead on local self-governing institutions and community involvement to improve the material conditions and autonomy of the poor."

The issue raised is the capability of the poor to organize their demands effectively and continuously; to some degree, this is the philosophy underlining the poverty program in Mexico, which has expanded rapidly in recent years and can be found elsewhere in other examples, like that of the Grameen Bank in Bangladesh. Equally, such an emphasis calls for a different role for the state: it is to play an activist part, but through its effective decentralization. Such a restructuring involves important changes, not least in the degree of concentration of public expenditure at the national level; in developing countries, decisions and public outlays are most frequently centralized. Also, the extent to which local elites can be pushed beyond their traditional roles as enforcers of a static order is obviously critical.

The role of community groups, assisted by the recent multiplication of nongovernmental organizations, has been an important positive component in the expansion of local authority in recent years. In particular, the capacity of these organizations to reach low-income groups, particularly in rural areas, should be stressed. Their growth rate has been quite impressive; it is now estimated that their coverage extends to a population of something like 250 million. Although still much short of total coverage, their rate of expansion in the last decade—more than doubling—has been quite substantial. But in the end, the issue comes back to central government capacity to reinforce and sustain decentralization. This next decade will test that capability.

It is useful to conclude this section by stressing that poverty reduction and income growth are not only compatible but are causally related. Improved quality of the labor force contributes fundamentally to continuing productivity gains. More adequate rural technologies have the same effect. Reduced pressure from migration to urban areas translates into smaller social outlays and, quite possibly, less unemployment. These are all good reasons to give emphasis not merely to ameliorating income inequality generally but to aiding the poverty population explicitly. That population is considerable, estimated by the World Bank to be of a magnitude of over 1 billion. What is worse is that even with appropriate policies, the size of the poverty group in sub-Saharan Africa continues to expand; to keep the number of the poor simply stable would require a realized rate of growth of income a full 2 percentage points higher than predicted over the next several years. This challenge, even in the midst of other pressing and immediate development problems, cannot just be ignored.

New Theoretical Advances

Some of the gains achieved in recent years in the analysis of growth have come from applying new models. Most prominent among them has been the theory of endogenous growth. One part of this neo-Schumpeterian literature starts from external increasing returns that drive continuing expansion; others have emphasized perfect competition, but permitting unlimited accumulation of capital with positive productivity; still a third has gone on to introduce either improved or new goods, invoking fixed costs as the limiting factor; and yet another group has introduced freer trade as a mechanism for growth, either through technological progress directly or indirectly by allowing for specialization in intermediate goods.

Some of these efforts have led to empirical estimation. Thus, models in which education, for example, plays a key role in explaining extended growth for a cross-section of countries have become common. Others have related trade policy to long-run growth in a similar fashion.[5]

A second and even newer element in the recent literature has been the explicit addition of political factors as important causal factors. The essence of such political economy is to recognize the important interaction between a willingness to accept less today in return for more tomorrow: democratic voters may be willing to forgo populism now in favor of increased investment and future growth. There is thus a combination of endogenous growth with endogenous policy in such efforts.

The key result so far obtained, exemplified by recent articles by Persson and Tabellini (1994) and by Alesina and Rodrik (1994), is that inequality is negatively related to growth. In the former piece, the effects of equality on growth are not only statistically significant but also quantitatively important. Thus an increase in equality with a standard devia-

---

[5]For an early empirical treatment, see Barro (1991). For a summary of work emphasizing trade, see Edwards (1993). For a critical evaluation of these initial empirical efforts, see Levine and Renelt (1992).

tion of 1, changing the share of income of the middle quintile of the income distribution by about 3 percent, is capable of increasing growth by $\frac{1}{2}$ of 1 percentage point. Moreover, and powerfully, this relationship seems to hold only for those countries that follow democratic policies; for those that do not—some 40 percent of the sample—the effect of inequality is not statistically different from zero. In the latter study, the Gini coefficient for a larger number of countries is employed as a key variable and turns out to be statistically significant. A reduction in the Gini coefficient with a standard deviation of 1 increases growth by more than 1 percentage point. But Alesina and Rodrik stress that they find no difference between democracies and nondemocracies.

As of yet, these findings, and still others in a similar vein, must still be regarded as tentative. The income distribution data in both studies relate to an early period, the 1950s through the early 1970s, and therefore are clearly doubtful, although Alesina and Rodrik do experiment with a slightly later set of observations. For a somewhat different sample of countries and slightly longer period, for example, as illustrated in Table 3, I find evidence of no statistical significance for inequality, especially when a dummy is introduced for the Latin American observations.

Table 3 utilizes observations both about the middle quintile of the distribution, as used by Persson and Tabellini, and the Gini coefficient chosen by Alesina and Rodrik. I have used more recent data to test the former, on the grounds that the income distribution seems to have shown little systematic change over a period as short as two decades; for the latter, I have used initial inequality dating from the 1960s and early 1970s but extended the analysis to a longer time frame.

In each of the three exercises, neither measure of inequality, the share of the income in the middle quintile, nor the Gini coefficient comes out as a statistically significant variable. This is true when all countries are utilized or developing countries only. Moreover, the conclusion is unaffected whether one uses the Gini coefficients selected by Alesina and Rodrik for three countries—Germany, Kenya, and Peru—where there are large differences between potential candidates, or excludes them altogether. The latter regressions involve fewer countries and are reported as well.

Additional conceptual issues about this new approach can also be posed. The mechanisms through which actual redistributive policies operated are not specified. The large place for developed countries in the sample may make the findings for developing countries more dubious. The implicit assumption of equilibrium can hardly hold in an interval in which the debt crisis had already begun and growth was significantly affected. And the model is still not dynamic and really only an imperfect model of reality.

Nonetheless, the Persson and Tabellini results, but not those of Alesina and Rodrik, contribute affirmatively to the notion that efforts combining

Table 3. Determinants of Rate of Growth of Product[1]

| | 1976–90 | | 1960–80 | | | | 1960–90 | | | |
	All countries	Developing countries	All countries[2]		Developing countries[3]		All countries[2]		Developing countries[3]	
Number of countries	63	44	46	43	29	27	46	43	29	27
Constant	-3.16	-2.41	1.37	2.86	3.27	3.11	2.40	2.87	3.46	3.22
	(1.1)	(0.85)	(0.88)	(1.87)	(2.01)	(1.79)	(1.74)	(1.92)	(2.01)	(1.77)
Initial real income	-0.00018	-0.00052	-0.00028	-0.00034	-0.00063	-0.00065	-0.00030	-0.00032	-0.00059	-0.00062
	(1.32)	(1.63)	(2.40)	(3.15)	(1.94)	(1.91)	(2.89)	(3.07)	(1.71)	(1.73)
Initial primary enrollment	0.045	0.048	0.039	0.038	0.026	0.027	0.036	0.036	0.027	0.028
	(2.91)	(2.75)	(3.34)	(3.50)	(2.15)	(2.09)	(3.45)	(3.37)	(2.13)	(2.10)
Share of income in middle quintile	-0.013	0.052	...	...	...	...	...	...	...	...
	(.09)	(.31)								
Gini coefficient	...	...	-1.50	-3.91	-3.44	-3.12	-3.77	-4.45	-4.74	-4.26
			(0.55)	(1.40)	(1.20)	(0.97)	(1.55)	(1.63)	(1.56)	(1.26)
Latin America[4]	-2.47	-1.47	-0.84	-0.76	0.28	0.35	-1.58	-1.49	-0.67	-0.56
	(2.94)	(1.35)	(1.32)	(1.26)	(0.37)	(0.45)	(2.78)	(2.53)	(0.86)	(0.68)
R squared	0.15	0.16	0.16	0.23	0.13	0.12	0.29	0.29	0.21	0.18

[1] t-values are in parentheses.
[2] The second regression excludes Germany, Kenya, and Peru.
[3] The second regression includes Kenya and Peru.
[4] Dummy variable to represent inclusion in Latin America.

greater equality with democracy may also yield higher rates of economic performance. They do so in this case because high income inequality motivates populist policies that do not contribute to the higher rates of investment required to ensure adequate growth. In the end, that conclusion conforms to good policy sense rather than being dependent on scientific demonstration. Let me cite the World Bank's *World Development Report 1991* (p. 139):

> . . . efforts to improve equity can sit comfortably within reform programs aimed at promoting growth. It is clear, however, that market-distorting and overzealous redistribution can quickly pose overwhelming financial problems . . . . Also, crude transfers through market-distorting interventions almost always end up worsening the distribution of income rather than improving it.

The difficulty comes in the practical implementation.

Final Remarks

We have come together to celebrate the fiftieth anniversary of Bretton Woods and to recognize the many advances made in dealing with international issues in the intervening years. These gains have been both technical and practical. Views on economic development have evolved, most strikingly within the past decade, moving toward greater consensus now in favor of market discipline combined with more limited, but more effective, government action. Gone is the faith in more complex planning models to regulate and control economic activity that was found at an earlier time. Gone is the commitment to overexpansive public expenditures. But gone as well is the initial belief that market forces by themselves could produce a social optimum.

Unequal income distribution, and its associated poverty problems, unfortunately remain central issues for the future. Other, and more immediate, adjustment concerns have held sway. While wide recognition now exists that there is need for both restored and continuing economic growth and renewed attention to the fate of the poor, the latter does not have the priority of the former. Even in democracies, the poor vote more infrequently, and then not always for their material interest.

Our real task in the future is to ensure that the new consensus for a market-friendly approach to development gives rise to a positive impulse for state activity where it is justified. Nowhere is it more so than in dealing with the poverty and income distribution problem. Social returns can be enhanced through much more attention to education, on the one hand, and to equitable rural expansion, including land reform, on the other. Safety nets must also become generally accessible. But to do so will require resources, and inevitably the burden will fall with greater weight on the domestic economy. External public funds are simply not available. A key requirement, therefore, is to ensure that this internal source is.

That requirement inevitably means an increased capacity for public savings in many countries, especially at the local level.

One of the lessons we have repeatedly relearned is that the miracle of equitable development requires adequate resources. At a time of increasing convergence in approach to the poverty problem, and that of development generally, it would be tragic to forget this need. It exists just as much for human capital as for physical, and for social services as well as for private needs. Reducing poverty is equally an investment for the future, and one whose time has surely come. If it is not pursued vigorously, the recent democratic emergence of many developing countries will not become permanent and enduring.

References

Adelman, Irma, and Sherman Robinson, "Income Distribution and Development," in Hollis Chenery and T.N. Srinivasan, eds., *Handbook of Development Economics*, Vol. 2 (New York: Elsevier Science Publishing Company, 1989).

Ahluwalia, Montek S., "Inequality, Poverty and Development," *Journal of Development Economics*, Vol. 3 (December 1976), pp. 307–42.

Alesina, Alberto, and Dani Rodrik, "Distributive Politics and Economic Growth," *Quarterly Journal of Economics*, Vol. 109 (May 1994), pp. 465–90.

Anand, Sudhir, and S.M.R. Kanbur, "The Kuznets Process and the Inequality-Development Relationship," *Journal of Development Economics*, Vol. 40 (February 1993), pp. 25–52.

Bardhan, Pranab, "Analytics of the Institutions of Informal Cooperation in Rural Development," *World Development*, Vol. 21 (April 1993), pp. 633–39.

———, "Poverty Alleviation," Overseas Development Council Occasional Paper No. 1 (1994).

Barro, Robert J., "Economic Growth in a Cross Section of Countries," *Quarterly Journal of Economics*, Vol. 105 (May 1991), pp. 407–43.

Behrman, Jere, "Investing in Human Resources," in Inter-American Development Bank, *Economic and Social Progress in Latin America, 1993 Report* (Washington: The Johns Hopkins University Press for the Inter-American Development Bank, 1993).

Chenery, Hollis, and others, *Redistribution With Growth: Policies to Improve Income Distribution in Developing Countries in the Context of Economic Growth* (London: Oxford University Press, 1974).

Edwards, Sebastian, "Openness, Trade Liberalization, and Growth in Developing Countries," *Journal of Economic Literature*, Vol. 31 (September 1993), pp. 1358–93.

Fields, Gary, "Data for Measuring Poverty and Inequality Changes in the Developing Countries," *Journal of Development Economics*, Vol. 44 (June 1994), pp. 87–102.

Fishlow, Albert, and others, *Miracle or Design: Lessons from the East Asian Experience* (Washington: Overseas Development Centre, 1994).

Kuznets, Simon, "Economic Growth and Income Inequality," *American Economic Review*, Vol. 65 (March 1955), pp. 1–28.

Levine, Ross, and David Renelt, "A Sensitivity Analysis of Cross-Country Growth Regressions," *American Economic Review*, Vol. 82 (September 1992), pp. 942–63.

Lipton, Michael, and Martin Ravallion, "Poverty and Policy," in *Handbook of Development Economics*, Vol. 3 (forthcoming).

Paukert, Felix, "Income Distribution at Different Levels of Development: A Survey of the Evidence," *International Labor Review*, Vol. 108 (August–September 1973), pp. 97–125.

Persson, Torsten, and Guido Tabellini, "Is Inequality Harmful for Growth?" *American Economic Review*, Vol. 84 (June 1994), pp. 600–21.

Psacharopoulos, George, "Returns to Education: A Further International Update and Implications," *Journal of Human Resources*, Vol. 20 (Fall 1985), pp. 583–604.

Robinson, Sherman, "A Note on the U-Hypothesis Relating Income Inequality and Economic Development," *American Economic Review*, Vol. 66, (June 1976), pp. 437–40.

Summers, Robert, and Alan Heston, "The Penn World Table (Mark 5): An Expanded Set of International Comparisons, 1950–1988," *Quarterly Journal of Economics*, Vol. 106 (May 1991), pp. 327–68.

United Nations Development Program, *Human Development Report 1993* (New York: Oxford University Press for the United Nations Development Program, 1993).

World Bank, *World Development Report 1980* (Washington: World Bank, 1980).

_____, *World Development Report 1990* (Washington: World Bank, 1990).

_____, *World Development Report 1991* (Washington: World Bank, 1991).

_____, *The East Asian Miracle: Economic Growth and Public Policy* (New York: Oxford University Press for the World Bank, 1993).

_____, *World Development Report 1994*, (Washington: World Bank, 1994).

Fazle Hasan Abed

We are gathered here to celebrate the completion of 50 years of the IMF and the World Bank. I feel greatly honored at having been invited to speak today, but first, my warm felicitations to the Bank and the IMF on this occasion. Celebrations are indeed in order today!

Bangladesh, my country, has nearly 120 million people living in an area of 144,000 square kilometers. This makes it one of the most densely populated countries in the world, a country characterized by pervasive poverty. Bangladesh's GNP per capita is only $220, life expectancy is a low 57 years, and the literacy rate is still a miserable 30 percent.

Yet in this ethnically homogeneous and geographically compact country, as a recent UNICEF report[6] says, "this grim portrait is slowly being redrawn." The report notes that per capita income has grown by almost 2 percent a year over the last decade in Bangladesh. Recounting the nation's progress, it acknowledges that Bangladesh's fourth five-year development plan incorporates most of the goals adopted at the world summit for children. It mentions that 80 percent of the rural residents are now within 150 meters of a source of safe drinking water, which, according to the report, is a feat unmatched by many richer nations. The report finds that noticeable progress has been made in the field of family planning. The contraceptive prevalence rate has risen from 3 percent in the early 1970s to 40 percent in the 1990s, and, in two decades, the country's total fertility rate has fallen from 7 births to 4.2 births per woman. In short, the report compliments the progress that is today noticeable in various sectors in Bangladesh. In all this, I dare say, both the IMF and the World Bank, in spite of the reservations one may have about their intervention in certain areas, have contributed in an increasingly effective manner. As these two institutions mature over the years and as they become enriched by their interactions with developmental problems, our faith in their playing an even more positive role in the transformation of the developing world takes firmer root.

At the Bangladesh Rural Advancement Committee (BRAC), we have a conviction that the main thrust for development of a country must come from within, where the poor and the deprived are empowered to alleviate their poverty and, as a result, that of the nation. But, then, we remain mindful that the world community is inseparably linked today through interdependent economies and shared sociopolitical views. Together, we confront such negative factors as malnutrition, illiteracy, the AIDS pandemic, and environmental degradation. For better or for worse, we share planet Earth together, and only through joint action will we overcome global problems. We therefore believe that cumulative actions, by both individual nations and the comity of nations, by institutions national and international, and by organizations great and small, can only accelerate the progress of humanity as we pass into the twenty-first century.

BRAC, a Bangladeshi nongovernmental organization, is but a small stitch in the huge tapestry of the saga of human development. It is to this that I have committed my life, and it is of its hopes, its endeavors,

---

[6]United Nations Children's Fund, *The State of the World's Children 1994* (New York: Oxford University Press for the United Nations Children's Fund, 1994).

and its possibilities in attaining sustainable poverty alleviation that I should briefly like to speak this morning.

BRAC's birth in 1972 followed that of Bangladesh. Its activities were then mainly directed at providing basic relief to a people ravaged by war. It soon became apparent that poverty was the biggest problem facing the newly emerged nation. BRAC thus set about designing a strategy to group the landless for their self-sustaining personal development through training, credit, and income generation, as well as through education for their children. Improving the health and nutritional status of women and children and developing and strengthening the capacity of communities to sustain primary health care activity also gradually became part of BRAC's development strategy. Today, BRAC is the largest national nongovernmental organization in the South, implementing several development programs all over Bangladesh, and employing over 12,000 full-time staff and 33,000 part-time functionaries.

Poverty alleviation, in our view, calls for a holistic approach. Poverty is a complex syndrome that manifests itself in many different ways. It is not only the lack of income that makes one poor but also the lack of good health, education, gender equity, access to resources, and an enabling environment.

It has been our policy to ensure effective participation of the people so that they may acquire the capacity to change their lives. With that end in view, we have given the highest emphasis to organization building, functional education, and training in human development. Our program beneficiaries, now numbering well over 1 million, organize themselves into cooperative groups at the village level. Members of the group undergo a course of functional education aimed at raising their awareness and at developing a sense of self-worth.

A village organization's initial task is to mobilize local and external resources to generate income and benefits for its members. Fish farming is developed in previously unused bodies of water; roadside verges, unutilized homesteads, and common lands are planted with trees and vegetables to meet the domestic needs of members. The members then turn to other resources in their locality, and their demand for the services of agricultural extension agents, health centers, and veterinary service centers for livestock is intensified.

Generating capital through savings is an important precondition for sustaining a village organization. BRAC group members are required to contribute a small sum weekly to a group savings fund. BRAC's revolving loan fund provides individual and collective loans to members participating in group activities and making regular savings contributions. A total of $120 million has been disbursed to date as small credits to group members, and their own fund—generated through savings— equals 40 percent of the loan fund outstanding with them.

Time and again, the poor have proved their creditworthiness. The loan recovery rate has been higher than 98 percent. The village organizations are gaining new confidence and strength, and they are venturing into new enterprises to create a more secure future for themselves and their families.

To improve income-generation opportunities for the poor, BRAC has moved into a number of new areas. One such area has been poultry development. We have trained 27,000 poultry vaccinators, 1 per village, who have been linked with the livestock offices. With a regular supply of vaccines from the Government, they provide vaccinations in their villages for a small fee, which has reduced the poultry mortality level. With the assurance of a regular vaccination service, large numbers of poor women have been encouraged to take up poultry rearing as a promising source of income; some 450,000 women have been trained. Hybrid varieties of birds with higher egg-laying capacity are also being introduced. We supply 500,000 day-old chicks every month to chick rearers who, in time, sell these to village poultry rearers. The livestock department, the vaccinators, the chick rearers, and the poultry farmers all form a supportive infrastructure for poultry development.

BRAC, as a leading organization, came to realize that in spite of all our efforts to empower the poor, the bottom 10 percent of the population was not being effectively reached. This, we felt, called for a separate strategy. The poorest among the poor were unable to create self-employment under the prevailing conditions. Employment opportunities needed to be created for them. Something more was needed, and this took us into new ventures. One intervention to reach that 10 percent is a program under which we have already planted 21 million mulberry trees all over the country. This also forms a part of our program target: to raise 40 million trees by 1997. This program is also an essential component in the development of BRAC's sericulture program, aimed at raising Bangladesh's silk production by the turn of the century from the current annual level of 60 tons to 1,200 tons and at creating half a million jobs for the most needy rural women.

In response to unacceptably high infant and child mortality rates in Bangladesh, BRAC took up a challenge in 1979—the International Year of the Child—to reduce childhood mortality from diarrhea by half. The efficacy of oral rehydration therapy to combat dehydration was well known among medical scientists. But how would a mother in a remote village in Bangladesh be informed that a solution of salt, sugar, and water, mixed in an appropriate measure, could save her child from dehydration and death? BRAC decided to go nationwide to show mothers face-to-face how to measure and mix an oral rehydration solution with home-based ingredients. It took as many as 1,300 staff ten years to cover 13 million mothers in rural Bangladesh. I am happy to say that oral rehydration therapy is now universally known in rural Bangladesh, and its use has risen to more than 60 percent. The result is that deaths caused by diarrhea have indeed been significantly reduced. Our success with oral rehydration therapy further made us aware of the need to change the national health statistics of the country and inspired BRAC to design a health program evolving through several distinct phases. BRAC's current Women's Health and Development Program, involving about 12.5 million people, integrates the various aspects of a community-based program in health, family planning, and nutrition.

Education is a basic element in generating what has been described as "social capital." The number of unserved children in Bangladesh runs into the millions. Among them, the number of girls is disproportionately high. There had to be a simpler way of tackling the problem of illiteracy! How could we hope to bring this massive population of non-schooled children to school? The simple answer was to situate schools near children's homes and to appoint a teacher from the immediate locality. Keeping the class size to a maximum of 33 helped the para-teachers with no previous teaching experience, and enrolling 70 percent female students in the school was our natural response to the appalling state of female education in the country. Sufficient parent involvement and participation strengthens the flexible design of the program, especially in setting school timing according to familial needs. Parents also form school management committees in every school, and all parents must meet with the school teacher every month to be informed of their child's progress. The school curriculum is specially designed to be relevant to the needs of rural children and is under continual revision based on feedback from the field. Working with simple program design, regular school visits by school supervisors, and intensive training and refresher courses for teachers, BRAC has been able to extend the nonformal primary education from 22 schools in 1985 to 24,000 schools today, reaching more than 750,000 children.

Access and equity have been long-standing concerns of education policymakers and practitioners. BRAC's nonformal primary education undoubtedly provides reasons for optimism—a hope that this may be a way to begin creating the social capital that we so seriously lack and so desperately need.

The limits of government development programs in bringing about a significant reduction in poverty, hunger, and illiteracy in most of the developing countries of Asia, Africa, and Latin America have provided impetus to involvement by nongovernmental organizations in national development. With their grassroots orientation and participatory approach, these organizations have been mobilizing and organizing the poor and the powerless to participate in the development process as subjects, rather than as the passive recipients of fragmented inputs delivered by the state.

Nongovernmental organizations' relations with their respective governments have, in many cases, stood on sensitive ground. I think a lasting answer to this problem lies in the realization by all concerned that these organizations are there to supplement and not supplant the development efforts that national governments undertake. Governments, however, believing in results achieved through privatization of development efforts, will only find it helpful to support and nurture programs undertaken by the organizations.

The World Bank's advocacy of structural adjustments calls for a comment. We think that the time has now come for the World Bank to consider making the network of nongovernmental organizations an element of that structural adjustment process. We believe that an authentic reform must direct resources to the rural areas, empower the poor, and democratize the purchasing power. If that is so, nongovernmental organizations can be effective partners in this task, if only because the successful ones among them have over the years developed mechanisms to reach the poorer sections of the community.

There is another point on which I should like to make my concern known. It is on the idea of *growth*, as promoted by the World Bank. In principle, no one can seriously dispute the need for growth, but to what extent it is "the necessary and sufficient" condition for poverty reduction needs, I think, to be examined carefully. We would do well to remember that growth-based development in East Asian countries has been successful in reducing poverty only in societies in which egalitarian and agrarian reforms preceded the present growth-oriented model of development. Those reforms in the countries of East Asia destroyed the power of the landed elite and thus created the ground for sustainable poverty reduction. In countries such as mine, not having gone through a meaningful land reform, access to the shared growth by the disadvantaged sections of the population remains limited, and it is this access that nongovernmental organizations like BRAC are engaged in developing. The World Bank and the IMF's advocacy of structural adjustment and policy reform should be aimed at facilitating this process.

Before I conclude, I wish to extend my appreciation to the organizers of this conference and would once again like to congratulate the World Bank and the IMF on the completion of their five decades of active support for the alleviation of poverty around the globe.

10

Establishing a Vision for Stabilization and Reform

The third and final keynote speaker was Jacques de Larosière, President of the European Bank for Reconstruction and Development, former Managing Director of the IMF, and former Governor of the Banque de France. Introducing Mr. de Larosière's speech on stabilization and reform of the international monetary system was Hans Tietmeyer, President of the Deutsche Bundesbank.

Hans Tietmeyer

Jacques de Larosière's speech will cover the central points on the issue of the reform of the international monetary system, an issue to which the work and the report of the Bretton Woods Commission have also made most valuable contributions. My own contribution to this exercise, therefore, can be a modest one. I should like to limit it to enumerating some factors of the global setting that are likely to be with us in the foreseeable future and that should be taken into account when thinking about the future role of the Bretton Woods institutions in the international monetary system and in global economics in general.

First, let me start with something self-evident, namely, that compared with our "needs" and aspirations, real resources are and will continue to be in short supply. This will be even more so if and when, in a global perspective, excessive population growth and ecological problems put question marks on traditional strategies for growth and employment. It follows that there should be an optimal mobilization of the resources available and that there should be an optimal use of the mobilized resources.

This leads me to my second point. Experience—costly experience for some of us—shows us that the task of mobilizing and using resources in an optimal way can best be performed by free markets, in a framework of monetary stability. This axiom also holds true of the special aspect for transferring scarce resources internationally, across national frontiers— an aspect of special importance for both developing countries and countries in transition. In other words, official channels for resource transfer, including the multilateral institutions, should encourage and supplement free markets as and when necessary, but not try to replace them. We all know that there are limits to official financing in the international field, no less than in the national context. It is therefore important for the IMF not to try to overplay its role in global financing—or to circumvent the economic and political limitations of the global transfer of real resources by ingenious financial engineering.

Third, any approach to stabilization and reform, and any approach to optimizing resource allocation globally, must take due account of the fact that, in our system, there is a dichotomy of globalized financial markets, on the one hand, and the continuing existence of traditional nation-states, on the other—notwithstanding regional integration and cooperation, as in the European Union. Together with the other factors I mentioned before, this dichotomy is of great relevance to the Fund's and the World Bank's role in our system.

I should like to mention only two aspects. First, by nature, nation-states' policies and priorities can and will often vary in direction and time—notwithstanding our countries' adherence to common principles, such as free enterprise, price stability, and full employment. Must we not conclude from that—whether we like it or not—that there are limits to what can be accomplished by efforts and arrangements to promote coordination and convergence of national policies and performance internationally?

If this is true of financial policies in general, it seems to be especially true of any attempts at "formalizing" exchange rate arrangements among the major currencies. As we know from experience in the European Monetary System, maintaining formalized exchange rate arrangements is already difficult on a regional basis. It would be all the more difficult on a worldwide basis. In any case, although experience tells us again and again that converging policies and performance with respect to "fundamentals" are a necessary condition for better exchange rate stability, they are unfortunately not always sufficient.

Second, it follows that in the foreseeable future there is no chance of establishing a world central bank, or of turning the IMF into such an institution. We have to realize that we are living and will continue to live in the future in a multipolar world, despite all our efforts at more and better cooperation. To my mind, this means that the chances of making the SDR the principal reserve asset in the international monetary system by substituting SDRs for the present multicurrency reserve system are rather slim.

Finally, if this analysis is correct, I wonder whether there are not some obvious conclusions to be drawn for the future role of our institutions.

First, the center of the purposes of the Fund must be monetary stability as the condition sine qua non for successful cooperation, sustainable liberalization, and integration, growth, and employment. That means there is no way of putting growth and development at the center, because that would not only be in conflict with the Fund's Articles of Agreement but would also harm the Fund's genuine role, namely, that of safeguarding an open payments system, balance of payments adjustment, and financial stability as *preconditions* for growth and employment.

Second, the role of the Fund in global financing should not be misunderstood. In the international as well as in the national field, creating additional liquidity cannot substitute for lacking capital. The Fund should stick to its proven role of providing "help for self-help" to its members in need by assisting them with conditional program lending and thereby catalyzing additional financing from other sources. In short, as the Fund's Managing Director has said, adjustment is more important than financing. For its part, the World Bank Group, in close cooperation with the regional development banks, should, of course, continue to provide capital for development and structural reform, ensuring its funding primarily on the private markets by maintaining its credit standing.

Third, we should also be realistic about the role of SDRs in the foreseeable future. Given the global framework I have just mentioned, pushing the role of SDRs in our system could be counterproductive and could destabilize rather than strengthen our monetary system. Obviously, there is no long-term global need for supplementing existing reserve assets. It is for these reasons that some members have expressed doubt about whether there is a factual justification for *general* allocations of SDRs in present circumstances. However, there are good reasons for being in favor of enabling the Fund's new members to participate fully in the SDR system through a *special* allocation of SDRs, ensuring the equitable participation of all members in the SDR mechanism.

Let me say one final word about cooperation and coordination. In view of the dichotomy, mentioned before, of globalized markets and traditional nation-states, stability-oriented cooperation, especially between the major countries, is an absolute necessity. At the same time, this dichotomy puts limits on what can reasonably be expected of cooperation and coordination. We should avoid overstraining this instrument.

Certainly, any formalized or quantified targeting, like any "automaticity," must be out of the question. If this is true of economic policy coordination in general, it is especially true in the field of exchange rate policy. Let us be realistic: in the foreseeable future, "formalized" exchange rate arrangements between the world's major currencies are not a viable route to follow.

Jacques de Larosière

Anniversaries—especially institutional ones—give rise to discussions and analyses of past and future. Set up half a century ago, the Bretton

Woods institutions are no exception, and over the past few months, many have attempted to review their performance.

This debate is well timed. During the 50 years since the Bretton Woods institutions were created, the economic and financial environment has changed radically, and the international monetary "system" set up at the end of the war has collapsed. Having had the honor to be associated with the fortunes of the Fund for some time, it is a great privilege for me to share with you today a few thoughts on the future of the monetary system. But before looking to the future, let us try to understand how we got where we are today.

How Did the Bretton Woods Monetary System Work?

The Bretton Woods institutions were founded on the following key principle: to establish a multilateral system of economic cooperation to promote free trade and monetary stability and thus foster economic growth. The mechanism created at Bretton Woods for monetary stability relied heavily on two factors that were crucial to the success of the system in the postwar years: on the one hand, a fixed but adjustable exchange rate system anchored to the U.S. dollar; and on the other, a monetary framework in which current account transactions predominated and international capital flows were limited. Let us look more closely for a moment at these two factors.

Regarding the first factor, the United States emerged from the war as the strongest economy. Owing to this unique position of strength, its currency became the anchor of the exchange rate system. The dollar was convertible to gold at a fixed price, and all other currencies were linked to it. No change in parity was allowed except to correct a fundamental disequilibrium and, even then, only after consultation with the IMF. The Fund was the institutional backbone of the Bretton Woods monetary arrangement. Its goal was the promotion of international monetary cooperation, exchange rate stability, and orderly exchange arrangements.

On the second factor, the system set up at Bretton Woods was based on the predominance of current account transactions. This reflected the reality that trade and invisibles made up the bulk of the balance of payments at the time. International capital movements remained of very limited importance because of exchange controls. At Bretton Woods, priority was placed on reducing restrictions on current account transactions, but little was said about the desirability of countries liberalizing capital movements. In fact, a clause in the IMF Articles expressly provided that if capital movements were ever to undermine the fixed exchange rate system, capital controls could be used to avert this danger.

What we must remember is that—unlike today—money had an essentially national characteristic at the time. It was accepted that currencies were for the use of residents. In general, exchange controls forced residents doing business abroad to repatriate funds, ensuring that holdings of a currency by nonresidents were an exception. For example, deposits of French francs by nonresidents in French banks amounted to only F 1.5 billion in 1960; by 1993 this figure had grown to over F 400 billion. National authorities thus enjoyed a large degree of autonomy over their currency. This had been of key importance to Keynes during the Bretton Woods conference. He is on record as telling the House of Lords in May 1944 that "we intend to retain control of our domestic rate of interest, so that we can keep it as low as suits our own purposes, without interference from the ebb and flow of international capital movements or flights of hot money."

While the two pillars of exchange rate stability and predominance of current account transactions remained in place, supported by the IMF, the postwar international monetary system secured remarkable achievements. It was a time of extraordinary economic growth in much of the world; an unprecedented level of cooperation and stability was achieved; and trade and exchange restrictions were substantially reduced. Many currencies became convertible and world trade grew dramatically: between 1953 and 1963, world trade grew at an average of some 6 percent a year, and between 1963 and 1973, at an average of some 9 percent a year. Those monetary problems that were inevitably encountered were overcome through cooperation and consultation, rather than through restrictions and reprisals.

How Did the System Collapse?

There are two basic reasons for the collapse of the system: first, the currency anchor was derailed; second, the financial and monetary context changed radically.

The success of the par value system based on the dollar depended on the internal stability of the anchor currency and on the quality of macroeconomic policy in the United States. The system worked well for two decades. However, the relaxation of fiscal and monetary discipline in the United States in the late 1960s to finance the Viet Nam war and the welfare state had two direct consequences: erosion of the domestic value of the dollar; and, as expectations changed, a growing tendency by holders of dollars to seek refuge in gold and currencies other than the dollar.

In parallel with the weakening of the anchor currency, capital account transactions came to dominate exchange transactions. Capital controls had been considerably relaxed in many countries by the mid-1960s, helping investors to invest in the money markets of their choice. This was further facilitated by the significant technological advances in global information flows. The outcome was that capital transactions increasingly overshadowed current account transactions. This trend has continued: in 1989, global foreign exchange trading was estimated at $650 billion daily, almost forty times the average daily value of world trade. By mid-1992, global foreign exchange trading had grown further—to $880 billion a day.

These factors meant that the whole concept of national currency became less focused. Currencies became international commodities rather than symbols of sovereignty. New actors, such as pension funds and mutual funds, entered the scene, closely followed by new financial instruments. These events served to "internationalize" portfolios and to make currencies more volatile and less geared to their equilibrium price. This internationalization of money had a knock-on effect on national monetary policies. Gone was much of the autonomy engendered by the postwar system, and, contrary to Keynes's wish, monetary authorities faced increasing problems in securing their desired monetary policy at home as international factors played an increasing role.

Inevitably, the collapse of the two pillars that maintained the system brought about the collapse of the system itself. In 1971 the United States decided to sever the dollar's link to gold, and then, following a period of devaluation within the fixed exchange rate system, the system broke down.

Search for New Solutions

Since then, the international monetary system has encountered many difficulties, as governments have sought to reconcile the principles upon which the Bretton Woods institutions were founded with the realities of the day.

The Floating Rate System

In the early 1970s, the immediate response after the collapse of the fixed exchange rate system was the adoption of floating exchange rates. That system has been disappointing. It was supposed to fulfill four key functions:

- protect countries from destabilizing short-term capital movements and speculation;
- allow currencies to respond to trade imbalances;
- preserve the freedom of international trade; and
- protect the autonomy of monetary policies.

In fact, the floating exchange rate system has fallen short of fully achieving these objectives.

Today, currency speculation is a huge business, and it has never been more intense. The name of the game for many institutions is to hedge their clients against exchange rate volatility—which is in itself a profitable operation—while themselves contributing to the volatility by taking positions on the markets.

High levels of exchange rate volatility and substantial currency misalignments have become increasingly frequent. I need only cite as good examples the sharp, sustained, and excessive appreciation of the dollar in the early 1980s, the real appreciation of some European currencies before the 1992 European monetary crisis, and the more recent appreciation of the yen. Of course, equilibrium exchange rates are difficult to define. Trade balance, year by year and country by country, is clearly neither desirable nor possible. Long-term capital flows from surplus countries to deficit countries have a crucial role to play in world growth and balance. But the problem is not long-term capital flows nor, to the extent that they are viable, current account imbalances, but rather the high frequency and magnitude of short-term capital flows and the ensuing erratic and distorted movements in the exchange rates of the major currencies.

Furthermore, in the field of monetary policy, national autonomy has been very limited, especially in those countries—mostly the norm today—that are largely open to international trade and finance.

Excessive exchange rate volatility and severe misalignments have had detrimental consequences for the real economy. Even if the gravity of these consequences is open to discussion, the reality of the phenomenon is widely accepted. Not only does business planning become very difficult in situations of high exchange rate volatility, but the costs and restricted horizons of hedging also tend to discourage investment, production, and trade. In addition, investors are reluctant to enter into long-term commitments if exchange rates look "wrong" over an extended period. Smaller companies have suffered relatively more; being less favorably placed to hedge currency exposures than multinationals, many have shied away from the international business arena. Currency misalignments also carry the threat of trade protectionism—a threat that we cannot ignore.

More pervasively, the apparent freedom and ease given to policymakers by the floating exchange rate system no doubt contributed to the laxity of economic policies and the surge of inflation we witnessed in the 1970s. Governments, freed from the sanction of devaluation, often decided to let their currencies slide. The world has not yet finished paying for the consequences of 15 years' disregard of the external stability of currencies.

Multilateral Surveillance

With the abandonment of the fixed exchange rate system, the institutional backbone of the postwar international monetary system, namely, the Fund, had to adapt to the new conditions and to redefine its role with regard to the exchange rate system. With the new Article IV, its tool became multilateral surveillance: the Fund was to exercise "firm surveillance" over the exchange rate policies of its members. Certain successes came from this new policy, but also many failures. During some periods, the instability of exchange rates was reduced, especially with the Plaza and Louvre agreements, but, in general, these achievements were limited. We did see the development of closer international cooperation between central banks, which is welcomed. And we have seen a remarkable convergence of mentalities on the need to fight inflation as a condition for sustained growth.

In general, however, it must be said that the policy of multilateral surveillance has been found wanting. A number of industrial countries have accumulated substantial fiscal deficits over the past 15–20 years. For example, if we look at the aggregate fiscal deficit for the Group of Seven countries as a percentage of GDP, including social security budgets, this figure has risen steadily from 2.6 percent of GDP in 1980 to a projected 4 percent of GDP in 1994. Many governments have lost control of their fiscal policies, and the succession of budget deficits over the past two decades has resulted in an unprecedented surge of public indebtedness. In the countries of the Group of Seven, the public debt-GDP ratio has increased by more than 30 percentage points since 1974, from 36 percent of GDP in 1974 to 67 percent of GDP in 1993.

The magnitude of the debt accumulated is such that policymakers in a number of countries are today deprived of their normal fiscal margin of maneuver in times of recession. Indeed, even if governments were tempted to have recourse to inflation as a means of taxation or as a way of reducing the real value of their debt, they now realize that this does not work any more: buyers of treasury papers today demand a real interest rate on their investment and are free to obtain it abroad if they wish; and central banks—being increasingly independent—have no choice but to counteract fiscal laxity by restricting monetary policy, thus only adding to the cost of treasury borrowing. Moreover, this mix of lax fiscal policies and tight monetary policies has tended to crowd some productive investment out of the markets and has thus hampered growth. The recent upheavals in the bond markets are connected to the markets' perception of this high level of public debt.

Finally, the stimulation, within the framework of multilateral surveillance, of Japanese domestic demand in the 1980s through monetary relaxation led to asset inflation (not price inflation) in one of the few countries to have attained a fiscal balance. When it later became necessary to burst the financial bubble, the result was further economic and financial strains.

Did the multilateral surveillance system successfully prevent these excesses? The answer is "no," and it is because of shortcomings in surveillance that the attempts to stabilize exchange rates had limited success. Although governments gave their word to cooperate and coordinate, domestic pressures often prevented them from delivering. Admonishment without sanction was not enough to make them perform.

The Future

What do we see on the horizon? On the one hand, we see an increasing integration of international trade and finance for reasons that pertain as much to social trends and technological development as to deliberate policy by governments; and, on the other, economic and monetary policies still being defined essentially in national terms.

We are all familiar with the dangers and abuses to which this situation has given rise. Unless something is done, international monetary relations will remain volatile and crisis ridden. Certain currencies will remain potentially destabilizing, owing to the size of the economies concerned and the extent to which they are used for foreign exchange transactions. This situation could lead to regional groups trying to defend themselves against the impact of currency fluctuations, which, in turn, could lead to a fragmentation of trade relations. Who could wish for such a situation, a situation so different from the spirit that prevailed, 50 years ago, at Bretton Woods?

Seeing the seriousness of the problem, I believe we must react against it and come up with solutions.

Historically, there have really been only two types of international monetary system: systems based on an anchor currency; and systems based on cooperation and commitment among states to abide by binding rules. Anchor currency systems are typical of periods in which one economic power dominates the international scene. Systems based on binding cooperation, such as the gold standard in the past and European Monetary Union in the future, are systems freely chosen by states that have decided to make their prime objective the external—and thus internal—stability of their currencies.

At the end of the twentieth century, the world has become more integrated, more interdependent, and more "egalitarian" than it was 50 years ago. The phenomenon of a dominant national currency is less common, and the use of reserve and transaction currencies tends to be more widespread. Furthermore, there is wide consensus on the dangers of inflation.

Logically, therefore, the future trend should be toward greater and closer international cooperation. As I have attempted to illustrate, "soft" cooperation based on pressure to emulate is no longer enough, and we must formulate and implement new approaches.

Views differ on whether such cooperation should be more or less ambitious. The more radical schemes have been described many times, and I will touch on them only very briefly. They involve global management of the international monetary system, with a central authority issuing and controlling an international currency. Under this type of system, external use of reserve currencies would be kept within set limits; above those limits, participants would have to settle their balances in the international currency managed by the central authority (asset settlement).

I do not believe that such proposals would be realistic at this juncture. I am afraid that the situation would need to be far more drastic for governments to accept such a far-reaching solution.

I do think, however, that a more formal mechanism of currency cooperation could be established to reduce misalignments and excessively volatile exchange rates. A system that would be suitably flexible while providing direction with exchange rates moving within bands, as described by the Bretton Woods Commission, seems to me to be an interesting possibility for the future.

It should be stressed, however, that a mechanism of this kind could work only if the participating states undertook to reinforce their macroeconomic policies and to cooperate closely with their partners. This was highlighted in the Treaty on European Union, which stresses the importance of precise and measurable economic convergence criteria as a precondition for fixed exchange rates and monetary union.

Thus, the quality of the economic policies of the main players in the world economy is the first requirement for greater exchange rate stability. Central elements of this are the progressive reduction of fiscal deficits and public debt burdens. As the recently published Bretton Woods Commission report concluded: "the major industrial country governments should take two successive steps: first, strengthen their macroeconomic policies, and achieve greater economic convergence; and second, establish a more formal system of coordination to support these policy improvements and avoid excessive exchange rate misalignments and volatility." I fully concur with its conclusion. This implies a set of objective rules by which all must agree to abide. But we must realize that the main players involved will de facto impose on themselves such rules only if they are truly committed to them politically. They will commit to them politically only if they are sure that it is in their own self-interest to do so. Furthermore, the domestic pressures to which they may be subjected will require governments not only to have strength of purpose but also to obtain the agreement of the main political groups. Without such a commitment, the market will start making its own guesses and presumptions; speculation could then even be intensified by the existence of bands, thereby undermining the necessary foundation for further coordination.

Role of the Fund

The Fund has a vital mandate to be the global monetary authority. It should be fully empowered once again to fulfill this role. Of course, I do not envisage returning to the IMF of the postwar years. Circumstances today have radically changed. Indeed, it is precisely because circumstances have changed so much that the Fund must revitalize and adapt its oversight function. To stabilize the system through greater cooperation, as I have suggested, countries will need to observe certain rules of the game. I believe the Fund should be the institution responsible for enforcing such rules. Essentially, this would mean two things: first, the Fund would have to ensure that the convergence criteria and rules pertaining to macroeconomic fiscal coordination between countries are respected by all; and second, once exchange rate bands are introduced, the Fund should be the agent responsible for their surveillance. But let me reiterate that political commitment will be the key to success. The Fund's shareholders—especially the major ones—must be willing to strengthen the Fund's monetary role and commit themselves to binding rules for this scenario to become reality.

In parallel to an enhanced role in monetary surveillance, what the Fund can achieve and has achieved in the area of conditional lending to restore balance of payments equilibrium should not be forgotten. If anything, this role should also be strengthened and the Fund given the necessary resources. The Fund's conditional lending throughout the period of floating exchange rates—and particularly since the foreign debt crisis—has greatly helped developing countries achieve macroeconomic stability, reduce debt overhangs, restore growth, and thus strengthen the international financial system. The experience of Latin America is eloquent in this respect. Now the challenge has turned to the transitional economies of Eastern Europe and the former Soviet Union, and much still needs to be done there. The IMF must continue to play a vital role in this area.

Conclusions

The volatility, speculation, and misalignments that have shaken the international monetary system in recent years must not be allowed to continue. Governments must recognize that it is in their best interests to take concerted action, both at home and internationally, to regain international monetary stability. Of course, the international monetary system is the reflection of the present and at the same time a product of the past. Such systems evolve with people and time. It would be difficult to imagine a totally new system emerging today. What we must do is learn, adapt, and evolve. As Fred Bergsten put it, "the overriding lesson [of the postwar years] is that systemic stability cannot be taken for granted. It must be nurtured and constantly renewed."

The problem we face is not so much with the technical difficulties of a new system, it is the acceptance by countries—especially the larger industrial countries—of the notion that they must adopt national policies that aim to attain a better international balance.

Strength of purpose alone, however, will not guarantee success in achieving effective international coordination and discipline. Indeed, systemic coordination and stability will also inevitably require a broadly accepted "oversight institution" with sufficient authority to sustain the rules of the game. It is undeniable that the professionalism, independence, and expertise of the Fund offer the attributes to be the natural source of authority; the difficult issue is enforcement. The challenge ahead is the design of, and commitment to, the incentive and sanction framework required to ensure that member countries abide by the rules.

Concluding Remarks: Hans Tietmeyer

Jacques de Larosière has given us a brilliant analysis, and he is absolutely right in stressing, on the one hand, the need for national policies that strive for stability both nationally and internationally and, on the other, the important role the Fund has to play in surveillance.

Cooperation is important and will be even more important in the future. Whether there is a chance to move into a more formal system or into a more formal cooperation is really an important question that has to be discussed further.

11

Surveillance and the International Monetary System

The final afternoon began with a session on the role of IMF surveillance and, more specifically, on the functioning of the international monetary system. Two of the featured speakers had served in the late 1980s as deputies to their country's finance minister for the international economic cooperation and surveillance activities of the Group of Seven: Canada's Wendy Dobson and Japan's Toyoo Gyohten. Ms. Dobson subsequently became Professor of Economics at the University of Toronto and authored a book on international economic cooperation for the Institute for International Economics; Mr. Gyohten became Chairman of the Bank of Tokyo and co-authored a book on international cooperation with Paul Volcker. The third speaker, Jacob Frenkel, participated in the work of the Group of Seven in his capacity as Economic Counsellor and Director of Research at the IMF before leaving that post to become Governor of the Bank of Israel. The session was chaired by Maria Schaumayer, Governor of the Austrian National Bank.

Introduction

Opening the session, *Maria Schaumayer* remarked that the issues to be addressed included the role of Fund surveillance in overseeing policy formation, the role of exchange rate policy in promoting sustainable economic growth, and the implications of the liberalization and international expansion of private financial markets. It was clear that it was neither possible nor desirable to return to a global system of fixed exchange rates, however defined. It was also clear that the free flow of private capital put a premium on credible monetary and economic policies. By the same token, under liberalized and globalized conditions, there was a heightened awareness of the need for consistent and flexible economic policies.

In her view, the future surveillance task of the Fund might usefully be oriented toward a "flexible stability strategy": activating national commitment, providing in-depth research capacity and advice on policy formation, and offering guidance on the execution of formulated policy commitments. The world economy was facing new challenges, and the

Fund should—and could—put greater emphasis on its qualitative role, advising members on the best policy mix to achieve or safeguard orderly conditions. Sound policies were not themselves the aim, but experience had shown that they were necessary to promote sustainable growth and prevent financial crises, which increasingly had a propensity to become global.

Wendy Dobson

> . . .the essential purpose of the international monetary system is to provide a framework that facilitates the exchange of goods, services, and capital among countries, and . . . sustains sound economic growth . . . a principal objective is the continuing development of the orderly underlying conditions that are necessary for financial and economic stability. . . .
>
> *IMF Articles of Agreement, Article IV, Section 1*

These words in the IMF Articles of Agreement provide a vision for the IMF's surveillance role—a role that continues to be appropriate today.[1] Yet the vision of a world of efficient markets, sustained growth, and financial stability has not been realized. Fifty years after the Bretton Woods agreement, the institutions exist in a paradoxical and volatile world. It is one in which the growing interdependence of national economies implies the need for effective surveillance. Yet the world is also one in which the significance and credibility of national governments and intergovernmental institutions appear to be declining before a proliferation of interest groups at home and multinational firms and financial institutions pursuing their interests abroad.

The effect of these paradoxes is apparent in three aspects of surveillance on which I will focus. First, the preconditions for successful surveillance and policy coordination are increasingly difficult to meet because of the role that domestic interest groups play, particularly in fiscal policy formation. Second, the perennial debate about exchange rate arrangements needs to be recast in the light of developments in international business and finance. Third, capital flows, freed by regulatory changes and technological innovation, are now so large and swift that markets, rather than international financial institutions, have become a major source of discipline on domestic policies. Yet surveillance still has a key role to play in providing advice on good policy that will sustain economic growth and promote stability; surveillance also still faces a challenge to adapt the process to take advantage of, rather than to be at the mercy of, interest groups.

---

[1]Valued research assistance by Walid Hejazi is gratefully acknowledged.

Let us step back briefly to consider some of the changes in the world economy that affect the transmission of economic policies across national boundaries and, therefore, the functioning of the international trade and financial systems. One of the outstanding characteristics of many of the changes is that they are market driven. As governments have made way for the private sector to be the engine of growth, firms have gained clout as international players.

New industrial competitors have emerged from low-cost industrial bases in middle-income developing countries and the former centrally planned economies. Business strategies of multinational firms based in the industrial countries to meet the competition, to take advantage of production cost differentials, to supply goods and services in these burgeoning markets, and to overcome trade barriers and exchange rate uncertainties have contributed to surges of foreign direct investment that are deepening the links across borders. According to the UN, there are now 37,000 multinational firms with 200,000 foreign affiliates. Sales generated by foreign affiliates totaled nearly $5 trillion in 1991, more than the world's total exports of goods and services (United Nations Conference on Trade and Development, 1994, pp. 4–7). These flows of direct investment reduce the independence of governments by tying the world's economies ever closer together. Paradoxically, however, such flows are a manifestation of the increased independence of multinational firms. With business units in several locations, they are better able to insulate themselves from exchange rate volatility than if they existed in only one location.

A second and similar paradox is that the ability of the international monetary system to provide a stable framework is reduced by the size and volatility of private capital flows and the emergence of multiple regional focuses of economic activity and of multiple currencies. At the same time, however, the emergence of sophisticated financial management techniques, such as hedging, is increasing the ability of firms to insulate themselves from financial market volatility.

In this context, there are several lessons to be learned from experience with surveillance in the postwar period.

Surveillance and Policy Coordination in the Group of Seven

Surveillance, or policy consultation, was essential to the functioning of the par value system. It was intended that IMF oversight would ensure that domestic policies conformed with negotiated rules. When the par value system collapsed, the surveillance process was continued in a more informal way; rules were replaced by consultation and peer pressure to monitor performance and to encourage remedial measures judged necessary to adhere to shared values of fiscal responsibility and monetary stability. In this informal system, the IMF required domestic allies to promote desirable remedial action; the large and influential players had to be willing to take the lead in adhering to shared values. If they refused, or reneged, the moral authority of the informal system would be eroded. Subsequently, the large players formed the Group of Five and then the Group of Seven, which, in the second half of the 1980s, attempted closer coordination of policies to achieve greater exchange rate stability than had prevailed between the breakdown of the Bretton Woods system and the 1985 Plaza accord. The IMF was invited to participate in this initiative in a limited way.

Theoretical work on coordination indicated that there were gains to be made, providing certain preconditions existed: that participants agreed on their goals; that they had an agreed institutional framework; and that policymakers could deliver commitments they made to their partners. This early work also indicated that the gains from coordination—even if perfectly implemented—would be small relative to the collective gains from countries individually pursuing good, rather than bad, policies.

Beyond these issues, participants must agree to participate in surveillance of economic performance and policies. Surveillance requires agreed objective benchmarks against which to evaluate performance and policies and to define when corrective action is required and what that action might be. Policy bargains must be identified, consisting of policy changes that provide net benefits to the participants. Finally, sanctions are required for failure to carry out commitments.

Recent evidence indicates that few of these preconditions were met in reality. The goal of Group of Seven policy coordination in the 1980s was to restore sustainable world economic growth by reducing the obstacles to growth posed by large external imbalances. Yet attempts to coordinate were undermined by differing views among participants about how the world economy works. Perhaps more important, these attempts were undermined by differing views among participants in the same country; by erroneous forecasts that undermined the credibility of coordination, such as occurred after the 1978 Bonn summit and following the stock market crisis in 1987; by asymmetry in policy commitments; by such institutional factors as lack of continuity among major players and lack of accountability or effective sanctions; and by political factors, such as breaches of confidentiality that revealed differing interpretations of goals and commitments.[2] And, as at this conference, disagreements persisted over *how* to coordinate. Was the exchange rate to be the point of departure for analyzing the consistency of macroeconomic policies as in the Bretton Woods regime or the European Monetary System (EMS)? Or was the objective to adopt consistent macroeconomic policies that would ensure exchange rate stability?

---

[2]For more analytical detail on these observations, see Dobson (1991).

In purely practical terms, the starting points for the fixed and flexible exchange rate approaches will differ, but the end point should be the same: if there is pressure on exchange rates, eventually there must be agreement to intervene in foreign exchange markets and, if necessary, to change monetary and fiscal policies. Much of the practical problem arises in reaching agreement on the circumstances that require a change in exchange rates, since currency markets are not fully rational and currencies move in response to financial as well as real factors.

Exchange Rate Policies

The fixed but adjustable exchange rate regime was the cornerstone of the Bretton Woods system. Disappointment with flexible exchange rates since the collapse of the Bretton Woods regime has been widespread. Costs of exchange rate variability are considered to be high, as illustrated in the recent report of the Bretton Woods Commission (1994, p. A-4):

> The Commission believes that the costs of extreme exchange rate misalignment and volatility are high. When current exchange rates are misaligned, resources are misallocated; when exchange rates are unduly volatile, it creates uncertainty and productive investments are inhibited. Exchange rate misalignment adds to protectionist pressures from vulnerable industries in one major country after another as their international competitiveness waxes and wanes. Exchange rate volatility can be hedged away in today's sophisticated financial markets, but hedging involves costs, not all risks can be hedged, and not all hedges are perfect.

> Since the early 1970s, long-term growth in the major industrial countries has been cut in half, from about 5 percent a year to about 2.5 percent a year. Although many factors contributed to this decline in different countries at different times, low growth has been an international problem, and the loss of exchange rate discipline has played a part.

The underlying concern is that the floating exchange rate regime fails to provide an anchor for expectations of future exchange rates, thereby amplifying volatility and undermining capital formation and economic growth.

Rather than extending these familiar arguments, I have chosen to examine more closely evidence of the costs of exchange rate uncertainty. Evidence of trends in production, trade, and investment suggests that exchange rates may have less impact on the real economy than is commonly assumed. The validity of this assumption is important because in a rapidly changing world economy, the fixed or managed exchange rate alternative imposes costs of its own, since other channels of adjustment must be found.

We begin with evidence at an aggregated macroeconomic level and then move to business decision making. It is true that we have seen misalignments in major currency relationships—both within and outside the EMS system of fixed but adjustable rates—since the collapse of the Bretton Woods par value system: most recently, the U.S. dollar against both the yen and the deutsche mark in the early 1980s. Since 1987, however, a fair degree of stability has existed in relationships between the dollar, yen, and deutsche mark, as nominal relationships in the Chart show. In the past seven years (1987–94), deviations from the nominal means of the yen/dollar and deutsche mark/dollar exchange rates are symmetrical and have been narrowing.[3] In addition, growth of world trade and investment has outstripped the growth of world incomes since 1983 (United Nations Conference on Trade and Development, 1991, p. 4).

More specific microeconomic evidence of the real costs of exchange rate variability is inconclusive. An extensive review of available empirical evidence published by Edison and Melvin (1990) failed to find a conclusive impact on trade flows or harm to international investors. Indeed, the authors suggested international investors may actually prefer the distribution of returns under floating rates to that realized under fixed rates. More recently, the search has focused on the relationship between exchange rate uncertainty and investment. New theoretical work by Dixit and Pindyck (1994) on investment decisions under uncertainty shows that the timing of real investment is affected by an increase in uncertainty. In marginal investment decisions, uncertainty raises the required return on an investment. We do not, however, know what uncertainty will do to the average realized return on investment in the long run, since uncertainty can mean an increased probability of higher, as well as lower, returns. Dixit and Pindyck observe that it does not follow that countries with greater economic volatility will have lower ratios of investment to GDP. And indeed, it can be argued that in some cases firms facing an increase in volatility may reduce, not increase, waiting time on investments if the increased volatility raises the expected profitability of those investments.

Another important dimension of the debate about exchange rate arrangements is the impact of exchange rate variability on business decision making. Do firms find nominal exchange rate flexibility a burden in their decision making? Or can they cope? Little systematic evidence beyond the costs and benefits of hedging is available on the net effect of exchange rate arrangements on long- and short-term business plans. As Caves (1989) has pointed out, one of the reasons is that the theory of

---

[3]Deviation of the nominal yen/dollar exchange rate from its mean in 1987–94 has been between 22 percent and 24 percent; deviation of the deutsche mark/dollar exchange rate has been about 18 percent in the same period (author's calculations).

Nominal Deutsche Mark-Dollar and Yen-Dollar Exchange Rates
(Weekly averages)

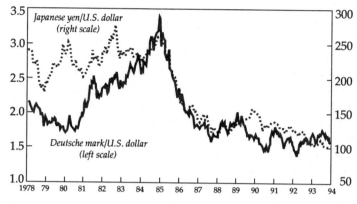

Source: Wharton Econometrics Forecasting Associates.

money neutrality implies that there is no real influence in the long run of a monetary variable such as the exchange rate. Nor are statistics readily available to study this aspect of behavior at the level of the firm.

To throw some light on this issue, I sought the views of nearly a dozen chief executive officers, corporate treasurers, and strategic planners in North American, European, and Japanese multinationals on their preferences and experiences with fixed and flexible exchange rate arrangements. Not surprisingly, they expressed a general preference for "flexible stability." Beyond that lay some interesting insights. Fixed and flexible exchange rate arrangements were viewed in terms of their impacts on short-term business behavior, such as trade, and on long-term direct investment decisions.

Beginning with fixed exchange rates, the perceived advantages included such factors as the absence of costs of currency hedging and the ability to set prices independently from monetary considerations. But the costs were reported to be considerable. Fixed exchange rates induce two illusions: one of the permanency of this key price, and another that it is a correct signal of purchasing power parities between any two economies. These illusions raise the risks of distorted price signals associated with misalignment, risks that are seen to be considerable, as investments made on the basis of false information can be disastrously wrong and difficult to change when currency revaluation eventually occurs. One of the issues here is the expressed lack of confidence in the authorities to make exchange rate corrections on a timely basis. As one chief executive officer put it, "I would prefer fixed exchange rates if I could be confident the authorities would change policies when this becomes necessary. But I do not have this confidence." The real implication of such distortions is that restructuring to raise productivity is deferred, and opportunities to relocate production in lower-cost locations are missed, with resultant loss of international market share and volume.

With flexible exchange rate arrangements, short-term decisions can be hedged. Hedging is costly, transferring profits to financial institutions in proportion to the magnitude of volatility. But the long-term implications are more favorable because corporations must form their own judgments about the overall economic environment and trends therein. With such a long-term view, they tend to stay more flexible and adaptable (since nothing can be taken for granted) than they do when exchange rates are fixed.

What about the role of exchange rates in longer-term decisions like foreign direct investment? Anecdotal evidence has its limitations, but, in general, exchange rate variability was not seen as a major factor in decisions on foreign direct investment. Rather, as in domestic investment decisions, what matters more are the prospects of future demand and the strategies of competitors. Foreign direct investment flows thus tend to vary with the business cycle. Although exchange rate variability adds to risks, it is only one factor among many considered, along with political and policy risks, such as changes in tax laws.

A further refinement refers to goods and services; exchange variability matters more when one is producing in one area and selling in another, which often happens with production of goods. In service industries, costs and revenues tend to be more closely matched in the host market.

It follows that exchange rate variability matters least to large multinationals. They can reduce many of the costs of hedging by internal matching. They can also locate production on both sides of major exchange rate relationships. Exchange rate variability matters more to small and medium-sized businesses, which have fewer financial options open to them and lack the experience, managerial capacity, and financial resources to anticipate and endure sudden changes in relative prices.

Other recent studies of the determinants of foreign direct investment are also instructive. Graham and Krugman (1993) searched for reasons for surges of direct investment such as have occurred periodically since the 1960s. Many observers have suggested that exchange rate changes, particularly the realignment of the yen and the dollar in the mid-1980s, triggered these surges. Graham and Krugman conclude that no single explanation is sufficient. Changes in corporate borrowing capacity and the availability of internally generated funds played a role, but follow-the-leader corporate behavior was also a factor, as was the existence of trade barriers and tax changes.

Other analysts have argued that yen appreciation in the mid-1980s triggered the surge of Japanese foreign direct investment into East Asia. Some argue that Japanese producers were forced offshore, which caused an undesirable "hollowing out" of Japanese manufacturing

(Ohno, 1994). Could it be, however, that the surge of outward Japanese investment was inevitable because of Japan's labor shortage and because of anticipated income and market growth in nearby Asian economies? Could it be that changes in relative prices resulting from exchange rate revaluation accelerated industrial restructuring and contributed to increased global welfare? The transfer offshore of labor-intensive operations has increased the overall efficiency and productivity of the Japanese economy. Flows of foreign direct investment into the Asian economies also have brought about transfers of technology and skills to the host economies and contributed to the diversification of their economic structures, creating higher-paying manufacturing jobs to replace jobs in traditional agricultural and service sectors.

The foregoing is a necessarily abbreviated discussion of the relationship between exchange rate variability and economic growth. The key point is that the evidence that exchange rate variability, per se, undermines economic growth is not conclusive. Indeed, recent IMF studies show how such a conclusion could be wrong (International Monetary Fund, 1994). Should we then be so certain that the world economy would be better off with managed or fixed rates? Perhaps more important is the fact that both growth prospects and exchange rate variability are affected by macroeconomic policies, and it is the challenge of achieving prudent policies on which our attention should focus.

The key concern for business and policy decision makers is that misalignments can occur with either floating or managed arrangements. When exchange rates float, the market can get it wrong. But when exchange rates are managed, the authorities can get it wrong. The difference is that when things are left to the market, firms are better prepared for uncertainty. As important, we have not eliminated uncertainty with managed rates; we have simply replaced the large probability of frequent small movements with a smaller probability of large movements. In addition, when we fix a major price like the exchange rate, we must find flexibility somewhere else in the system to ensure that adjustment occurs. Resorting to flexibility in the real economy through greater adjustment in labor markets or industrial and spatial distribution of economic activity is not easily obtained, as European experience attests; looking for flexibility in fiscal policy presents an even greater challenge, as the recent Group of Seven experience attests.

This skeptical view of the costs of exchange rate variability is not meant, however, to be a defense of the status quo. Rather, the skepticism relates to an appreciation of the costs of abandoning exchange rate flexibility in a world of rapid change in which the ability of governments and central banks to act quickly and decisively is waning. A system of generally floating rates among the major countries can help to cope with divergent cyclical positions and with real shocks. While major exchange rate movements have occurred, there is evidence that most of these movements could have been avoided if individual countries had followed sound fiscal policies. The key challenge is to find ways to encourage pursuit of good policy to anchor expectations of future exchange rates.

Implications of Financial Market Developments

Good policy becomes ever more important because of developments in financial markets. Today, financial markets are increasingly integrated and deregulated; one of the concerns for surveillance and the international monetary system is that although part of these capital flows represents investment in wealth-creating productive capacity, speculative activities have increased enormously, and skepticism of the ability of national authorities to maintain orderly markets has also increased.

Several major developments lie behind the rapid expansion of capital flows since the late 1960s. One is rapid developments in microcomputing and telecommunications technologies. Another is financial deregulation in the major countries and innovations in the supply of financial instruments. Another is the growth of investment demand and related developments in financial markets in China, India, and the middle-income developing countries.

These developments imply several issues for the future. The first issue is the prospect of a global shortage of capital as world growth momentum picks up in the mid-1990s. While industrial countries will grow at annual average rates of 2 percent, the developing economies are growing at average rates that are more than twice as fast. Huge investment requirements in infrastructure and enterprises are forecast; the IMF expects that investment in all developing countries from domestic and foreign sources will rise to 27 percent of GDP in the years ahead (International Monetary Fund, 1993). These countries, because of their current status of capital scarcity, will be attractive hosts for equity and portfolio flows from capital-intensive developed countries. But while some of this capital will be sourced in the industrial countries, many of these countries are struggling with heavy public sector indebtedness. Thus many of these savings requirements will have to be generated locally and channeled through nascent domestic capital markets. Equity and bond markets will have to be developed that are reliable and safe, and these markets, in turn, will have to be integrated into the global system of capital markets.

The second issue, in established capital markets among the industrial countries, is a different one. In these markets, much of the capital flows that influence exchange rate movements is speculative and moves in volumes that far outweigh capital flows that actually allocate the world's savings. Private speculators operating through the so-called hedge funds, which invest borrowed funds in high-risk, often highly speculative activities, distort exchange rate signals that influence trade, direct investment, and long-term portfolio investment.

These developments imply reduced macroeconomic policy autonomy for national authorities because of the magnitude and speed of capital flows. Central banks and international financial institutions like the IMF collectively lack the resources to offset speculative bets on weak currencies. Some senior observers have called for intervention to regulate and moderate such flows to restore a degree of national autonomy and to lengthen markets' time horizons. James Tobin's call for a tax on international currency transactions is one such proposal (for a recent statement, see Tobin, 1994). Henry Kaufman's call for intervention to lengthen the commitment of mutual fund investors is another (Kaufman, 1994).

But the deeper implication is that those who allocate private capital for speculative purposes are no longer particularly impressed by exchange market signals. The weakness during 1994 of the U.S. dollar against the Japanese yen is a case in point. Some participants believe the alignment of the two currencies is about right. Others point to two expectational factors about underlying policies to explain the persistent weakness of the dollar. One factor is nervousness about the possibility (however unlikely in fact) that the U.S. Administration might depreciate the dollar in reaction to the intractability of U.S.-Japanese trade frictions rather than move to correct the underlying saving-investment imbalance. The other factor is inflation expectations. The heavy public sector indebtedness of a number of industrial countries, including the United States, is a continuing concern. Although more industrial country central banks are gaining independence, financial market participants share a deep suspicion that governments will succumb eventually to the temptation to reduce the real value of their indebtedness by reflating. To anchor expectations, a credible combination of concerted intervention, coordinated interest rate changes, and more action on fiscal consolidation would probably be necessary.

Implications for Surveillance

What are the implications of these observations for surveillance and the international monetary system? I have argued that because market participants have more clout than national authorities, stability of exchange rates must be anchored in prudent and flexible domestic policies and in credible arrangements for international cooperation. I have also emphasized that because domestic interest groups are increasingly influential in democratic decision making, these arrangements should operate in ways that promote coalitions of interest between international financial institutions and domestic allies. The challenge for the future, therefore, is to redesign the IMF's system of surveillance to increase the credibility and weight of international peer pressure for sound domestic policies. I see six practical attributes of a future system that recognizes these realities and that observes the preconditions for successful cooperation identified at the beginning of this paper: agreed goals, institutional framework, and ability to deliver.

Surveillance Should Be Formalized Within the Fund

One of the main practical goals of a system of surveillance should be to promote among senior government officials the awareness of, and commitment to, good domestic policy. This important function should be taken out of the Group of Seven economic summit framework and rolled into a restructured IMF.[4] Private capital markets are now so prominent that the IMF has a diminishing number of instruments at its disposal to require policy changes, and these instruments tend to be most effective in managing rather than averting crises. Much, therefore, depends on the quality of debates and opportunities for exercising peer pressure. Treasury ministers would still participate in summit meetings, but on an accountability, rather than on a decision-making, basis (exchange rate decisions are almost always excluded from summit discussions anyway). Depoliticization in this way would also strengthen the case for greater central bank and treasury involvement in surveillance discussions. To encourage governments to accord the process the necessary credibility, surveillance discussions—as the Bretton Woods Commission has noted—should be reduced in frequency to ensure that the most senior officials with direct responsibility for policy formation and implementation participate, as well as carry out their responsibilities in capitals.

Exchange Rate Arrangements and Surveillance

As I have argued, the focus of surveillance should be good policy. Time and resources should be spent on understanding fundamentals. This is not to deny that exchange rates do move in ways that do not reflect economic fundamentals. Such circumstances, however, are difficult to recognize, especially during periods of rapid structural change. As Peter Kenen (1994, p. C-15) has pointed out:

> We return ineluctably to the quest for a system of stable but adjustable exchange rates—one that will preclude or minimize the risk of large

---

[4]The OECD would continue to focus on its review of industrial countries' overall economic performance, recognizing its heavy reliance on peer pressure to achieve changes in policies.

swings in real exchange rates due to interactions between policy mistakes and volatile expectations, but one that will not lead to the ossification of nominal exchange rates characteristic of the Bretton Woods System and of the European Monetary System in the late 1980s.

Kenen's goal is a sensible one, which takes account of the decision-making constraints that democratic governments face. Several proposals exist for stable but adjustable exchange rates, including Kenen's pragmatic approach. Another is Bergsten and Williamson's (1994, pp. C21–29) target zone proposal. As I have argued elsewhere, sophisticated proposals like Bergsten and Williamson's require levels of technical and operational involvement by national decision makers that it is not yet practical to achieve. In addition, attempts to maintain target zones would require a degree of linkage among monetary policies that does not exist. Indeed, current evidence suggests the opposite: national authorities accord greater weight to domestic than to international objectives in the conduct of monetary policy. Thus, we face a situation where exchange market intervention will continue to be ad hoc; where policy changes to restore order are possible but will also be undertaken on an ad hoc basis. In these circumstances, the quality of analysis and advice will be a critical factor in achieving consensus to act.

Surveillance Should Be Backed by Credible Analysis and Advice

The quality, credibility, and accuracy of policy advice will matter very much. A high priority of a future system of surveillance should therefore be to improve the basics of analytic capability, continuity, and accountability. The IMF has a respectable track record on this score. The credibility of its advice and its ability to act as an "objective referee" will be among the few levers it has to encourage good policy and performance in the large economies. Its analysis should also make greater use of scenarios that demonstrate the consequences of adopting or continuing undesirable domestic policies.

While much emphasis will be placed on policy analysis and discussions, exchange market developments will also be analyzed, but on a confidential basis. Actions to restore order in the markets involving the three major currencies would be even more confidential and directly involve the responsible authorities.

Surveillance Results Should Be Publicized

The Fund currently provides its technical and analytical advice on a confidential basis. Although confidentiality is necessary in exchange rate matters, when it comes to macroeconomic and structural policies, it may be a costly luxury. Informal surveillance requires domestic allies drawn from those groups that accept international responsibilities. When IMF prescriptions are kept confidential, it is difficult to build coalitions supportive of good policies. Surely, the time has come to make public the results of Article IV consultations. It has been argued that publicity can introduce moral hazard into the process because national authorities will hesitate to be candid. But it is possible to envisage that the prospects of publicizing Article IV consultations would have the opposite effect—especially when national authorities recognize that policies that contribute to international balance are also good domestic policies in the long run.

An alternative way to address this issue is for the Managing Director to create an independent global economic panel of wise people acting in their personal capacities to carry out analysis and issue public assessments of, and prescriptions for, desirable policies and performance among the Group of Seven countries. This mechanism would enhance the Managing Director's clout, help to depoliticize forecasts, and augment peer pressure with public pressure, possibly after a waiting period following confidential consultations.

Participation Should Be Broadened

Delegating surveillance to the IMF, reducing its secrecy, and increasing its professionalism are ways to increase the credibility of its policy advice. But surveillance also suffers at present from insider-outsider tensions. Since the world's largest economies and most dynamic markets include East Asian economies that are outside the Group of Seven and that are already developing cooperative mechanisms among themselves in the Asia Pacific Economic Cooperation (APEC) forum, the IMF should respond to these developments by creating mechanisms for including them more extensively in surveillance and in peer review. As participants in the Group of Seven have found, informality and frankness are the most valued aspects of the process, yet these attributes tend to decline as the size of the group increases.

The process should have two stages: one, which is decentralized, for consultation among groups of neighboring countries; and a second one at the global level for decision making. The constituency structure should be revised to promote consultations structured around two evolving groups: the Europeans (including the emerging economies of Central and Eastern Europe and Africa) and the APEC group (the United States and Japan and including Canada, Mexico, Latin America, China, and the other East Asian economies). Although the danger is that such structures increase regional awareness at the expense of the world economy, network structures of this kind would allow for more involvement and commitment to global consultation and policy coordination.

Crisis Management

One 30-year veteran has observed that the challenge is to create structures that are small enough to take action but large enough to involve all that wish to be involved. In order to take decisions or to act collectively in a crisis, the surveillance body would probably require an executive committee composed of the largest economies. At present, this body would be the Group of Seven, but provision will have to be made for it to evolve to include China, India, and other large economies that emerge as market-based economies in the next quarter century. If such a formula is not found, informal structures, operating outside the Fund, will inevitably spring up to fill the gap.

Conclusion

I believe I can conclude on a positive note. We are moving in the right direction, not away from it. National authorities have learned important lessons in the past 20 years. Central bankers know the value of price stability and are determined to contain and reduce cyclical inflationary pressures even if they are not ready to link monetary policies. Fiscal authorities are learning that, even though they would like to believe that fiscal policy is one of the last bastions of national sovereignty, persistence with bad domestic policies will eventually be disciplined by financial markets; such discipline provides much rougher justice than would peer pressure and cooperative action applied in preventive ways.

To adapt to the realities of a world in which the significance of national authorities is declining before interest groups and market participants, the political will in the large countries to cooperate is a necessary condition for successful management of the international monetary system. Such cooperation will be possible only when these countries are willing to adopt domestic monetary and fiscal policies that contribute to international balance. Unless they do this credibly, market participants will test their resolve, and the case for a more sophisticated system, in which exchange rates are managed on a systematic basis, will remain an elusive one.

References

Bergsten, C. Fred, and John Williamson, "Is the Time Right for Target Zones or the Blueprint?" in *Bretton Woods: Looking to the Future,* Vol. 1, *Commission*

Report, Staff Review, and Background Papers (Washington: Bretton Woods Committee, July 1994).

Bretton Woods Commission, *Bretton Woods: Looking to the Future*, 2 vols. (Washington: Bretton Woods Committee, July 1994).

Caves, Richard, "Exchange-Rate Movements and Foreign Direct Investment in the United States," in *The Internationalization of U.S. Markets*, ed. by David B. Audretsch and Michael P. Claudon (New York: New York University Press, 1989).

Dixit, Avinash, and Robert S. Pindyck, *Investment Under Uncertainty* (Princeton, New Jersey: Princeton University Press, 1994).

Dobson, Wendy, *Economic Policy Coordination: Requiem or Prologue?* (Washington: Institute for International Economics, 1991).

Edison, Hali, and Michael Melvin, "The Determinants and Implications of the Choice of an Exchange Rate System," in *Monetary Policy for a Volatile Global Economy*, ed. by William S. Haraf and Thomas D. Willett (Washington: AEI Press, 1990).

Graham, Edward M., and Paul Krugman, "The Surge in Foreign Direct Investment in the 1980s," in *Foreign Direct Investment*, ed. by Kenneth A. Froot (Chicago: University of Chicago Press, 1993).

International Monetary Fund, *World Economic Outlook* (Washington: Internatinoal Monetary Fund, 1993).

_____ , *World Economic Outlook* (Washington: International Monetary Fund, 1994).

Kaufman, Henry, "Structural Changes in the Financial Markets: Economic and Policy Significance," *Federal Reserve Bank of Kansas City Economic Review*, Vol. 79 (No. 2, 1994), pp. 5–15.

Kenen, Peter, "Ways to Reform Exchange-Rate Arrangements," in *Bretton Woods: Looking to the Future*, Vol. 1, *Commission Report, Staff Review, and Background Papers* (Washington: Bretton Woods Committee, July 1994).

Ohno, Kenichi, "The Case for a New System," in *Bretton Woods: Looking to the Future*, Vol. 1, *Commission Report, Staff Review, and Background Papers* (Washington: Bretton Woods Committee, July 1994).

Tobin, James, "A Tax on International Currency Transactions," in *Human Development Report 1994* (New York: Oxford University Press for the United Nations, 1994).

United Nations Conference and Trade and Development, *World Investment Report 1991: The Triad in Foreign Direct Investment* (New York: United Nations, 1991).

United Nations Conference on Trade and Development, *World Investment Report 1994: Transnational Corporations, Employment, and the Workplace* (New York: United Nations, 1994).

Toyoo Gyohten

Surveillance is not an invention of the 1980s and 1990s. Since the 1950s, it has been the main instrument to ensure the effective functioning of the international monetary system. Under the Bretton Woods regime, surveillance was conducted by the Fund as the key operation to restore international equilibrium and thereby ensure the stable functioning of the adjustable peg system of exchange rates; when a member country ran a serious external deficit and its currency came under pressure, the Fund conducted surveillance and—as it does now—urged the country to adopt the macroeconomic policies necessary to rectify the situation.

Until the early 1970s, because most countries except the United States were still vulnerable in their balance of payments positions and the financial support of the Fund was critically important, it was natural that member countries felt obliged to comply with the suggestions and the advice given by the Fund. In other words, a country in a state of imbalance agreed to give priority to the stability of the exchange rate over short-term domestic considerations.

Since that time, however, a series of events has taken place, such as the collapse of the Bretton Woods exchange rate regime, the important development of the EMS, and the end of the Cold War. These events brought about fundamental changes that altered the environment in which surveillance was expected to be performed. What were these changes? In my view, there were four.

First, the maintenance of global exchange rate stability, namely, the maintenance of the adjustable peg system, ceased to be the main objective of surveillance; we lost the clear target for the exercise.

Second, the international economic balance of power changed dramatically. Particularly, the position of surplus and deficit countries was reversed, with the United States becoming a major deficit country while other industrial countries and some newly industrializing countries became surplus countries. This change brought about a new problem. We now have to redefine how the burden of adjustment should be borne between surplus and deficit countries.

In the heyday of the Bretton Woods regime, with the United States virtually the only surplus country and with its overwhelming economic power, we took it for granted that the main burden of adjustment should be borne by deficit countries. However, what we see today is quite a different situation. Although the United States has become a major deficit country, the general tendency is to ask the surplus countries to bear the burden of adjustment because of the "benign neglect" policy of the United States and the global concern about slower growth and higher unemployment. This asymmetry, in my view, is a major cause of confusion for the surveillance process, particularly among major industrial countries.

Third, the U.S. dollar's predominance as the key international currency, with guaranteed value, has been eroded. The international monetary system has lost its anchor. Major currencies are floating against each other. Therefore, when we talk about exchange rate stability as a main objective of surveillance, we need to redefine what we mean by exchange rate stability.

Fourth, international financial markets have grown enormously in size, breadth, and fluidity. As a result, the monetary authorities' power to control the market has been seriously undermined. In that sense, the surveillance exercise among authorities is now faced with a new challenge, because surveillance was intended to achieve its objective through macroeconomic and exchange rate policies conducted by the authorities.

In these new circumstances, our first task is to redefine the purpose of surveillance. In order to argue that surveillance is still necessary in the new environment, we need to make the following three assumptions.

First, all countries want to maintain noninflationary and sustainable growth so that they can ensure a steady improvement of their people's welfare and contain unemployment. This assumption is a very valid one, and I think we can endorse it without reservation.

The second assumption is that all countries want to maintain the free flow of goods, services, and capital. I am not so sure about this second assumption, as we see some ominous signs of protectionism looming in different corners of the world. But, in a broader context, I think there is agreement on this point as well, at least in principle.

The third assumption is that all countries agree that excessive volatility and prolonged misalignment of exchange rates should be prevented. Again, I am not so sure that this assumption is valid. As we learned from the interesting exchange of views between Fred Bergsten and Stan Fischer yesterday, and as Wendy Dobson has just pointed out, there are different views on this point. But again, I think that there is a broad consensus that this assumption is accepted in principle.

If these three assumptions are endorsed, the purpose of surveillance in the new environment should be, first, to try to establish reasonable balance in each national economy so that serious international imbalances can be avoided and, second, to prevent systemic risk to the international financial market. As was the case in the aftermath of Black Monday in October 1987, there is no doubt that we need some mechanism to conduct surveillance rapidly and agree on prompt action to cope with such crises. Third, surveillance will be needed to cope with the excessive volatility and prolonged misalignment of exchange rates. The mechanism of surveillance for that purpose should be a kind of crisis management. It could well be different from the surveillance mechanism for the first and second purposes I mentioned.

It is a difficult practical problem to decide on the nature and number of mechanisms or forums we should establish to conduct surveillance for those purposes. In any case, I believe the Fund needs to perform the central role as a strong leader and a trusted umpire. In a broad context, we need three different forums: broad multilateral surveillance, within the framework of the Fund in the form of meetings of either Executive Directors or something like the Interim Committee; an improved Group of Seven or summit-type forum that will conduct surveillance for the largest, most important economies; and a forum established specifically for crisis management of exchange rates and financial markets.

In any of these forums, I believe that three basic requirements need to be met for the successful performance of surveillance. First, all participants must acknowledge the benefit of being a member of the surveillance mechanism. This may sound obvious, but it is an important starting point. Second, all participants must be prepared to accept surveillance and give it priority over short-term national policy objectives; in other words, they need to accept the disciplinary feature of surveillance. Third, recommendations produced as a result of the surveillance exercise should be at least intellectually convincing and should be practicable, provided that there is an adequate amount of political will.

Unfortunately, these assumptions and conditions are not fully endorsed at present. Therefore, we cannot take it for granted that, in today's circumstances, surveillance can function as the main instrument to support a stable international monetary system as it did in the heyday of the Bretton Woods regime.

Having said that, I do not want to sound too cynical or pessimistic, because as long as we agree on the need for closer international policy coordination for the global benefit—and I believe we do—we need to encourage efforts to conduct surveillance in a realistic way as an important and effective means of building mutual confidence and exerting peer pressure. In fact, we are already in that process. What is critically important now is to accumulate successful instances of surveillance. If and when we succeed in proving the usefulness of surveillance, we can create the environment in which it will function with greater authority and effectiveness.

I would like to put forward two practical suggestions to facilitate this process. First, participation of officials in the surveillance exercise should be as senior as possible, so that conclusions reached in the surveillance process can carry greater weight with policymakers and taxpayers in the country concerned. I can endorse fully what Wendy Dobson pointed out in this respect. The second suggestion is to explore ways to make surveillance more an issue of national interest. Unless a critical mass in the country concerned is convinced of the need for, and benefit of, surveillance, we cannot expect a meaningful outcome.

For this purpose, I would argue that some disclosure of the discussions held in the process of surveillance would be useful and necessary. If people at home are informed of what their representatives argued for at the surveillance meetings and how these arguments were received by other participants, they may recognize their country's position in a global context. The success of surveillance hinges on the crucial condition that voters and taxpayers understand the international implications of domestic policies.

In conclusion, in the increasingly interdependent and ever-evolving world economy, we should not simply dwell on the status quo.

Jacob Frenkel

When the great Princeton University economist Fritz Machlup started addressing a topic, he usually spent the first few minutes analyzing the title and going through a textual analysis of what was on the minds of those who suggested it. The topic of this session is surveillance and the international monetary system. One could speak about surveillance; one could speak about the international monetary system; one could speak about multilateral surveillance; and one could speak about Fund surveillance. I would like to address all of these topics, because each one of them has implications for the subject at hand.

To begin, I think that "surveillance" is a terrible word. Most of us who are used to speaking this language are not aware of all the connotations that this concept and this word carry. Surveillance gives the impression of a policeman chasing criminals. Surveillance means that somebody is looking after somebody, typically in a patronizing way. It means that one needs to coerce somebody who does not implement a commitment of one sort or another. It conveys the notion of dictatorial intervention, intrusion, arbitrariness, and an atmosphere of competition and rivalry between the policeman and those who want to run away. At least, these are the connotations in the English language, and I am told by my linguistic friends that surveillance carries a similar, although perhaps not as strong, connotation in French and other languages.

With this in mind, and if one looks at the Fund's history, one can detect that in the past, we have seen situations where the Fund allowed itself to be put in the position of an overzealous policeman, a "bad guy" from the perspective of those being treated like criminals, someone who always wanted to impose something. Therefore, criticizing the Fund became the norm and a legitimate style of intellectual exchange. Authorities negotiate with the Fund and then issue extreme criticisms domestically of this immoral, heartless, senseless, technocratic institution. More than one government has chosen to take the easy way out, telling the population that the Fund has forced it to take measures against its will. These are bad mistakes, economically and politically.

The fact is that economic programs, to be successful, require stamina. Therefore, governments that are not strong enough to sell the economic program as their own undercut their authority in the eyes of their own population and cannot be relied upon to implement the details of the program. This creates a syndrome in which the government cannot be relied upon to implement and therefore somebody must coerce it. This is not a constructive atmosphere for an ongoing effort, unless one believes that the job of the Fund is to offer a quick fix: to come in, make its point, and get out. History suggests that that is the wrong perspective.

I would say that surveillance should give way to concepts of cooperation, partnership, and consultation; of bringing on board the rest of the world's considerations. With this perspective, many questions that the Managing Director raised in his opening remarks and that have come up in the discussions throughout this conference also can be cast more constructively.

Why should the Fund be so deeply involved in surveillance? I think this is so because it is the organization with institutional memory—an asset of considerable value not only to historians but also to member countries' authorities, who tend to repeat mistakes and tend to forget the lessons of the past. The Fund is there with its objective capacity to bring about institutional memory. The Fund brings to the process experts, an extensive data base, and the like.

This brings me to the subject of Article IV consultations. First, should one publish consultation reports? I do not see why not. In my view, the Fund should publish reports but give member countries the prerogative to ask the Fund not to publish a specific report. I think we would see an interesting competition, in which most countries would have their Article IV consultation reports published, and outliers would feel embarrassed to ask the Fund not to publish. Much less secretive elements would come into play, and there would be much broader knowledge of what the Fund is really doing.

Those of us who spent our professional lives at university before coming to public service really did not know how the Fund operates, because of its low-key, behind-the-curtains approach. I think that we can create a club of those who are proud to have their consultation reports published, and it will be a universal club in the long run.

Second, the impact of Fund policy advice ultimately depends on its quality, and therefore there should be a sharper distinction drawn between the Fund as a financial resource and the Fund as a resource for knowledge and professional expert advice. I think that, in the long run, the financing aspect of the Fund will need to diminish as the other elements will need to come to the fore, because there is no way that, in serving the financial needs of the future and facing the development of private capital markets, the Fund can have a strong enough impact.

If that is so, there may also be a way to bring the Group of Seven back into the Fund in the fundamental sense of using the Fund's expert advice in a more operational way. For a long time there has been a feeling that somehow, perhaps because of developments in the 1970s and 1980s, the Fund moved away somewhat from being a major partner, a major player with the industrial countries. A country had to be a user of Fund resources in order to be in an ongoing relationship with the Fund. But if one defines resources not in a financial way but in a more conceptual way, as knowledge and expert advice, then the industrial countries will also become users of Fund resources. This will bring back the importance of Article IV consultations and will move the Fund closer to its original purposes.

One way to elevate the role of the Article IV consultations would be to introduce it more explicitly into the discussions within the Group of Seven. As those countries are both major shareholders in the Fund and major participants in the international monetary system, they should be the first to take an interest in having at their disposal the conclusions of the Article IV consultations with member countries during their own deliberations. At the present time, this information is not introduced as explicitly as it should be.

A second way to strengthen the role of consultations is to promote continuity. Even for a country that is a user of Fund resources, although there is an ongoing consultation, there are on-and-off negotiations, ministers come and go, and the staff comes and goes. For a nonuser of Fund resources, the consultation is an annual event (now that, fortunately, the bicyclic procedure has been dropped).[5] To promote greater continuity, I would propose that each Article IV consultation start with a more detailed analysis of the previous year's consultation. The discussion could perhaps be opened with a scorecard of where the country is, compared with the recommendations of the previous round. Is the economy moving forward? The reality is that ministers change, governors change, but the Fund is always there. Institutional memory is required, and this would be one way to improve it.

The Managing Director asked yesterday morning how growth-generating features of Fund-supported programs can be strengthened. I think we should begin by dispelling four interrelated myths. When one talks about the Fund, it is often suggested that there is a distinction between the short and the long run; between crisis management, which is said to be the role of the Fund, and long-term development, the role of the World Bank; between the Fund's role in macroeconomic matters and the Bank's involvement with structural policies; and, similarly, between stabilization and growth.

These are fallacious distinctions. One cannot start a stabilization program that will generate growth unless, from the beginning, one keeps in

---

[5]The bicyclic procedure, which was introduced in 1987 for a limited number of countries, provided for a discussion by the Executive Board only every other year, with a simplified consultation in the intervening year. It was dropped in 1993 in response to concerns that it might have weakened the continuity and evenhandedness of Fund surveillance.

mind that the goal is not just extinguishing a fire but resuming growth later. To do this, some concerns need to be redirected. The Fund has exerted a lot of effort in assessing budget deficits. Clearly, excessive budget deficits are a serious problem. But a budget deficit means very different things depending on the composition of government spending and of taxes. Government outlays on investment in infrastructure or education have a very different impact on the economy and on generating growth from outlays on consumption and wasteful activities. Similar considerations apply to taxes, such as whether they are levied on the business or the personal sector.

When the Fund started focusing more on the design of programs and on the composition of government spending and taxes, the question naturally arose whether it was too intrusive for the Fund to express a view to governments about those intimate domestic matters. I think that the very way of posing this question—of being too intrusive—belongs to the old regime, under which surveillance meant the policeman pursuing the criminal. If, on the other hand, surveillance means partnership, cooperation, advice, and expert know-how, there is nothing too intrusive when the institution draws on the lessons that it has learned from its own experience and that of its member countries.

Should the Fund encourage further moves in capital market liberalization, the Managing Director asked yesterday. The reality is that most links between countries today operate through the capital account: this is where the massive flows occur and where most of the action takes place. Therefore, I would put the question somewhat differently, taking for granted that countries are linked through the capital account.

I remember the days when it was felt that perhaps countries are linked too closely, and that we should "put sand in the wheels." That was a mistake then, and I believe it is also a mistake now. As every mechanic knows, if you put sand in the wheels, it is very difficult to take it out. The solution, if traffic is moving too fast and accidents may occur, is not to close the roads but to widen and open them. If we are worried about accidents, then safety belts are called for. So, if we are opening up—and we should be—obviously the regulatory system has to be in place, and the supervisory system has to be in place, but we should not put sand in the wheels.

What then should we add to our policy advice as we take it for granted that openness is going to be the basic focus of the advice? That brings us to the question of protection. A lot of attention is devoted to reducing trade protection: through the General Agreement on Tariffs and Trade (GATT), the North American Free Trade Agreement (NAFTA), and similar efforts. In a world in which exchange rates are flexible (if I may take the extreme case to make the point clear), the capital account is just the mirror image of the current account. Therefore, in principle, if a country is worried about sanctions imposed by the GATT or the World Trade Organization if it enacts protectionist trade measures, it can achieve the same results by putting restrictions on the capital account, because the two are just mirror images. I am not necessarily proposing here a new institution, an analog to GATT, but the concept of capital account protection is clearly the counterpart to normal trade protection.

Moving to the next topic, I will make just two brief remarks about the concept of the international monetary system. Incidentally, although some people refer to it as a nonsystem, there is a fundamental contradiction in the concept of a nonsystem. A system merely links parties or components into something that may be more or less synchronized, but it is nonetheless a system.

The international monetary system, or the exchange rate system, has n currencies and, as Robert Mundell told us long ago, n minus 1 exchange rates. There is always one degree of freedom in a system that links n currencies. Only n minus 1 countries can choose what exchange rate they want to pursue, and the nth country is the extra. The Bretton Woods system was very explicit about how the world would use this degree of freedom: all countries would peg to the U.S. dollar, and the system would use its degree of freedom by having the dollar pegged to gold. So the system had consistent features. I would suggest that any system, whether based on target zones or some other key, must be explicit about how to use the degree of freedom that is left. If we are not explicit about it, something is missing in the characteristics of the system.

How do we judge whether a system is good or bad? There are basically two perspectives. Either we could say that a system is good if it normally works acceptably well, or we could presume that any system normally works and conclude that the proper test is whether a system can handle crises and other abnormal situations. This second perspective will give us a very different criterion. The analogy here is the story of the architect who, having noticed that under normal conditions, all buildings stand very solid and rigid, concluded—with disastrous results—that in order to withstand storms he must build very rigid buildings. The criterion for judging the merit of a system is how it operates in a crisis; what is the safety valve that will absorb severe disturbances? I am also reminded in this context of U.S. President Truman's dictum: "If it ain't broke, don't fix it." There is a real question of whether to fix the present system and of how to know whether the system works or not.

I will conclude with a quote from John Maynard Keynes. Fifty years ago, at the closing ceremony of the Bretton Woods conference, he said, "I am greatly encouraged, I confess, by the critical, skeptical, and even carping spirit in which our proceedings have been watched and welcomed in the outside world. How much better that our projects should *begin* in disillusion than that they should *end* in it!" That was 50 years ago, and I think that we are ready for the next round.

General Discussion

Jacques Polak remarked that Frenkel's reference to Fritz Machlup's methodology raised an interesting point about the Fund and surveillance. The original Articles of the Fund did not mention surveillance. There was a very good reason for that: the original Articles embodied a system, the par value system, that countries had been expected to obey; thus, the system had included punishments for nonobedience, as France had discovered in 1948. It was only after the par value system had disappeared and the Fund had, to a large extent, lost its surveillance power over its members that it had introduced into Article IV the dictum that "the Fund shall exercise firm surveillance over the exchange rate policies of members . . . ." Since then, it had been trying to find a way of exercising that firm surveillance.

The bravest attack on Fund surveillance was the period during which it had appeared as if the Group of Seven was exercising surveillance over its own members. He was grateful to Wendy Dobson, who had written a book on that issue, for her recognition of the fact that the Group of Seven countries had not been able to exercise firm surveillance over themselves, and for her conclusion that the surveillance function should be taken back by—not given back to—the Fund.

It was an illusion to believe that the Group of Seven would conduct its meetings by reviewing carefully the policies of the members of its group and, through peer pressure, exercise surveillance. At its most effective, the Group of Seven had succeeded only in an occasional case of arm-twisting, not surveillance as such. The Fund's acceptance of its role of exercising surveillance over all its members did not mean that there was no role for the Group of Seven; as Dobson had correctly said, there was an important role for the Group in pursuing common purposes with respect to the system, and he was confident that it would continue to do just that.

With that in mind, it was regrettable that Dobson had retreated somewhat from her earlier position, namely, the primacy of Fund surveillance over all its members. In her presentation, she seemed to suggest that surveillance should be decentralized, with surveillance over Europe by one group and surveillance over Japan and the United States by another group. There was a strong case for arguing that if the Fund were to have responsibility for surveillance, it should be conducted by the Fund, not by a subcommittee.

Dobson replied that shortage of time had forced her to be a bit cryptic in her presentation. She had not retreated from her earlier position on surveillance. Rather, she had suggested a two-stage process, the first of which might be based on regional consultation, given that learning and sharing were valued elements of the surveillance process. She did not see surveillance decisions themselves, evaluative or otherwise, being taken in regional groups. Formal surveillance would still be conducted at a senior level in what she would expect to be a revamped Fund, by a body analogous to the current Executive Board.

Peter Kenen observed that the focus of the discussion had been on Article IV consultations, essentially a bilateral process of consultation between the Fund and the individual member and a subsequent discussion of that consultation in the Executive Board. Another issue was involved, however, which Dobson might have had in mind: the exchange rate relationships among the large industrial countries must be discussed with them jointly.

It was one thing to discuss with a small country its exchange rate vis-à-vis its largest trading partner, which was, in a sense, a one-sided story. It was not meaningful, however, to talk about "the" dollar rate: there was a dollar/yen rate, a dollar/deutsche mark rate, and so on. In every case, a collectivity of exchange rates among a group of major countries was involved. The same was true within the EMS. Thus, it was not enough to contemplate an intensification of the bilateral process; it was necessary to consider a strengthening of the process of consultation between the Fund and those countries, whose exchange rate relationships, together, were key to the functioning of the system.

Frenkel considered that the perspective that Kenen had provided was correct. To assess exchange rates among the major industrial countries, it was necessary to include all parties in the discussion. In a sense, that structure was approximated by allowing for the participation of the Managing Director of the Fund as the representative of the rest of the world.

Implicit in the present discussion was an idea that Fred Bergsten had touched on earlier. In the early days, the discussions on exchange rates among major industrial countries had focused on the management of exchange rate intervention—issues largely of a technical nature. As time passed, it came to be recognized that it was not sufficient to focus on exchange rate intervention without discussing the basic economic policies underlying exchange rate behavior. That realization had brought about the discussion of economic policy coordination.

The semantic debate about cooperation versus coordination, illustrated most vividly by contrasting the German and French views, was also very telling. The view of some officials was that they could not deliver on commitments that were made in such a forum, or that they did not believe that such a forum was appropriate for discussing the details of economic policymaking. In their view, the aim was not coordination but rather cooperation—exchanging views, data, assessments, and objectives.

That debate was still open, in the sense that some of the countries participating in those discussions believed that there was more to coordination than just cooperation. Some, however, believed that all that could be hoped for was cooperation. Since the strength of the chain depended on the weakest link, the fact that one of the major countries believed that the coordination mechanism meant cooperation ensured that that view would prevail, which was the situation today.

Toyoo Gyohten commented that Kenen was right in pointing out that there were several aspects of surveillance. It was probably not possible to cover all its aspects in one forum, which was why he had put forward the idea of a three-level surveillance mechanism. In dealing with exchange rates in the context of a financial market crisis, for example, the forum would need to be more compact, efficient, and flexible than other, somewhat larger forums.

Salvatore Zecchini, referring to Frenkel's comments on the evolution of the Fund toward being a provider of expert advice rather than financing, wondered how effective such advice could be if it were detached from financing.

On the issue of publicity, a policy of openness should be phrased in terms of providing either full and adequate information or no information at all, since partial information might be misleading, particularly to the markets. Markets did not always have full information, of course, which occasionally led to market-induced misalignments. In the case of the exchange rate mechanism of the EMS, for example, the exchange rate relationship between the French franc and the deutsche mark had been put under pressure on occasion, owing perhaps to a lack of adequate information.

With respect to Gyohten's point about the goal of the international monetary system, namely, to prevent imbalances vis-à-vis other countries, it was useful to bear in mind that imbalances could be good or bad. Gyohten's point hinged on the concept of the sustainability of imbalances and, in particular, the extent to which the exchange rate mechanism was part of a process aimed at making good imbalances sustainable.

Klaus Engelen recalled that, among the themes to emerge from the May 1994 conference organized by the Institute for International Economics, two specific points stood out in the context of the present discussion. The first, which might come as a surprise to some, was that Germany's relationship with the Fund in the early days was not without problems. The second point was that some German officials had felt that a careful reading of the original Articles of Agreement of the Fund suggested that the Fund would be in existence for only a limited time. Perhaps that perception changed with the establishment of the General Arrangements to Borrow in 1962.

In looking at the more recent history of the Fund, one was struck by the extent to which the Fund had not been able to put pressure on the major European or Group of Seven countries on such key issues as exchange rate misalignments, whether in the context of the recent EMS crises or the earlier overvaluation of the U.S. dollar. With that experience in mind, he wondered whether the Fund would be able to find a way, as de Larosière had proposed, to convince the major countries to accept an international role for the Fund. In a sense, the Group of Seven was acting in much the same way as the United States had done under the Bretton Woods regime. Although the Group of Seven might well be reduced to a Group of Three, key countries, and not the Fund, would probably continue to make the rules for the next 50 years.

Gyohten, responding to Zecchini's point about the link between the exchange rate and sustainable internal balance, observed that while exchange rates could produce changes in economic performance, they also reflected economic performance. Thus, there was a two-way relationship. In urging that countries aim to improve the internal balance, he had in mind that each country should try to maintain a reasonable balance between domestic savings and investment at the highest possible level. If each country were successful, the exchange rate would reflect the fundamentals, namely, the inflation rate and the productivity of the respective countries.

Dobson remarked that the persistent differences of view on surveillance among participants in the present conference were informative. In her view, the way forward was very much through what Frenkel had usefully relabeled a cooperative process, facilitated by the Fund. The process would remain informal until the major countries were willing to accept a role for an objective referee.

Frenkel said that he would not be surprised if participants in a conference commemorating the one hundredth anniversary of Bretton Woods were to have a discussion along the lines of the present debate. The difficulty in reconciling the two sides of the debate had less to do with the inability of academics and other observers to design elegant solutions than with the realization that, in the end, international monetary relations involved an element of judgment. The standard debate about fixed versus flexible exchange rates, for example, would probably always be characterized by proponents of one system pointing to the weakness of the other. Thus, among the chief executive officers expressing a preference for "flexible stability" to whom Dobson had referred in her presentation, no doubt there were those who really preferred "stable flexibility." Therefore, it would be naive to believe that further, even exhaustive, discussion of the issues would point to a single system; the solution to the dilemma had to be earned, so to speak, through good economic policies.

12

Preparing for the Future

This session brought together a distinguished panel of senior policymakers from different regions of the world to discuss the lessons that had emerged from the conference for the future work of the Bretton Woods institutions. Kenneth Clarke, the Chancellor of the Exchequer of the United Kingdom, introduced and moderated the discussion. His opening remarks were followed by statements from the four panelists, each of whom played a key role in major economic transformations in his own country: Kwesi Botchwey, the Minister of Finance of Ghana; Moeen Qureshi, who has served both as a Senior Vice President of the World Bank and as Prime Minister of Pakistan; Leszek Balcerowicz, former Deputy Prime Minister and Minister of Finance of Poland; and Paul Volcker, former Chairman of the U.S. Federal Reserve System.

Introduction

Kenneth Clarke noted that the challenges currently facing the Bretton Woods institutions were as demanding as any they had faced since their establishment, although the institutions themselves had already changed a great deal. The issues under discussion in the present session promised to dominate much of the agenda of the ministerial meetings in Madrid.

A number of issues touched on in earlier sessions remained to be resolved, such as the extent to which the Fund should be actively involved in encouraging the liberalization of capital markets throughout the world. In addition to asking the panelists to make progress in dealing with that issue, he asked for reactions to his recent proposals for alleviating the multilateral debt burden of the poorest, most severely indebted countries, proposals that were intended to build on the advances that had already been made to secure Trinidad terms for those countries burdened with bilateral debt. It would also be useful to explore the more general issues related to the development work of the Fund and the World Bank—conditionality, structural adjustment, and so on, that had been frequently debated. Finally, he suggested that panelists might also wish to consider whether both the Fund and the Bank should enhance their efforts to encourage private capital inflows and activities of the private sector more generally, alongside the development and support of public sector activities in developing countries.

Kwesi Botchwey

It is an honor and a privilege to have been invited to speak at this conference. Ghana, as is well known, was not represented at the Bretton Woods conference whose fiftieth anniversary we are celebrating here. Indeed, it was not to become a sovereign nation until a full 13 years after the conference. Therefore, in a certain sense, my very participation in these proceedings is testimony to the great transformation that the Bretton Woods institutions have undergone. But more important, it is a pleasure to participate in these proceedings because Ghana has benefited immensely from 12 years of very close relations with the Fund and the Bank in terms of both financial and technical assistance. We therefore know firsthand that there is more than ample cause for celebration.

Let me begin by associating myself entirely with all those who have rightly applauded the authors of the Bretton Woods system and the great achievements that have been recorded over the past 50 years in world output, trade, and the quality of life in general. But even as we applaud these achievements, it is important that we critically review the working of the system as we prepare for a future laden with so much promise and yet so much challenge. I should like in this connection to offer an African perspective.

But first, I would like to make a few general remarks. There clearly is an urgent need to strengthen international coordination of macroeconomic policy. The case for such coordination is in my view self-evident and compelling. As many commentators have noted, the consequences for global economic activity and interest rates of uncoordinated monetary contraction among the Group of Seven countries in the early 1980s contributed, in no small measure, to the Third World debt crisis. Developed countries, whose domestic policies have such a trenchant effect on the world economy and thereby on other countries, must not be allowed to do what they please merely because they do not draw on Fund resources. Some mechanism for monitoring and enforcement must be part of the coordination system, and I agree with those who suggest that the institutional agency for such coordination should be the Fund—a more democratic Fund—and not the Group of Seven.

I also support the view that for low-income countries, especially those in sub-Saharan Africa, the Fund and the World Bank will need to provide more, not less, vigorous financial support to compensate for private capital flows, which for these countries are likely to continue to be weak for some time to come. The Bank and the Fund can also offer useful advice to these countries to help them reduce their vulnerability to commodity price instability through more aggressive use of futures and options markets.

Now, let me turn to the role of the World Bank and the Fund in sub-Saharan Africa. By most accounts and assessments, including the World Bank's, the medium- to long-term outlook for Africa is one of unrelenting gloom. As the Bank's President, Mr. Preston, reminded us yesterday, the sub-Saharan region is the only one in which poverty is actually projected to increase by the end of this century. It is almost as if this is the working of some iron law, as if the African lion is condemned perpetually to lag behind the general advance, to surge forward at best occasionally, but then quickly to relapse helplessly into some predestined backwater. But we know that no iron laws are at work. Indeed, not too long ago China and the East Asian countries, whose miraculous successes we now cite with such salivating approval, were themselves regarded with the same pessimism. Today, their successes are considered so rapid and so grand that even their mistakes are sometimes presented as "creative" policy responses.

That sub-Saharan Africa is a subregion in travail, no one can deny. But it is important to appreciate that in this subregion too, a change or turnaround is not just possible, it is happening in many countries, thanks in part to the active support of the Bretton Woods institutions and the donor community at large.

The experience of Ghana over the last 12 years—and Ghana is not alone in this regard—offers an excellent example of this turnaround. Through sustained domestic policy reform designed to stimulate growth and ease impediments to factor mobility and productivity, and with international support from multilateral and bilateral sources, we have succeeded in reversing more than a decade of negative growth, which saw incomes fall by over a third and saving and investment ratios decline to negligible levels. Real GDP growth has averaged about 5 percent a year, imports and exports have more than doubled, and revenues have expanded many times over, enabling us to increase expenditure on education and health. Comprehensive structural reform covering the civil service, and the public sector as a whole, as well as a major overhaul of the financial sector, is under way. Thanks to a rapidly growing stock market and a highly successful recent international flotation, Ghana is today cited among the world's most promising emerging markets. Contrary to the fears of the skeptics, these fundamental changes have not been imperiled in any way by the transition to multiparty democracy, which was successfully accomplished in 1992.

In listing these gains, my purpose is not to hawk the glory of Ghana's adjustment experience. Indeed, a great many difficulties remain. It is to say that change is possible and also to acknowledge the role of the Fund and World Bank in the achievement of Ghana's turnaround.

Let me now conclude by looking at some specific areas in Fund and Bank practice where improvements are needed to expedite the delivery and enhance the effectiveness of assistance to reforming countries.

First, it is important to appreciate that reform or adjustment programs do not, and indeed cannot, define the entire context of the national development effort. If things are done right, they must be located in and therefore be informed by a long-term national vision defined by the country itself and anchored in a broad national consensus. Again, it must be left to the country itself to decide how this consensus is to be forged.

Second, the programs must be "homegrown" or "owned" by the adjusting country. This is now widely agreed, but there is a danger of this perfectly agreeable aphorism simply being intoned by the parties as they walk to the negotiating table, like an incantation, designed—as most incantations are—to free them from the tedious obligation to think through what they are saying. Fund and World Bank staff and the authorities must understand and accept this idea of ownership with all that it implies for program content, timing, and sequencing. But what does ownership mean exactly? It must mean above all that the authorities agree with and see the program objectives as being fully consistent with their goals, as something that they need to do on their own, not as some imposition they must accept because they "need the money" and have no other choice. If differences exist between, say, the Bank and the country over any particular aspects of the reform package, they must be resolved through dialogue.

These observations are particularly relevant in adjustment lending, and the worst case of derogation from country ownership is where the World Bank seeks to lure the country into accepting the Bank's preferred package by promising additionality or front-loading of tranche releases or some other incentive. When this happens with an adjustment loan and its financial flows are built into an entire macroeconomic program, it follows that macroeconomic projections are made based on an agreed growth target, export projections and import elasticities, and capital flows. The adjustment operation then becomes in a sense the channel through which financing is provided; if there is any delay in the fulfillment of tranche conditionality for whatever reason, the whole macroeconomic program is thrown off balance. As all adjustment loans have a general macroeconomic stability condition, the macroeconomic imbalance caused by the nondisbursement of a "main" tranche from a principal adjustment loan cascades through all other adjustment loans by means of the general conditionality. If in the mean time bilateral grants are attached to this principal adjustment loan, the crisis affects not only the foreign exchange cash flow but also the financing assumptions of the budget as grants become unavailable for financing. The program is then crushed under the weight of a labyrinth of cross-conditionality and multiple conditionality as lawyers and country economists haggle over whether conditions have been met. This is no way to run an economy, and the World Bank especially should explore less disruptive ways of tying in financing gaps with policy reform over a medium-term framework, and in ways that make these flows more predictable.

Third, there is a more general need to review the entire concept and working of conditionality, especially if the Bank's preoccupation with slow disbursements should lead to an intensification of the conditionality hassle instead of its rationalization. The least we should do then is to make conditionality less susceptible to mechanical legal interpretation. In this connection, privatization targets, for example, can be very awkward indeed. When do we say, for instance, that a state enterprise has been divested? When a sale agreement is signed with a willing buyer? When he pays the purchase price in full? What if he changes his mind? What if no buyers come at all? Where conditionality is not met, there must not be a rush to blame it on a lack of political will by the authorities. Instead, a principled appraisal of all the relevant conditions that affect program implementation must be undertaken, and the result accepted by all parties. Waivers must then be granted where the circumstances warrant, without any hidden costs to the country or indeed to the staff arguing the case before the Executive Board of the institution!

Finally, there has been a certain surge in bilateralism through tied-aid export credits and donor funds, which, for whatever reason, have to be allocated administratively rather than through the market. A frank review of these arrangements by the Bretton Woods institutions and donors is called for.

I should like to conclude by saying that there is a welcome process of change under way in Africa that needs to be deepened and accelerated, especially in the areas of domestic resource mobilization, through further work on nonbank financial intermediaries and more aggressive private sector promotion. The World Bank especially will need to clear its resource delivery channels to improve their effectiveness.

Moeen Qureshi

We all agree that the world has undergone dramatic changes over the past 50 years. What is less clear is how these changes should affect the mandate and the operations of the Bretton Woods institutions.

I believe that the fiftieth anniversary of the Bretton Woods institutions is first and foremost an occasion for celebrating their contribution toward shaping the world as it is today, and toward improving the welfare of its people. The world community owes them an enormous debt

ıe. As Prime Minister González said yesterday, "if these insti-
did not now exist, they would have to be created" (Chapter 2).
however, is not the issue before us. The issue is how these institu-
s should prepare to respond to the emerging issues and challenges
oı the future.

What are those challenges? For the World Bank, I would list five key
areas.

First, I believe it is becoming more and more necessary for the Bank to
define more clearly how it intends to pursue its fundamental mandate
in the future. The World Bank's task, as originally defined in its Articles,
was to foster long-term development. It did this by providing access for
developing countries to long-term capital for development, together
with some useful advice on how to use that capital. Now, the agenda of
the Bank appears to be increasingly influenced by the political preoccu-
pations and concerns of some of its shareholders. These shareholders
would like to see the Bank become much more proactive in advancing
the cause of democracy or human rights, or curbing military spending,
or promoting whatever worthy objective seems most appealing to the
more vociferous of their domestic political constituencies and lobbies.
In most cases, these are desirable objectives, but, however laudable they
may be, they tend to diffuse the Bank's central development thrust, po-
liticize its image, and diminish its effectiveness.

The World Bank is a global institution with many members, and its
programs must be responsive to their diverse requirements. In many of
the poorest developing countries, the alleviation of poverty through investment in people and the pursuit of comprehensive reforms that promote broadly based growth must take the highest priority. In some of
the more advanced developing countries, the Bank has a somewhat different role and priority, which is not dissimilar to that which it performed after World War II: to reinforce their private sectors and to facilitate their access to capital markets. In all countries, the Bank must
promote the cause of the environment. The important point, however, is
that in each country the Bank must remain focused on the strategic tasks
that will advance its central development role and not pander excessively to the many political pressures pushing it to cover a broad canvas
of ill-conceived sociopolitical causes.

Second, I believe that the greatest future development challenge for
the World Bank lies in Africa, where the intensification of poverty and
the related environmental degradation threaten the breakdown of societies and heighten the potential for civil conflicts. By virtually every measure of human well-being, the African continent ranks the lowest. The
world community must come to grips with this problem, and the World
Bank must prepare itself to play a leading role in such an endeavor.

Third, I agree very much with Mr. Preston that development is not
just about economics, it is also about governance. The World Bank must

continue to insist on a process of reforms—where these are need̲ pecially in the area of governance, as a precondition for providing ı̲ sistance. The best-laid economic plans and policies will be frustrated̲ poor governance. The Managing Director of the Fund has put it very incisively. He has said that the bottom line of development is to reform the government. The Bank must be prepared to take a strong position on governance issues and to deny its support to those governments in which an unwillingness or inability to improve governance is an obstacle to economic progress.

Fourth, the World Bank needs to devise new ways of promoting and supporting the private sector. This is a part of the Bank's mandate, and the Bank was constitutionally endowed with instruments such as "guarantees" to act as a catalyst for cross-border capital flows. However, after an initial burst of activity in the late 1940s and early 1950s, the Bank has done little in this area except sermonize.

The World Bank and the regional development banks are in a position to play a major catalytic role by providing partial guarantees or by taking a small participation in large private investments, thereby raising the threshold of confidence and making possible very large private capital flows into emerging markets in infrastructure, environment, and privatization programs.

Fifth, the World Bank's greater emphasis on lending for human resource development and poverty alleviation—which I applaud—raises the question of whether it is currently organized and equipped to perform effectively in this area. The Bank is a highly centralized institution with most of its multinational staff stationed in Washington. It will not be able to maintain the quality and effectiveness of greatly enlarged lending for the social sectors and for poverty alleviation unless it changes into a different type of institution, with a much higher proportion of its staff located in the field to work in tandem with local authorities, communities, and nongovernmental organizations.

Turning now to the Fund, it also has had superb leadership in recent years, and it has acted with the right blend of flexibility and decisiveness in becoming an emergency source of financial support and the purveyor of financial advice and discipline for developing countries and for economies in transition. But given the development of international markets and the access that the industrial countries have to these markets, as well as to each other, these countries have had *no* recourse to Fund facilities for nearly two decades. More important, as so many speakers have pointed out, the Fund is not drawn into the policymaking councils of the major industrial governments, and it does not serve as the central clearinghouse for the discussion of international monetary issues as its founders had intended.

By a curious turn of events, the Fund appears to have been defrocked in its own parish. It is even more curious that, on the one hand, we talk of an increasingly global and interdependent world monetary system while, on the other, we refuse to use the *only* multilateral instrument that is available for its surveillance. As the Managing Director has noted, there is an intellectual but not a political acceptance yet of the role of the Fund in multilateral surveillance. Since governments generally tend to act only in times of crisis, I fear that we may stumble toward a political acceptance of the Fund's role only after we have suffered the pains of another major financial crisis. We desperately need—to quote Mr. Duisenberg—"mutually agreed rules. . . . providing an incentive for stability" (Chapter 7). The Fund is clearly the place to forge them.

The future challenge for the Fund can therefore be very simply stated. It is to allow the Fund to play the same role with respect to the industrial countries that it has been able to perform with such effectiveness in the developing countries. The challenge is to give the Fund a more central and credible role as the main forum for discussion and resolution of international monetary issues, including the management of the system. Its capacity to create additional international liquidity through the allocation of SDRs is of particular significance in developing the linkages between international stability and development.

Last year, when I took over as Prime Minister of Pakistan for a brief period, I had personal experience of dealing with the Bretton Woods institutions as a client. At that time, Pakistan faced a severe financial and economic crisis, which necessitated that I seek the assistance of the Fund and the World Bank. After taking some immediate steps to stabilize the situation, I initiated a dialogue with their leadership. I informed them that I would announce to the nation a comprehensive program of economic, social, and political reforms within three weeks after assuming office, but that they should be prepared to act expeditiously and provide support to the program. I was delighted to find that within a month after I had announced the program, both the Fund and the Bank Executive Boards were able to approve a stand-by arrangement and adjustment loans, respectively, in support of Pakistan's reform program.

The program that I announced included major improvements in governance, in attention to minority rights, and in movement to free and fair democratic elections, as well as some reduction in military spending, but there was no prior discussion of these items with the Fund or the Bank. The reason that I was able to take sweeping measures in the governance area was precisely because it was clear that these were *not* taken at the behest of the Fund or the Bank. However, the support provided by the Fund and the Bank provided the critical elements of confidence and bridge finance that were essential to the successful implementation of the reform program in Pakistan.

Over the last 50 years, some changes have been made in the organization and institutional structure of the Bretton Woods institutions, but their basic architecture and decision-making processes remain rooted in the economic circumstances and political realities of the world of 1944.

Both institutions have an outstanding tradition of leadership at the top, which continues to this day. But just as in their organizational structure, the current arrangement by which the President of the World Bank is always an American and the Managing Director of the Fund is always a European detracts from their international character and global legitimacy.

Furthermore, since their inception, the World Bank and the Fund have functioned largely outside the purview of the UN system, of which they are specialized agencies. If the UN system is revitalized and restructured to reflect current world circumstances—for which there is increasing political support—it will become necessary to re-examine how the Bretton Woods institutions can be realigned with that system to form a more dynamic alliance to preserve and promote "human security," in the broadest sense of the term.

It is time, in my view, to look again at the mandate and organizational structure of the Bretton Woods institutions to see whether they can be brought closer into line with the imperatives of a vastly changed world environment. We shall not achieve it in one fell swoop overnight. To use Jacob Frenkel's phrase, we shall have to "earn it" through intensive negotiations, especially among the larger countries, and by the demonstrated excellence of the work of the Fund and the Bank.

Leszek Balcerowicz

When I was thinking about the topic of this session, I came to the conclusion that there are at least three factors that are both relevant for the future and related to the topic at hand: first, domestic policies of the respective countries; second, international economic cooperation, including the international monetary system; and third, the Bretton Woods institutions in relation to the first two factors. I will not discuss the second factor, but I would like to say a few words about the domestic policies of the developing countries, with a view to the future, including the transition economies; a little about the Bretton Woods institutions; and, at the end, a small remark about the transition problems of developed countries.

Let me start with the developing countries. In thinking about policies, it is useful to distinguish the vision of a target system and the transition to this system, given an initial situation that is usually very bad.

With respect to the target system, I think that there is now what is sometimes called a new development paradigm: a vision of the economy defined by a set of fundamentals that, if implemented, ensure a given country the possibility of fast and sustained economic growth. These fundamentals include a market-friendly state, which is limited and focused on those activities that the private sector cannot do, outward orientation, limited ratios of taxes and expenditures to GDP, dominance of the private sector, and political stability. Of course, political stability is not a solution in itself, but only if it serves as a basis for good economic policy.

One may remark that this development paradigm is not new. It is not very new. To a large extent, it is a return to old truths, and the paradigm of development through a state-dominated economy can be seen now as an historical aberration. We are largely returning to the classical truth, with some additions and modifications, such as environmental regulations, more focus on human capital formation, and so on. So perhaps this so-called new development paradigm should be called a neoclassical development paradigm.

Let me turn now to the second topic, to the transition from usually bad economic conditions to this target system. This issue is burdened with much more confusion and misunderstanding, and I think I have to be a little polemical on this point. I would like to refer to yesterday's intervention by Richard Portes, which I think conveyed some bad advice to the transition countries in his criticism of their policies. I found it ironic that in stipulating certain mistakes, he committed mistakes of his own. Without going into detail, let me mention only a few examples. First, it is not true that there was a deliberate premature dismantling of the Council for Mutual Economic Assistance (CMEA). Quite the opposite. All the smaller countries of the CMEA tried to maintain some transitional arrangements but failed in the face of the opposition of the Soviet Union. Second, treating the countries of Central and Eastern Europe as a homogeneous group disregards very important policy differences that can be linked to differences in economic situations. Third, it is misleading to sum up all the illnesses of the member countries, all their alleged mistakes; no one attributes the sum to each country. It is as though one counted all the illnesses of the members of mankind and attributed the sum total to each person.

But these are only examples. More generally, I think Professor Portes implied that less emphasis should be put on stabilization. This is bad advice for countries burdened with a very high inflation rate at the beginning of reform—which was typical of post-Soviet economies—where stabilization should be decisive enough to break inflationary inertia and inflationary expectations. Furthermore, I think it is dangerous to suggest that more emphasis should be put on microeconomic policies, which, although a very obscure term, is usually interpreted as more detailed state intervention. To be very brief, what is needed in transition economies, which face very difficult economic situations at the beginning of the reform process, is a decisive and comprehensive program of stabilization, liberalization, and rapid privatization.

This would be, in my view, the main message to those countries that are either in the process of transition or about to launch this transition. These countries should not neglect their efforts at stabilization or at liberalization and privatization for the sake of microeconomic policies.

Let me now turn to the role of the Bretton Woods institutions and start with some givens. I take as a given that the World Bank should continue to play an important role in concessional finance, especially with respect to the African countries, and that the Fund should be focused, among other things, on the issues of monetary and macroeconomic stability. But beyond these givens there are some questions regarding the future role of these institutions.

In thinking about this future role, I think one should be guided by two criteria: first, the activities of these institutions should be focused on their comparative advantage; and second, they should continue to try to improve the economic policies of their member countries.

When one puts these criteria together, I think one comes to the conclusion that the comparative advantage will continue to reside in policy-related lending, which requires conditionality. One can have discussions about the details of conditionality, but one should not reject the principle of conditionality. Lending is linked to discussions about policy and is dependent on the implementation of certain policies.

However, I can see at least two problems in this comparative advantage. One problem can be perceived as the price of success, and this is the decline in the share of finance provided, especially by the World Bank, because some developing countries have been successful enough to attract more private capital. The second—already noted many times during this conference—is that the Bretton Woods institutions, especially the Fund, come into the countries concerned mostly in times of crisis, crises that very often are brought about by bad economic policy. This is why the Fund in particular is regarded by the domestic populace as a whipping boy.

Against this background, one could think about the response to these two problems, which I can only sketch. The first element of this response is that the Bretton Woods institutions should think about restructuring their activity in such a way that they focus more on crisis prevention activities to help countries stay on course to prevent the crises—which I know is very difficult, but worth thinking about. Second, they should then realize that their voice over time would depend less on the financial factors and more on the recognition of their expertise, which has already been stressed in the previous discussions.

What would be the practical implications of these general suggestions? First, it is worth thinking about a program of mass economic education, financed and launched by these institutions. There is a lot of talk about human capital formation as a very important activity, but the capacity to comprehend better what is good and what is bad economic policy belongs clearly to human capital formation of a very special type. This is a very important input into democratic decision making, and this democratic decision making may, in turn, be an important input into better economic decisions and better economic policies. So perhaps it is worth thinking about setting up a joint research tank charged with helping to improve the public's understanding of good and bad economic policy.

Second, it is important to realize that most countries today are democratic and have more open societies. So it is important for the Bretton Woods institutions to realize that they should shift from their roles of being a sometimes secretive negotiator and advisor to the governments concerned to becoming agents for positive change in open and pluralistic societies. They should not see governments as their exclusive partners. It is important that Bretton Woods institutions see that they are partners with the mass media, nongovernmental organizations, and all other representatives of open societies, and that governments do not always best represent the interests of society. This implies that in selecting personnel one should look not only at technical skills but also at communication skills. This is very important, especially in countries that need a lot of convincing.

Let me finish by noting the transition problems of developed countries. Transition problems are not the monopoly of transition economies and of developing economies. I would like to mention two transition problems that seriously affect some developed countries. First, protectionism is still prevalent, especially in agriculture, as is very well known. Second, in some Western European countries there has been an oversocialization of the economy, creating a crisis of the welfare state and related high unemployment.

These transition problems should be solved for two reasons: first, in the interests of the countries concerned, and second, in the interests of other countries, because, as we very well know, dismantling protectionist devices is extremely important for the development of developing countries. It is also very important from a political point of view, because what exists now in this form in developed countries quite often gives a very bad example, and it is used by the opponents of reform in other countries to argue that this is the way to go.

Paul Volcker

In purely human terms—and here I can speak from personal experience—fiftieth birthdays inevitably are bittersweet affairs. It is much too soon for an autopsy but much too late for any sense of real celebration. I have to tell you, after participating in three or four conferences this year commemorating the fiftieth anniversary of Bretton Woods, I am struck by the parallels to the human condition. No one seems to actually contemplate the demise of the one being honored; at the same time, it is undeniable that there has been a certain loss of youthful enthusiasm and vigor. The conversation often seems to involve too many might-have-beens, too many opportunities missed, too few agreed victories. There is indeed a condition that some might interpret as encroaching arteriosclerosis, while others, more positively, would perhaps suggest there is a mature recognition of the complexities of the world and of the powerful forces beyond governments and maybe even beyond human control. I have to remind myself, and I remind you, that unlike human beings, institutions are not governed by biological realities. As we look to the future, the question is: What are the chances for a rebirth, a reconstruction, a new vigor for the Fund and the World Bank?

I have listened to all the debate this year, and it seems to me there is a strange dichotomy in thinking. On the one hand, there is a widespread sense of dissatisfaction with the performance of the world economy. A contrast is constantly drawn between the first 25 years after Bretton Woods and the second 25 years, and you know the story: slower growth, more inflation, more unemployment, slower productivity, lower savings, lower investment—all the rest. It is also quite clear that that reduced economic performance has been paralleled by much greater volatility in financial markets domestically and internationally: volatility in the sense of extreme price fluctuations, compared with the first 25 years of Bretton Woods, in financial markets; and volatility in the sense of surges and withdrawals of capital internationally. Jacques de Larosière pointed out some of the implications this morning. But it is also a fact that any relationship between the poorer economic performance and a breakdown of what used to be called the Bretton Woods system is hotly contested.

It seems to me that however one judges some of the technicalities of this debate, one might think the correlation between diminishing economic performance and increasing financial volatility would inspire more radical thinking about the role of the Fund and the World Bank. But what we seem to find instead—and I am making a simple observation from other conferences—is that any real challenge to the institutional status quo has been turned back with relatively little argument. Indeed, the case is hardly strongly pressed. This is not to say that we do not all want the Fund and the Bank to stay around. We want them to learn around the edges from experience, we want them to do a little more concentration in this area and a little less in another area, but none of it strikes me as very fundamental from a systemic point of view, posed against the evident problems of the world economy.

What is going on here? Do we have a collective lack of imagination or a lack of will? Or does it all reflect a simple wisdom and appropriate modesty, a recognition of reality? Well, part of it, I have to say, is a simple matter of human nature, which has been referred to a number of times today. We simply have not had a world-scale crisis to motivate action—certainly nothing on a magnitude of the 1930s. But in making that point, I also have to say promptly that we certainly have had some close calls in this 25-year period, and in a number of those instances the Fund and the Bank have played a key role in preventing the potential crisis from becoming a real catastrophe. In the process, success contributes to a sense of inertia.

More positively, we can all point to some important and really brilliant successes: successes in economic development, most notably in Asia, but very good grounds for hope elsewhere—in Latin America and potentially in Africa. More broadly than that, we are all aware that there has been a profound shift from the earlier postwar period to faith in market-oriented approaches. Although a faith in the market is not exactly antithetical to all government and to international institutions, in many minds they exist somewhat uneasily together. We are aware, at least in industrial countries, of a generalized lack of faith in government itself, a profound skepticism in almost all our countries about the ability of our governments to get anything very right for very long, and that skepticism inevitably spills over to the international institutions that those governments control.

Some of the implications are clearly seen, for instance, in the work of the World Bank. There are in fact, it seems to me, inherent difficulties in a public bureaucracy lending to private enterprise. If that is where the action is—and the action clearly is there much more than in the earlier postwar period—it obviously poses a problem for the Bank in how it rearranges its operations in that kind of environment.

More broadly, in this new world of private markets and many more international capital flows, the idea of managing floating exchange rates is more difficult; to some, managing exchange rates today is almost an oxymoron. We are told time and again that the volume of capital flows makes all the old possibilities in that respect nonfunctional.

Maybe it is a generational difference, but all that implied passivity does not strike me as justified. There is, of course, the view that the instability is related to economic difficulties in individual countries, that reform is fine, but nothing can be done without a better convergence of national policies. I cannot tell you how many times I myself have made a speech that we will see no stability internationally with high and volatile rates of inflation in important countries. But I used to make those speeches 20 years ago, and I still hear some of those speeches, which are almost oblivious to the fact that rates of inflation are today very low and converging—converging in a way we have not seen since the creation of the Bretton Woods system. I point out to you that we have had a remarkable movement toward the independence of central banks, which presumably brings at least a potential ability to maintain control of economic policy in that very important area. I realize that it is much harder to say favorable things about fiscal policy, but I am almost inclined to say we have had a convergence; it may be bad policy, but there is convergence.

I really do not think we can look to the excuse of lack of convergence anymore or lack of stability, or we cannot do it for much longer, if we continue to have the kind of success we have had recently. I think the problem lies elsewhere. I can understand the skepticism of public officials themselves about stabilizing exchange rates if they have a sense of lack of control over the instruments of economic policy nationally, because it is hard to conceive of stable exchange rates unless there is an ability to control national policies in a way consistent with that objective.

We are not going to be able to solve the problem of how to get more flexible fiscal and other policies here, but I think that is an important concern. Fiscal policy is a major source of pessimism, but it does not seem to me to be an excuse for passivity in the world economy. I have emphasized the importance of price stability. I think we are making remarkable progress in that direction, and that certainly should get us thinking about how we can move from domestic price stability to greater stability in exchange markets.

How can we strengthen the institutional structure? This has been what most of the conversation today has been about. I would certainly agree that, as a matter of political legitimacy—and, in less high-flown terms, as a matter of political and public support—we must be moving, if we want reform in this area, toward a more prominent role for the international institutions, as opposed to bilateral or ad hoc discussion and bargaining among major countries.

This all points toward a central role for the Fund and the World Bank, and I do not have to go through the arguments here. It seems to me that the issue resolves in part into what we do to strengthen the Interim Committee and the Development Committee. I point out that the mere fact that we are still using the word "Interim" 20 years after this Committee was created suggests a certain lack of commitment to that presumably central body governing the Fund. I think it is fair to say that criticism of the Development Committee has been greater. But I think there is a great potential—I will not rehearse it all here, because you have heard a lot about it—for bringing the management of the Fund and Bank and the organizations themselves more closely into the process of cooperation or coordination. To the extent that the process exists, it now largely revolves around the Group of Seven or the old Group of Five. You are not going to eliminate major countries talking among themselves and coordinating positions as best they can, but I think there is a difference when you bring those discussions, after whatever discussion there is among other groups of countries, more clearly into the organized, legitimate body of the Fund and the Bank, if we really want to get serious about getting action.

I have listened to all this talk about surveillance, and it reminded me a little bit—it always does—about a conversation I had 20 years ago when I was involved in trying to reform the system after the fixed rates fell, and we had all kinds of elaborate rules for this system, all kinds of surveillance mechanisms. I visited a wise official in one of the developing countries to "sell" him this story and to tell him how he ought to support these reforms, and he had an answer that always impressed me. He said, "I know all about surveillance in the Fund. When we disagree with the Fund, we get in line. When a big country disagrees with the Fund, the Fund gets in line. When the big countries disagree among themselves, the Fund does not function." Well, I think we can all recognize some reality in that description, and I would suggest, if you are going to have successful surveillance—and I cannot go into all the details—you had better have at least some simple core of agreed rules and measures that can serve as a measure of performance applied to one country or another, big and small, difficult as it is to get any real symmetry in that process. I would suggest to you also what seems to me obvious—that if you are going to have a focus for surveillance internationally, exchange rates had better play a very large part in that process.

It is easy to point out in that connection the holes in the target zone approach, or however you want to label it. Fixed rates or floating rates are much more intellectually satisfying in the textbook and in description. Someday, we may have fixed rates, more generally. Maybe we will have a floating rate system that seems to work in a more stable way. I certainly think fixed rates are possible regionally, but I do not think we are ready to go there internationally for a very long time. But I would ask whether it is beyond the wit of man to suggest there are ranges of exchange rates that would be generally agreed to be grossly misaligned. If the answer to that question is "yes," then we have to proceed to the next question: whether we can, with the best institutional arrangements possible, manage—and I would emphasize the word "manage"—to avoid those misalignments. I happen to read experience favorably in that connection. But, whatever your judgment is on that point, I think we can agree on some points. Success will require clear recognition of the importance of the effort; importance, let us say, at least comparable to the importance of maintaining open markets, getting GATT agreed, avoiding unjustified retaliation in the trade area, and all the rest. It will also take effort and a willingness to conduct monetary policy, in particular, with an eye to the objective of avoiding extreme misalignments in exchange rates. I am well aware that success in that endeavor will require a reasonable—maybe not perfect, but reasonable—medium-term position with respect to fiscal policy.

Furthermore, avoiding excessive exchange rate stability will take a national commitment to that objective, supported by a few agreed rules. Not least, it will take a resolution to stop meeting to celebrate the past or to discuss the problems of the present or the old problems. It will take a willingness to move from discussion to action. I would suggest, frankly, that all of those qualities heretofore have been lacking.

But I have another, prettier picture in mind. Suppose we do succeed collectively in restoring expectations about price stability—and that is a supposition that, it seems to me, we are indeed in the process of achieving, not just because of its importance internationally but because of the priority given to it domestically. Suppose we do make progress on fiscal policy and achieve a reasonable medium-term position most of the time in most of our countries—also something we should be doing for its own sake. Then, suppose we take the further step of a commitment to take the objective of stable exchange rates seriously to avoid gross misalignment. I would simply conclude with unaccustomed optimism. Under those conditions, we might be surprised at how easy it is.

General Discussion

Nancy Alexander felt that it would be useful if the panel could join some of its thinking to that of the earlier session on poverty. Some of the points emerging from the discussion of poverty were particularly striking, such as the observation that the benefits of economic growth could often be canceled out by poor income distribution and that inequality of income was a significant drag on governments' ability to achieve the poverty reduction goal that was at the heart of the World Bank's mandate. Given the fact that the Bank had been very deliberate about its anticipated greater role in promoting free markets in developing countries, she wondered how the market could be made to be friendly to the poorest segments of the population, which needed to be reached in a way that reduced not only poverty—indeed, earlier speakers had said that poverty reduction was not enough—but inequality as well. She asked the panel to address that question in the light of the need to deepen partnerships with a variety of players throughout society. She hoped that the vision of a people-friendly market and a participatory society could be fed into the session of the conference devoted to establishing a vision for the future.

Kwesi Botchwey replied that it was widely recognized that trying to achieve growth with equity in the distribution of benefits raised difficult issues. A key element in Ghana's structural adjustment program was the inclusion at the outset of the program of specific measures targeted at the most vulnerable groups in society. Those kinds of measures, which in Ghana had included labor-intensive programs and direct credits to vulnerable groups to allow them to engage in productive activity, were not on their own sufficient. The resources required to achieve the desired results were large, and programs of intervention were at best a temporary expedient, designed to smooth the path of adjustment. In the end, it was necessary to ensure that growth itself was robust and that it generated a significant amount of employment.

Paul Volcker, responding to a query from the moderator, remarked that from the perspective of the United States, one of the principal issues that had to be faced squarely was that, in providing funds for development initiatives, there was no substitute for budgetary resources. If the World Bank had a role to play in fostering private sector activity in developing countries, which it clearly did, highly concessional finance would be required, which did not come easily from any donor country, including the United States.

At the other end of the spectrum, the problems that needed to be addressed were not likely to be solved in a fundamental way by infusions of money, even on a concessional basis. Many more elements had to be put in place, as experience had shown. There was currently much less optimism than in the early days of the Bank and the Fund about the benefits of lending or cash grants as the key to the process; there had been a healthy recognition of the importance of the many other factors, including the role that private markets could play. In that sense, the World Bank might fall back into what could be a very important advisory role, both in poor countries and in those providing finance.

Layeshi Yaker felt that the World Bank and the Fund deserved praise for having helped a number of developing countries achieve satisfactory rates of growth in recent decades, one of the most encouraging aspects of global economic trends in recent years. As major sources of multilateral development finance, the Bretton Woods institutions played an important role in supporting and even influencing Africa's development programs, not only through financing programs but also through influencing the orientation of economic reforms and the overall attitude of Africa's development partners toward the continent.

Within that context, he suggested a review of the current international monetary arrangements, particularly the strategies used in promoting economic growth and development and the mobilization of financial resources for development. The emergence of a generalized system of floating exchange rates had brought about increased volatility in the exchange rates of major currencies, which had contributed significantly to the severe economic and social adjustment costs in many countries in Africa. Africa was especially vulnerable in that respect, as many countries in the continent had moved progressively toward more flexible exchange rate arrangements in line with general developments in the world economy—hence, Africa's interest in the establishment of a stable international monetary system.

Moeen Qureshi responded that he would not want to elaborate on the excellent discussion of those issues that had taken place in earlier sessions, particularly the previous session in which Jacob Frenkel and others had considered at some length the relative merits of fixed versus flexible exchange rates. His own sense was that, as developing countries were not able to influence developments elsewhere, the best approach from their standpoint would be to concentrate on managing their own monetary and financial affairs in an orderly way and to forget about the exchange rate system. Exchange rates would work out quite well if the monetary policies were right.

13

Closing Statements

The conference concluded with evaluations of the issues by the two heads of the Bretton Woods institutions, along with statements by Jean-Claude Milleron, the Under Secretary-General of the United Nations (UN), who looked at the international agenda from the viewpoint of the UN, and by Pedro Solbes Mira, the Minister of Finance of Spain.

Jean-Claude Milleron

I should like first to express my personal appreciation to the hosts and organizers of this conference. My only regret is that I may not be able to enjoy your one hundredth anniversary. The Secretary-General of the UN, Mr. Boutros Boutros-Ghali, has asked me to convey to you his warmest greetings, to offer you best wishes for the years ahead, and to assure you of the UN's continued support for your endeavors. More generally, all of us in the Secretariat of the UN would like to congratulate our sister organizations on their golden anniversaries. As has been indicated over the past two days, they have been 50 years of which the World Bank and the Fund—and all of those associated with them during the past half century—can justifiably feel proud. The world is a better place as a result of your achievements.

Mankind's progress over the past 50 years has probably been beyond even the remarkable foresight of the founders of our institutions. It has become a platitude to emphasize the extent to which the world has changed—even in the past few years—and to point to the new challenges that the international community is facing. It is, I believe, universally accepted that, in a world that has become increasingly globalized and interdependent, there are new responsibilities that must be assumed by international institutions. At the same time, the international community has to recognize where it has failed to accomplish some of its long-standing objectives and to rededicate itself to those tasks of global concern that remain. The aims of both the UN and the Bretton Woods institutions in the years ahead must be to ensure that the progress of the past 50 years is not only continued but enhanced in both depth and breadth.

It would be a rewriting of history to pretend that the World Bank, the Fund, and the UN have worked closely together over the past 50 years. To a large extent, each has focused on its own responsibilities and constituencies and has acted independently. Increasingly, however, there are commonalities between the three organizations and a need for them to work more closely together. All three organizations now have almost universal membership, there is a large measure of agreement on the key items on the international agenda, and—most important of all—there are growing interrelationships between the traditional responsibilities of the different organizations.

We have heard today many proposals for the future work of the two Washington organizations. I should like to take a somewhat different approach and identify what I see as some of the key issues on the agenda of the UN for the immediate future. I think you will agree that these matters also concern both the World Bank and the Fund. I therefore hope that a new dialogue on these subjects will take place between the "northerners" in New York and the "southerners" in Washington. In many cases, such a dialogue could lead us to act more collectively, which is in the spirit of the Agenda for Development that the Secretary-General is currently finalizing.

Nowadays, there is a very wide, almost universal, convergence of views on the desirable nature of many key national economic policies. We agree on the need for a sound macroeconomic framework, for greater emphasis on economic efficiency, and for individual countries to integrate themselves into the global economy. However, there is less agreement about the division of responsibilities between the government and the market in this process, in particular with regard to equity questions, social issues, and the environmental challenge. These are all areas in which government has a crucial role to play and which are, in my view, becoming of increasing relevance at the international level. They are topics that should be on the agenda of the international institutions, hopefully not for the next 50 years but for the immediate future.

Globalization and greater interdependence among countries are increasing the range—and our awareness—of international public goods. There are, to start with, the "global commons," and the Rio Conference on Environment and Development in 1992 was a major attempt to address many of the questions in this area. The forthcoming entry into force of the Law of the Sea will be another step forward. On such questions, it is agreed that government at both the national and international levels has an important role to play. Nevertheless, many difficult issues remain to be resolved before we can declare that we have a consensus on the extent of that role. Addressing these questions must continue to be a priority item on the international agenda.

A second international public good is global peace and security. Internal law and order and national defense have long been recognized as quintessential public goods: all members of society benefit, and almost nobody argues that meeting these essential foundations of society should be left solely to the market. In most countries, therefore, meeting these needs has long been a public responsibility. At the international level, however, we are far from finding an adequate solution to the problems of peace and security under the changed global circumstances.

We in the UN firmly believe that peace and development are inextricably intertwined: peace provides a foundation for long-term development whereas conflict is often brought about by a lack of development. Here, I refer to development in its broadest sense, meaning not only economic well-being but the ability of all individuals to participate fully and freely in society. It is only too apparent that a lack of such development is one of the threats to the global peace and security that we all seek. It is in our collective interest both to invest in peace and to foster the development that will assist in securing it.

One new aspect of this challenge lies in dealing with what are frequently called post-chaos situations—cases where economies have been devastated by war or civil unrest. Here again, it is in the global interest—as well as a moral imperative—to ensure that these countries return to a path of political stability and sustained development and regain their place in the world community. However, these economies are unlikely to achieve these goals if left to fend for themselves, as was recognized when the World Bank was established to assist in the reconstruction of Europe following the Second World War. More recently, the international community should be applauded for its efforts to date in such countries as Cambodia, El Salvador, and Namibia. Nevertheless, we are still in the learning phase of dealing with such situations, and this is one area in which our organizations have to work together more closely.

A similar challenge arises with respect to the burgeoning number of international refugees. Some—but far from all of them—are the result of conflict. It has long been accepted that the responsibility for these downtrodden people should not fall solely on the host country. In this case, I think we can all agree that the Office of the United Nations High Commissioner for Refugees can be proud of the way in which it has responded to the immense new burdens placed upon it. Looking ahead, however, it seems likely that there will continue to be millions of people who will feel under pressure to leave their homes, either as refugees or as long-term migrants. Here again, a collective international response is required.

I do not mean to belittle the large amount of attention and resources that are already being devoted to peacekeeping, post-conflict peacebuilding, and refugees. Rather, the principle that underpins both the Secretary-General's Agenda for Peace and the Agenda for Development is that global peace and security and an improvement in development prospects would reduce the need for such activities. Such preventive measures are an international public good whose value should not be underestimated.

Preventive diplomacy is essential and continues to be a major endeavor of my colleagues on the political side of our organization. But diplomacy is unlikely to be sufficient. Global peace is at best tenuous while such a large proportion of the world's people live in misery. Distribution is a second broad area in which there is a question of the division of responsibilities between government and the market. Even at the national level, there is, almost inevitably, disagreement on the trade-off to be struck between efficiency and equity. We seek to achieve efficiency through competition, and yet the very objective of competition is to drive out the weakest. Consequently, there is no guarantee that the benefits of progress will be properly distributed, and some form of intervention is called for to pay sufficient attention to the weakest and disadvantaged.

For most of the past 50 years, the industrial countries were largely successful in such efforts—they countered this tendency toward the marginalization of some segments of society by instituting a system of what were widely known as "social safety nets." However, holes have begun to appear in these safety nets, with the result that even in these countries an increasing number of people are falling below the level at which they can re-establish themselves economically or socially. The concern about distribution is now receiving greater attention in many developing countries. Nevertheless, there continue to be very wide disparities in individual well-being in many of these countries, where hundreds of millions of individuals live in poverty and social deprivation.

The conclusion of the Uruguay Round was an important step toward applying at the international level the principles of competitive markets that are increasingly being adopted at the national level. Although the gains to the world as a whole will be significant, it seems inevitable that some of the countries that are already the most disadvantaged are likely to face further difficulties as a result of the agreements reached in the Round. There are, of course, new opportunities to be seized, but it is becoming increasingly difficult for "latecomers" to penetrate the world market. There is a risk that some countries will fail and be further marginalized. To some extent, this has already occurred: in the words of Ambassador Somavia of Chile, Chairman of the Preparatory Committee for the World Summit for Social Development, "a globalization of prosperity is accompanied by a globalization of poverty." The old development question of "dualism" persists: the difference between the "haves" and the "have-nots"—at the level of both the country and the individual—may even be more pronounced than ever.

Over recent years, all our organizations have allocated a greater share of their resources to Africa and to other lagging countries that face the threat of marginalization. This focus must continue. At the same time, both national governments and the international community must give more attention to the disadvantaged within countries. In this instance, experience suggests that part of that effort must be devoted to achieving greater understanding of the issues and to devising more effective means of responding.

One key area in which knowledge has improved concerns the interrelationship between poverty, population, development, and the environment. However, this is only a starting point; the real success lies in the agreement of member states to address the corresponding challenges both individually and collectively. The Program of Action that was adopted by the International Conference on Population and Development in Cairo earlier this month was an important building block toward an overall consensus on the challenges currently facing the world community and on the actions that need to be taken.

Looking ahead, the World Summit for Social Development that will take place in Copenhagen next March is an explicit recognition by member states that many questions of distribution remain unresolved. The three themes of the summit are the alleviation of poverty, the expansion of employment, and the enhancement of social integration. We expect the summit to agree on a plan of action in each of these areas, with the result that they will become more important on the international agenda in the years ahead.

An important cornerstone of the Program of Action adopted in Cairo is the recognition that it gives both to the role of women in the development process and to their needs. This half of the world's population continues to find itself in a disadvantaged position, and its potential contribution to development remains constrained. This situation cannot be allowed to continue. A further opportunity for new and more wide-ranging initiatives will arise in Beijing one year from now when the Fourth World Conference on Women is held.

A final challenge lies in mobilizing the necessary resources. At present, the outlook in this respect is mixed: additional resources have been forthcoming for emergency needs, while development assistance has been faltering. But it is short-sighted to reduce efforts to foster development, because development reduces the need for emergency assistance. Mobilizing resources for development must therefore continue to be the overriding challenge facing the international community and international organizations.

I hope that what I have said here will not be interpreted as another call by an international bureaucrat for more international bureaucracy. Clearly, I believe that there are areas where more should be done at the international level. But I should like to underline that I subscribe fully to the principle of subsidiarity—that local problems should be addressed at the local level, national problems at the national level, and only international problems at the international level. I believe we have to make greater efforts to devise methods of applying the principle of subsidiarity to the priorities I have identified this evening. We need to establish a consensus on our international responsibilities, the means of accomplishing them, and the resources that are required. If we can do this, our successors may credit us with the same sense of vision that we attribute to those who established the institutions that we are celebrating here this week.

Michel Camdessus

This has been a most interesting conference. We have been treated to a rich feast of statements and discussions. The proceedings will make an important contribution to our work and help our constant efforts to improve our approaches and methods. We are grateful to all participants and discussants for their contributions.

The conference has, if anything, made it even clearer to us that the Fund has a lot to do as it enters its second half century. I am well aware of our full agenda, and I have been highly encouraged by the support that has been expressed for the Fund to continue pursuing actively the purposes for which it was established—purposes that all agree are so highly relevant to the needs of today.

I have also been impressed by the additional evidence I have seen at this conference of the strong consensus that now exists on the policy strategies that all countries need in order to pursue the objective of sustainable, equitable economic growth with high employment—what I like to call "high-quality growth." It seems that few here would disagree that high-quality growth requires five ingredients: sound macroeconomic policies; structural policies that promote the efficient use of resources and a responsive supply side; an open trade and exchange regime; active and effective social policies; and good governance.

The formation and strengthening over the past decade or so of this consensus on the policy strategies needed by all countries—industrial, developing, and transition economies—is surely one of the most significant developments in the history of economic policy in the postwar period. It lies behind policy improvements in many countries, which have borne much fruit; those successes have in turn helped to strengthen the consensus. Many of those successes have, of course, occurred in developing and transition economies with policy programs supported by Fund and World Bank financial and technical assistance. Here, I include a number of countries whose reliance on Fund financial support at critical times in their development, in the 1960s and 1970s, is now sometimes forgotten. If, as suggested by several speakers, the Bretton Woods institutions have contributed to this new consensus—I call it the "silent revolution"—this is certainly something of which we can be proud.

But the Fund has also seen disappointments and setbacks. Let me share with you some thoughts on how the failings we see can be corrected, and on how the Fund can help its member countries—which is to say the world—achieve stronger and more consistent progress. I shall consider the two areas of Fund activity that have received most attention in the past two days.

First, let me consider financial assistance for adjustment and reform in the developing and transition economies. Although there are many examples of outstanding growth performance in countries that have persevered with structural adjustment strategies, some countries that have begun to implement Fund-supported programs have apparently seen little early reward in terms of growth and little early improvement in saving and investment performance. This is frustrating, but it is not altogether surprising. Experience shows that two of the essential requirements of improved growth performance are effective and wide-ranging structural reforms to enable markets to work and time to establish a track record of better policies and build the confidence of potential investors. Boldness in reform and perseverance often provide the key to better growth performance for these countries.

It is, of course, also disappointing to see that a number of countries have failed, for political, administrative, or other reasons, to implement programs with enough consistency even to establish a sufficient degree of macroeconomic stability to make sustainable growth possible.

What can the Fund do to help in these cases?

First, to speed up the growth-generating effects of our programs, we can encourage the earlier and more effective introduction of structural reforms in the programs we support, as well as the pursuit and strengthening over the medium term of these demanding but essential efforts. I referred yesterday (Chapter 2) to the ways in which the Fund's financial facilities have been adapted to take account of the need for medium-term programs and structural reforms. The extended Fund facility and the extended ESAF (enhanced structural adjustment facility) are now in place as the key instruments for programs appropriately front-loaded with structural measures, institution building, and social safety nets.

Second, in our technical assistance, training, and surveillance work, we must intensify our efforts to help countries establish the expertise and administrative capacity they need both to implement and to design the policies that are appropriate to their circumstances. We are strongly in favor of countries having their own "homegrown" policy programs, as long as they meet the necessary conditions. In fact, there is a remarkable variety of features among the programs to which the Fund has given, and is giving, its support. This fact is not always fully appreciated.

Third, the Fund's financing instruments must be strengthened further, and we have been working toward this end. I am confident that the Interim Committee will this weekend endorse a "package" that has been put together to help meet the financing needs of many members. This package will, I hope, comprise a rise in access limits on Fund financing, an extension of the availability of the systemic transformation facility, and an allocation of SDRs that will ease the reserve constraints on members and ensure that each member has a fair stake in the SDR system.

Fourth, far from weakening its conditionality, the Fund must seek to strengthen the programs to which it gives financial support. This is not only because the Fund is required by its Articles to lend only "under adequate safeguards"; it is also because it is through conditionality that Fund financial support has acquired the credibility that is the foundation of its ability to catalyze parallel financial support from other creditors and donors. We cannot allow this credibility to be weakened. And conditionality must be maintained also, of course, to catalyze the domestic support required to implement the necessary measures; let me assure you that some of the strongest support of Fund conditionality that I hear comes not from within the Fund but from policymakers striving for adjustment, reform, and progress in their own countries.

In sum, I believe that the Fund must work to provide and obtain stronger financial and technical support for stronger growth-oriented adjustment and reform programs.

Let me now turn to the second area of Fund activity—the Fund's role in the international monetary system. Here also, there have been failures and disappointments. I continue to consider that the exchange rate volatility and misalignments we have seen under present arrangements are too costly and destabilizing to be acceptable; I attach importance to exchange rate stability as part of the environment of monetary stability essential for the effective working of market economies. Moreover, I am attracted by the objective of carefully designed systems of formal exchange rate commitments because of their potential advantages in terms of macroeconomic discipline, as well as of reduced exchange rate instability. But we know from experience the difficulties: we know the limited power of intervention and the limited role that fiscal policy can play. And we also know that such a system could work at the global level only if certain conditions were to be met. Now, for sure, the time is not ripe for it, partly because the countries issuing the three major currencies are not convinced at this stage that they must be ready to go an extra step—to subordinate their monetary policies to exchange rate objectives. We therefore have to approach the task of fostering a more stable system of exchange rates in a different way. And that way is to strengthen Fund surveillance. What you have told us yesterday and today has been an unambiguous call for a stronger and indeed central role for the Fund in surveillance, in particular of industrial countries. I have heard the message, and I welcome it.

We must go beyond business as usual. Your message has many aspects. Effective surveillance must be backed by solid, high-quality analysis. I was heartened to hear a number of you refer to the technical competence, professionalism, and objectivity of the work of the Fund's staff. We shall continue to strive to improve it. Participation in the surveillance process should be at a very senior level: this was another call. I agree, and indeed we have an Executive Board consisting of competent individuals. We must keep it that way and achieve the highest possible level of national government representation to give weight and authority to the Fund's views and to ensure that they translate into action. We must publicize the results of surveillance: this was a recurrent theme in the speeches yesterday and today. I know this is a sensitive matter, but we must be more transparent and open in our work than we have been so far. We will carefully consider this and every other part of your message, and I intend as Managing Director to undertake new initiatives. Sometimes our efforts in this area have been frustrating, but we will try again with steadfast determination, and I am sure that the inspiration of the meetings in Washington (of the Bretton Woods Commission) and Madrid will help us find proper responses to your calls.

Ultimately, of course, what the Fund can do in any field depends on its members' will to cooperate; what the Fund can do to foster a more favorable exchange system depends above all on the political will of the major industrial countries to cooperate. I strongly hope that this cooperation will be forthcoming.

International cooperation is all the more important because the process of globalization is making the Fund's task of surveillance even more essential, as a means of preventing negative spillovers of policy mistakes from one country to others, and indeed of preventing all forms of weakness in policies, which often lie at the root of exchange rate volatility and misalignment. Through our efforts to sharpen our analysis and surveillance, we must also seek to provide the world with an even more reliable early warning system of emerging economic risks.

Also in the context of globalization, I would say that the progress that has been made toward greater freedom of capital movements invites the Fund to give early consideration to the appropriateness and modalities of a fast-disbursing, very short-term financing mechanism that could help cushion the reserves of countries experiencing short-term balance of payments pressures in spite of sound fundamentals and policies.

In these remarks, I have focused on growth and stability—two key objectives of economic policy that the Fund was founded to serve. The past 50 years have shown how multilateral cooperation can serve these objectives. In the years ahead, the Fund, together with the governments that form our membership, must ensure that the benefits of multilateral cooperation are exploited more fully. After 50 years, the spirit of Bretton Woods, so alive at this conference, has a great deal more to offer.

Lewis T. Preston

My colleagues and I have been listening with great interest to the issues raised during the past two days. I would like to thank everyone for the time and thought they have devoted to the future of the World Bank Group. Your presence here reflects your genuine concern for the development of our member countries—and for the important role you see for the World Bank Group in that process.

We will need some time to absorb the many useful ideas put on the table. I will not therefore attempt to provide specific reactions at this stage but rather try to convey some of my thinking on the broad issues raised. I will focus on three points.

First, the World Bank needs to change both what it does and how it does it. The Bank has been flexible over the past 50 years in responding to diverse challenges; it must continue to change in response to the changing needs of our members.

We are already seeing some profound changes in the composition of our lending program, for example, with a substantially enhanced focus on private sector development, environmental sustainability, and human resource development. Many of you have urged us to continue aggressively in this direction. Let me assure you that we will.

We are also changing the way we do business. The guiding principles we outlined earlier this year in our vision statement reflect the broad directions of change, and they are part of the ongoing change in management practices and institutional "culture." As Gerry Helleiner, among others, noted yesterday afternoon (Chapter 5), a number of measures are under way to increase the development effectiveness of our operations, enhance country focus and client orientation, and increase participation by beneficiaries in project design and implementation. These changes will help us to get better results on the ground—which is what really matters.

A second set of issues relates to the World Bank's cost-effectiveness. I am committed to ensuring that the Bank becomes a more agile, more responsive, and leaner institution. Actions have begun to be taken to bring that about. For example, we are on a zero-growth budget this year—and sizable budget reductions are planned for fiscal years 1996 and 1997.

But I also want to sound a note of caution here. As we make an increased effort to be even more cost-effective, it is important to recognize that the Bank cannot be all things to all people. It will need to be increasingly selective in the things it does, and to seek partnerships with others.

This will not only reduce some of the burden on the Bank but also help to maximize everyone's different strengths.

I am all too aware of the danger, to which Manmohan Singh alluded (Chapter 3), of the risks of a diffused pattern of lending that can result from pursuing too many objectives. This is precisely why selectivity is the first of our guiding principles. However, for it to be applied effectively, we will need the support of our shareholders. And on this point, let me just echo what Moisés Naím and others have said (Chapter 5) about the need for our shareholders not to be "absentee landlords." It is in the institution's interest for our shareholders to play an active role in helping to shape our future direction.

A third set of issues relates to accountability and openness. The World Bank has had a long tradition of openness in analyzing its own performance—including through the publication of our evaluation reports. In other areas of the external dialogue, however, we have not been as forthcoming, and we have paid a high price for an institutional culture that Moisés Naím has described as "inward looking." We are trying to break this down.

Recent changes, such as enhanced access to information, increased interaction with nongovernmental organizations, the emphasis on participation, and the establishment of an inspection panel, will help to increase openness and broaden the World Bank's outreach efforts. Openness permits outside scrutiny of our policies and operations—and thus helps to strengthen accountability and performance. Given our new policies, I think it is fair to say that the Bank is among the most—if not the most—open development institution in the world (including nongovernmental institutions).

The dialogue that this permits with our friends and critics is vitally needed. But it must be a genuine dialogue, based on mutual respect and intellectual honesty on all sides. A few failed projects, for example, should not be allowed to define an institution that has undertaken some 6,000 development operations. Development is a risky business. All institutions seriously engaged in that business will inevitably make some mistakes. But mistakes must be seen in context. In the case of the Bank—as many of you have noted—that overall context has been highly positive.

At the end of the day, all of us must remain focused on how we can best help the 4 billion people in the developing countries to reduce poverty and improve their quality of life. The World Bank Group will continue to concentrate on this goal—and we call on all our partners in development to work with us in this great endeavor.

May I conclude by thanking Finance Minister Solbes and the Spanish authorities for the excellent arrangements for this conference. We have learned a lot these past two days—and the Annual Meetings will have been enriched by your many thoughtful contributions.

Pedro Solbes Mira

This conference commemorating the fiftieth anniversary of the Bretton Woods agreements is an excellent opportunity to take an in-depth look at the lessons we have learned from the past and, more important, to consider the future of our institutions. Although we have not taken any formal decisions, I do not think it would be an exaggeration to characterize the discussions of these past two days as historic, inasmuch as the proposals that have been discussed and the ideas they have prompted will be fundamental in predisposing us to face the reforms that may be needed to improve the functioning of the IMF and the World Bank.

Although it has been said repeatedly during these two days, I have no hesitation in once again stressing the importance of the moment in which we live. The ongoing changes in international relationships are of transcendental importance and are having profound consequences for all our societies, when, for the first time in many years, the economies of many of our countries are experiencing broad economic recovery.

The IMF's half-yearly report on the world economic outlook, presented two days ago, contains—also for the first time in several years—an upward revision of the last previous projections. The world economy is moving strongly out of an economic recession likely to have been the worst in the last 50 years. Not only the developed economies but also a large number of Asian and Latin American countries now find themselves in much more favorable economic circumstances than they experienced even a few months ago.

We must not forget, however, that important exceptions to this favorable economic situation remain, including the poorest countries in Africa and several countries in transition to a market economy.

We must put this relatively widespread economic boom to good advantage. We must not forget that the economic recession left significant aftereffects, such as the unemployment rate in many European countries—of which Spain is a clear illustration—and the sizable budgetary deficits we have incurred as a result of the recession.

We are indeed coming out of a very deep crisis, which requires that economic policies be designed with a view to ensuring the sustainable economic development that is the ultimate objective set for the IMF and the World Bank at the time of their creation.

Increased economic interdependence and the resulting need for closer coordination of economic policies are two basic concepts on which our cooperation efforts must surely be based. From this standpoint, the roles to be played by the Bretton Woods institutions are further strengthened, even as they are constantly adapted to the new realities.

During this fiftieth anniversary conference, we have had the opportunity to listen to comments of every kind on the evolution and functioning of the IMF and the World Bank. The balance of the first 50 years in the life of these institutions may be regarded as a positive one, even if it is not devoid of aspects that are not fully satisfactory. This brings up the irrevocable need to introduce or consolidate, as the case may be, reforms that in some cases have already begun.

The evolution of both the Fund and the World Bank has also entailed gradual changes in their functions, as would be expected. These changing functions may have made it appear at times that the roles of the two institutions were beginning to overlap, giving rise to seemingly inefficient situations at first sight. The shift in the functions of the two institutions is an issue that has been discussed ever since the Bretton Woods agreements came into effect. Let us look at some of the aspects of their evolution.

The IMF has been taking an increasingly closer interest in the problems of developing countries, especially since the debt crisis of the 1980s, and has played a fundamental role not only in its policy advice but also in the solution of the problems of adjustment and indebtedness. This has led to an image of the Fund as rather more distant from its original role of overseer of exchange stability, which had such a great influence on developed countries under the system of fixed but adjustable exchange rates. I am in agreement with some of the opinions expressed these past few days, to the effect that the IMF, without ceasing to play a fundamental role in its relations with developing countries, should try to recover some of the influence it used to have on the design and coordination of economic policy in the developed countries.

From this standpoint, the review of the role of the Interim Committee, which will mark its twentieth anniversary on October 2, may be a fundamental issue. The Committee's current Chairman, Philippe Maystadt, has taken the timely initiative of having us propose that the Governors of the IMF take up this review of the Committee's role, and of its working procedures as well, with a view to making them more efficient. Revitalizing the Interim Committee as a forum for discussing not only problems stemming from the increased vulnerability of the exchange system in a context of full capital mobility but also problems related to economic policy coordination will contribute to a useful exchange of ideas, as well as to achievement of a multilateral commitment that may enhance the efficient functioning of the international economy.

What we are talking about is the Fund's ability to reassume some of the powers assigned to it by the Articles of Agreement, which it should put into practice now more than ever.

Turning now to the evolution of the World Bank, we see that major changes have taken place in its organization and behavior as it has adapted to the changing nature of the problems associated with economic development. The World Bank Group has not only modified some of its thinking but also gone further and introduced major institutional reforms. The creation of new institutions within the World Bank Group, such as the Multilateral Investment Guarantee Agency, the growing emphasis on the essential role of the private sector in the Bank's activities, and the increasing attention given in its studies to the environmental impact of its projects illustrate the continuing evolution of thought within the Bank itself as it adapts to new requirements in developing countries.

During these days of the conference, as also during the similar meeting held in Washington in July, opinions have been voiced about the advisability of creating new international institutions to deal with specific topics. The decision to create a new institution, such as the World Trade Organization, gives us an idea of the strengthened power of multilateral approaches. I continue to think that, in a more global world, multilateral approaches must indeed coexist suitably with purely regional arrangements. In such a context, coordination of functions among the various existing institutions will be fundamental to preventing interference among them and to permitting each to specialize in the area for which it was created.

We can find an example of enormous significance in the approach we took to solving the huge problems faced by countries with economies in transition.

The relatively recent creation of the European Bank for Reconstruction and Development (EBRD) was a bold initiative. Having gone through its start-up phase, and largely thanks to the wise management of its President, Mr. de Larosière, the EBRD now focuses on increasingly efficient policies to support the transformation of economies in transition. Thus, the gradual strengthening of the EBRD should take into account the policies we ourselves decide should be implemented through the IMF and the World Bank for these countries, which are so much in need of support by the international community.

The conclusion, then, is that a review is needed of the functioning, role, and coordination of multilateral institutions as a group, whose design should never be accepted as fixed in a changing world. Given the nature of this forum, I would be so bold as to state that we need a review that will make use of the positive aspects of the experience of recent years and of the changes already made, but that can be thought of as a kind of refounding of our institutions, amounting in some cases to a return to their origins. If Keynes and White were called upon today to propose plans for organizing the international monetary system, how would they do so? It seems evident that the problem of development, which was not on the original Bretton Woods agenda, is today a basic priority, as is the situation of the countries in transition, now that the Cold War is over.

We would have to adapt to the challenge of the global economy, with no exclusions or self-exclusions, consistent with strong, consolidated areas of regional integration. And all this would have to be suitably reflected in the organization, functioning, and decision-making mechanisms of our institutions, which would play a new role in driving and guiding a new concept of global multilateralism with a political and economic weight distribution different from the one that prevailed at Bretton Woods.

This means being prepared to change the existing pattern, keeping in mind the goal of properly defining the appropriate functions for each institution and ensuring proper coordination between them. These changes will not be effective unless the political will is present. But I am convinced that, sooner or later, they must be taken up, and I believe that this anniversary is a good occasion to begin doing so.

In conclusion, I wish to thank you again for your presence in Spain and to congratulate you on your work. I would like to make special mention of the Managing Directors and Presidents who have led the IMF and the World Bank, respectively, and particularly of Michel Camdessus and Lewis Preston, under whose batons expert staffs representing all our countries are working most effectively.